William Sproston Cain

A trip Round the World in 1887-8

William Sproston Cain

A trip Round the World in 1887-8

ISBN/EAN: 9783744728331

Printed in Europe, USA, Canada, Australia, Japan

Cover: Foto ©Andreas Hilbeck / pixelio.de

More available books at **www.hansebooks.com**

A TRIP ROUND THE WORLD

IN

1887—8

A

TRIP ROUND THE WORLD

IN

1887—8

BY

W. S. CAINE, M.P.

ILLUSTRATED BY

JOHN PEDDER, H. SHEPPARD DALE, GEO. BICKHAM,
And the AUTHOR

LAHORE GATE, DELHI FORT.

LONDON
GEORGE ROUTLEDGE AND SONS
BROADWAY, LUDGATE HILL
GLASGOW AND NEW YORK

1888

LONDON:
PRINTED BY WILLIAM CLOWES AND SONS, LIMITED,
STAMFORD STREET AND CHARING CROSS.

TO

MY CONSTITUENTS AND FRIENDS

AT

BARROW-IN-FURNESS,

TO WHOM THESE LETTERS WERE ORIGINALLY ADDRESSED,

THIS VOLUME

IS RESPECTFULLY DEDICATED.

PREFACE.

THIS volume consists of a reprint of letters addressed to the *Barrow News*, the leading newspaper of the constituency I represent in Parliament, dating from August 1887 to March 1888. The letters were written during idle hours on board steamers, for the amusement and information of my constituents and personal friends, but with no intention of adding to the many volumes of travel which deal with the various countries I have seen in my rapid tour round the world.

I have, however, found by experience, that the *obiter dicta* of other travellers have been of so much greater service to me during my own journey than the recognized guide books, many of which have been put quite out of date by the rapid developments of transit, and the equally rapid changes in Eastern customs, that I venture to add my modest contribution to the literature of travel. I hope it may prove of value to some of that increasing number of English and Americans to whom a tour round the world is becoming a matter of course, and perhaps also of some interest to the general reader. I have tried to make my letters readable by old and young alike.

In one respect this volume differs—so far as I am aware—

PREFACE.

from any other of the kind which has yet been published. It is profusely illustrated. I trust more to my pictures than to my inexperienced literary powers, to make this volume acceptable to the public. I wish to acknowledge gratefully the assistance I have had from my old friend, Mr. John Pedder, of Maidenhead, who has evolved the greater portion of the illustrations, with accuracy and artistic skill, from a heterogeneous collection of rough sketches and photographs made by me on my journey; and also to Mr. H. Sheppard Dale for the excellent architectural drawings of Japanese and Indian buildings which bear his name.

The journey taken by my daughter and myself has entailed no hardship or inconvenience, with the not very serious exception of our voyage across the Pacific. Sir William Pearce's steamers can be avoided by other travellers, without losing the enchanting scenery of the Canadian Pacific route, or incurring extra expense. The Canadian Pacific Railway Company will book passengers from Quebec or Montreal, through to San Francisco, at slightly higher rates than the direct American Pacific Railroads; the sea passage from Vancouver to San Francisco is for the most part in smooth water, the coast being extremely beautiful, and the steamers comfortable. The only really good line of steamers crossing the Pacific are those chartered from the White Star Line sailing from San Francisco; their names all end with "ic," and if tourists take care to secure this last syllable, they will be sure of fine ships and comfortable accommodation.

None of the trans-continental railways of the United States can compare with the Canadian Pacific either for beauty of scenery or comfort in travel. It is easy, however, for those wishing to see the Yellowstone Park, to cross over *viâ* Winnipeg to the Canadian Pacific route.

It is important on all American lines of railway to secure sleeping-car berths the day before starting on the journey—they are generally crowded. I know no bed of little ease to compare with a night spent in the ordinary American car.

I advise travellers to resist all temptations to travel by steamers not flying the British flag. Their ways are not our ways.

There is absolutely no remedy for sea-sickness, but to go to bed and stop there till it runs its horrid course. The best food to take is beef-tea absolutely free from fat, with crisp dry toast, and grapes. There is an excellent preparation which can be made ready in a moment with boiling water, called Bovril, and another equally good, Johnson's beef-tea. I have often seen well-meaning but misguided folk, coming on board to see their loved ones off on a voyage, loading their friends' cabins with hot-house flowers. A basket of hot-house grapes instead, with six pots of Bovril, would bring grateful memories the third day at sea. Above all things to be avoided are quack remedies, or such dangerous drugs as cocaine, nitro-glycerine, or bromide of potassium. In ninety-nine cases out of a hundred, every passenger is ready for a good breakfast the third morning out, without any remedy but Nature's recuperation, and the odd hundredth is best left to the ship's doctor.

Clothing sorely exercises the intending traveller round the world, and, as a rule, twice too much is taken. I advise plenty of good woollen underclothing, two new tweed suits, light and

PREFACE

strong, a thin dress suit, a light overcoat, a good ulster, and a mackintosh, with three or four pairs of shoes of different strengths, buying tropical clothing on the spot as required.

It is much more costly to pay fares from place to place, than to make up your route before starting, buying a through ticket from Thos. Cook & Son. Wishing to be free to select my own routes and steamers, I took the former course. Here follow the fares I had to pay:

	£	s.	d.
Liverpool to Montreal (Allan line)	18	18	0
Montreal to Vancouver (Canadian Pacific Railway)	15	8	3
Vancouver to Yokohama (Sir Wm. Pearce's steamer)	36	9	2
Yokohama to Colombo (P. & O. steamer)	52	0	0
Colombo to Calcutta (ditto)	12	0	0
Calcutta, Benares, Lucknow, Cawnpore, Agra, Delhi, Jeypore to Bombay, by rail	12	0	0
Bombay to Brindisi (P. & O. steamer)	63	0	0
Brindisi to London (by rail)	12	8	0
Total	£222	3	5

Messrs. Thos. Cook & Son can supply through tickets covering all these journeys for £155 18s. 8d., so that if I had booked through at starting, I should have saved £66 on each of my fares. I have not included in the list of separate fares the extras I paid for securing whole cabins for my daughter and myself.

I advise intending travellers round the world to fix their route, and take a through ticket from Cook. The £66 saved would more than suffice to secure the unspeakable comfort of a whole cabin, when the steamers were at all crowded. We indulged in this luxury crossing the Atlantic and Pacific, at an extra cost of £30 each, and felt it to be the most profitable expenditure made on our whole journey.

It is well to have a small medicine chest. Ships' doctors are often very young and inexperienced, and in out-of-the-way places native doctors are not to be trusted, and the drugs are bad. In remote Japan, the almost universal treatment for disease of any kind is to stick the patient's body, in all safe places, full of needles. Any family doctor will be able to give a list of tinctures and compressed drugs, such as those manufactured by Wyeth, or Burroughs Welcome and Co., obtainable through any good chemist, with simple instructions for treating the ailments incidental to travel. They will pack into a small box about six inches cube. It is true I presented my own box intact to a medical missionary just before leaving India, but the knowledge that in cases where doctors were available, I had the best quality of drugs likely to be required, added greatly to my comfort of mind all through the journey.

A six months' tour round the world can be done economically, travelling first-class throughout, for about £350; luxuriously, with exclusive cabins, for £420 to £450.

I can confidently recommend to travellers in Japan my two guides, Mr. Ito and Mr. Hakodate, both of whom are to be found at the Grand Hotel, Yokohama.

CONTENTS.

CHAPTER I.

FROM LIVERPOOL TO QUEBEC.

The "Sarmatian"—The Antrim coast—Our fellow passengers—Atlantic bills of fare—Belle Isle Strait—The aurora borealis—The Seamen's Orphanage—Miss Macpherson and her lambs—Contumacious anti-vaccinators—Quebec 1

CHAPTER II.

MONTREAL.

Par ici—British swagger—Old Quebec—The St. Lawrence—Mount Royal—The "Windsor"—The Lachine rapids—The two bridges—The president of the Canadian Pacific—Protection and the iron trade 14

CHAPTER III.

NIAGARA.

Our first journey on the C. P. R.—Toronto "side"—Its university—Its churches—Niagara—American advertising horrors—The falls—The rapids—The whirlpool—Niagara in winter—The Welland canal and locks—Railway *versus* canal—A Canadian homestead—A farmer's life — Apples — New London — Lake Huron — The "Alberta"—Soult St. Marie—Lake Superior—Thunder Bay .. 25

CHAPTER IV.

WINNIPEG.

Port Arthur—Once more on the C. P. R.—Camping out—Trout and grasshoppers—Night in the train—Thirteen babies—Winnipeg—Who should emigrate—Wages and cost of living in Winnipeg—Farming prospects—Glenbeigh *versus* Manitoba 41

CHAPTER V.

CALGARY AND THE RANCHING COUNTRY.

The great Canadian prairie—The Assiniboine valley—Brandon—The Bell farm—Regina—The prairie fauna—Blackfeet—Natural gas—Calgary—Ranches—Stimson's Ranch—Cowboys and their prospects—The Sarcee Indians—Bull's Head—Indian swells—Eagle rib—The Leland Hotel—The Salvation Army—" Bravo, Ted !"—Prohibition of the liquor trade—The fire brigade—Electric light   .. 52

CHAPTER VI.

THE CANADIAN NATURAL PARK.

The Gap—Canmore—Dr. Brett's sanitarium—The panorama of the Rocky Mountains—The hot springs—An aristocratic boatman—The Bow river—Trout—Canoeing—Vermilion lake—Sunday at Banff—A prairie bishop—The national park and its ranger—The Spray river—Deer, bears, beavers, catamounts, panthers, and other fearful wild fowl—Fish—Forest fires—The Indians—The C. P. R. Hotel   68

CHAPTER VII.

THE SELKIRKS.

An early start—Silver city—Mount Lefroy—Summit lakes—Kicking Horse pass—Field—Mountain goats—Our bear hunt—Glacier House—Mount Sir Donald and its great glacier—The Hermit range—Stoney Creek—Avalanches and snow sheds—Roger's pass—Comfort on wheels—The great bend—The gold range—Thompson river—Fraser river—A train burnt—The Cariboo road—Agassiz—Harrison lake—Vancouver 93

CHAPTER VIII.

BRITISH COLUMBIA.

Five years ago and to-day—The Great Sound—Salmon runs—The candle fish—Herrings—Oysters—Dog-fish—Cod—Coal—Gold—Iron—Silver—Timber—The Douglas fir—The lumberer—The farmer—Climate—The Japan current—Victoria—Esquimault—Work and wages—The heathen Chinee   119

CONTENTS.   xvii

CHAPTER IX.
THE TEMPERANCE MOVEMENT IN CANADA.

PAGE

Sober habits of Canadians generally—Women—The churches—History of legislation—Prohibition for the North-West—The Scott Act—Has it succeeded?—A stepping stone to prohibition   132

CHAPTER X.
ACROSS THE PACIFIC.

Bad management of Sir Wm. Pearce's steamers—Delays—The "Port Victor"—Confusion and overcrowding—Extra Chinamen—Cockroaches—A popular captain—Life on the Pacific—Chinamen's meals—"Chin-chin Joss"—A typhoon—A volcano—Japan at last   145

CHAPTER XI.
YOKOHAMA.

The "City of Sydney" in a typhoon—Yokohama—The bund—The bay—Ships of all nations—The Grand Hotel—Jin-rickishas—Shops—Flower-sellers—Bed!—England v. America—Funerals—Railways—Agriculture—Utsunomiya—The merry Jap—Babies—A tea-house—The bath—Food—O-hy-o—Straw-clothes—Jin-rickisha men—Cryptomeria Avenue—Road-side incidents   153

CHAPTER XII.
NIKKO.

A Japanese hotel—Curio dealers—Nikko the "sunny splendour"—Nantai-san—Images of Amida Buddha—Nikko the holy—The sacred lacquered bridge—The Torii—The pagoda—The gate of the two kings—The holy water cistern—The library—The Korean lantern—Yo-mei-mon—The cloister—The carved panels—The Chinese gate—The inner sanctuary—The tomb of the mighty Shogun—Iye-mitsu's temples—The Wind God—The Thunder God—The Kara mon—Iye-mitsu's tomb—Enno Shokaku, the sturdy-legged—Chiu-sen-je—Travelling in Kagos—The Mikado's birthday—Kamakura—The great Daibutz or Bronze Buddha—A Japanese feast—Sea-fishery—Sunday at Yokohama—Christianity in Japan—Fuji-yama—A Japanese mail steamer—Vries island—Kioto   ..   173

b

CHAPTER XIII.

SOCIAL LIFE IN JAPAN.

Population—Work and wages—Cost of living—Education—The Dragon pond school—A pretty picture—**Little maids** from school—The university—The Emperor and his ministers—Local government—Religion—Justice—Army—Navy—**Exports and imports**—Foreigners—Amusements—Music—Dancing—**Theatres**—The children's street—Singing and dancing girls—Holidays 205

CHAPTER XIV.

JAPANESE ARTS AND MANUFACTURES.

The Mikado's palace—The old castle of the Shoguns—Marvellous paintings and carvings—Decorations—A tea garden—Mr. Gladstone's portrait—"Waiting for the young Mikado"—Lacquer working—Porcelain—Inlaying in gold and silver—Bronze—The inland sea—Nagasaki—Japanese martyrs—Pappenburg island .. 219

CHAPTER XV.

HONG KONG.

The Ladrones—Piracy—The harbour—Typhoons—"Too much piecy top-side"—Stick—English town—China town—Shops—The Hill of Great Peace—Street scenes—The Governor and Government House—Kowloong—Chinese fishing—Revenue and expenditure—Water—The council—Missionaries—Shipping and commerce—Work and wages—Crime 232

CHAPTER XVI.

SINGAPORE.

Coolie swindlers—The tropics at last—The heat—Singapore—The botanical gardens, an open-air hothouse!—The cathedral—The sailors' rest—English town—Malay town—China town—The twenty-five nationalities of Singapore—Dress—Locomotion—Markets—Ducks—Fish—Fruit—Whampoa's garden—**The harbour** and docks—Fortifications—Revenue and expenditure—Opium and drink—The Government—Missionaries—Trade and commerce—Sir Hugh Low—Penang—A curry breakfast 246

CHAPTER XVII.

KANDY.

Spicy breezes—Ceylon in sight and smell—Point de Galle—Adam's peak—Colombo—Catamarans—The Kandy railway—Country sights—A 6000-feet railway climb—Sensation Rock—Kandy—The sacred tooth of Buddha — Horrible beggars — Kandy—The Peradenia Garden—Dr. Triman—Keep off the grass—leeches and snakes—Palms of all sorts—Jack-fruit—Ferns—Creepers—Giant bamboos—Squirrels—Tropical birds—Tipsy flying foxes—Nuwera Eliya—An imitation England—The Hakgala gardens—The jungle—Elephants—Leopards—Cheetahs—Eagles—Rest-houses—Ramboda 261

CHAPTER XVIII.

COLOMBO.

A. M. and J. Ferguson—Princely hospitality—Sir John Coode's great breakwater—The Grand Oriental—Pedlars and precious stones—Market place—Cingalese men and women—Bullock carts—Street scenes—Population—Religion—The devil dancer—Missionaries and Christianity—The Salvation Army—Education—Mrs. Pigott's school for Cingalese girls—Arabi the exile 277

CHAPTER XIX.

THE RESOURCES OF CEYLON.

The blessings of seventy years of British rule—Crops—Exports—Coffee planting—Tea — Chinchona—Cacao— Cardamoms—Plumbago mining—Condition of the poor—Trade and commerce—Government—Work and wages—Governor's monuments—Intoxicating drink—Licensing system—Consumption of liquor—Intemperance and crime—Madras—Surf boats 291

CHAPTER XX.

CALCUTTA TO BENARES.

Thomas Cook and Son, benefactors!—Calcutta—The Hooghly—Our Christmas dinner — Beadon Square — Young Bengal — Indian railways—Country scenes—Benares—Dr. Lazarus—The Hindoo

gate of heaven—Buddhism—Sarnath—1454 temples—The bathing
ghâts—The Rain God—The Goddess of Small Pox—The observatory
—The Maharajah's launch—The well of healing—The well of
knowledge—The golden temple—Pictures from the "Arabian
Nights"—The sacred bull—Fakeers—The goddess Durga's temple
—Her monkeys—The mosque of Aurungzebe—The Ganges .. 307

CHAPTER XXI.
THE CITY OF THE GREAT MOGULS.

Agra—The river Jumna—The fort—The Delhi gate—The pearl
mosque—The great divan—The courtyard—The harem—The
Jasmine tower—The three pavilions—The glass palace—The view
from the terrace—The Taj-Mahal—Its beauty—The gardens—The
mausoleum—Moonlight—The jewelled tombs of Shah Jehan and
his beloved wife—The marble trellis—The great gateway—Sikandra
—Akbar's tomb—The gateway at Sikandra—Mausoleum of Prince
Etmad Dowlat—Fattehpur Sikri—The royal buildings—Akbar's
palace—The divers—The Fakeer's grave—Birbul's house—The
peacock throne—Mission work in Agra—Village life—Roadside
scenes—Work and wages 325

CHAPTER XXII.
DELHI.

One of the ancient cities of the world—Toglakabad—Timour the Tartar
—The Kutab-Minar—The mosque of Kutab-ul Islam—The iron
pillar—The tomb of Humayoun—Indrapat—Firozabad—Asoka's
pillar—The great Jumma Musjid—The fort of Delhi—The Chandni
Chowk—Merchants 350

CHAPTER XXIII.
JEYPORE TO BOMBAY.

Rajputana—Jeypore—The stables—Man-eating tigers—The Maharajah
—His park—Palace—Museum—Art gallery—College schools—
Hospital—School of Art—Prison—Picturesque street scenes—The
deserted city of Amber—An elephant ride—Alligators—Hindoo
Ascetics—The palace—Ajmere—The Dargah—The Mayo college

—The tank—The bazaars—Ahmedabad—Its trade—Sidi Said's marble window—The mosques—Rani Sipri's tomb and mosque—The Jain temple—Lonely Sarkhej—Bombay—The Parsees—The towers of silence—The caves of Elephanta 359

CHAPTER XXIV.

SOCIAL PROBLEMS IN INDIA.

The struggle for existence—Race differences—One of the poorest countries in the world—Average annual income of the people—Famine — Cholera — Taxation — Land tax — The usurer — The zemindar—The ryot—Education : primary, intermediate, University—Mission schools—Cultured natives and social reforms—Technical education—Loyalty of educated natives—Their desire for a share in the government of their country—The National Indian Congress—The Civil Service—The Indian Council 380

LIST OF ILLUSTRATIONS.

	DRAWN BY	PAGE
Jin-rickisha travelling in Japan	*John Pedder*	Frontispiece
Lahore Gate, Delhi	*H. Sheppard Dale*	title-page
Aurora Borealis	*W. S. Caine*	8
Quebec, from Point Levis	*J. Pedder*	16
Horse Shoe Fall, Niagara	,,	29
Whirlpool Rapids, Niagara	,,	31
Emery Hall, a Canadian Homestead	*W. S. Caine*	35
Sault St. Marie Lock, Lake **Superior**	*J. Pedder*	39
Thunder Cape, **Lake Superior**	*W. S. Caine*	40
A Manitoba **Homestead**	*J. Pedder*	49
Threshing **out Wheat-stacks** on the Prairie	,,	53
Railway Depôt, Brandon	,,	55
Calgary, with distant view of the Rocky Mountains	*W. S. Caine*	59
Bull's Head, the Sarcee Chief	*J. Pedder*	61
Sarcee Squaw and Pony Cart	,,	63
Eagle Rib, a Sarcee Chief	,,	64
"Bravo, Ted!" a Salvation Army incident	,,	65
The Gap: Entrance to the Rocky Mountains	,,	69
Canmore Rocks	,,	71
Castle Mountain	*W. S. Caine*	72
View of Banff from above the Sanatorium	,,	73
Bridge of Boats and Twin Peaks, Banff.	*J. Pedder*	77
Cascade Mountain	*W. S. Caine*	80
On the Bow River, Banff	*J. Pedder*	81
The Bow Falls	,,	83
Vermilion Lake, National Park, Banff	,,	85
A Forest Fire, National Park, Banff	,,	89
Canadian Pacific Railway Hotel, National Park, Banff.	,,	91
View in the Selkirks	*W. S. Caine*	92
Summit Lake	*J. Pedder*	93
Kicking Horse Pass	,,	95
Field Station	,,	97
The Monarchs of the Rocky Mountains	,,	99

LIST OF ILLUSTRATIONS.   xxiii

	DRAWN BY	PAGE
The Bear Hunt	J. Pedder	103
Snow Sheds	,,	105
Mount Sir Donald and the Great Glacier	W. S. Caine	107
The Great Bend of the Canadian Pacific Railway	J. Pedder	110
Roger's Pass: the Summit of the Selkirks	,,	111
An Indian Salmon Cache	,,	113
Salmon Cannery on the Fraser River	,,	116
Harrison Lake	W. S. Caine	117
The "Yosemite" leaving Vancouver	J. Pedder	119
Indians Salmon Fishing on the Fraser River	,,	121
Douglas Pines, Vancouver	,,	125
Esquimault Harbour	,,	129
The "Port Victor"	J. Pedder	146
Vries Volcano, Yokohama Bay	W. S. Caine	151
Tea House, Yokohama Bay	J. Pedder	154
Yokohama Harbour	,,	154
A Street in Yokohama	,,	155
Buying Chrysanthemums, Yokohama	,,	157
Group of Children, Utsunomiya	,,	162
Doll and Fan	,,	163
Interior of Tea House, Bedroom Floor	,,	165
Jin-rickisha Man in his Straw Rain-Coat	,,	167
The Road to Nikko	,,	168
The Hotel at Nikko	,,	174
Row of Buddhas at Nikko	W. S. Caine	176
The Pagoda, Nikko	H. Sheppard Dale	179
Holy Water Cistern, Nikko	,,	180
The Kio-zo, or Library, Nikko	,,	181
Korean Bronze Lantern, Nikko	,,	182
The Yo-mei-mon Gate, Nikko	,,	184
The Yo-mei-mon Cloisters, Nikko	,,	187
The Nio-mon Gate, entrance to the Temples of Iye-mitsu	,,	189
The Kara-mon Gate, Iye-mitsu's Temples	,,	190
The Chinese Gate, Iye-yasu's Temples	,,	191
On the Road to Chiu-sen-je	W. S. Caine	195
The Great Buddha, Kamakura	J. Pedder	197
Fuji-yama, the Sacred Mountain	W. S. Caine	201
Shooting the Rapids, Kioto	J. Pedder	203
A Shinto Priest	,,	211
Music, Japan	,,	214
Dancing Girl, Japan	,,	215
A Street Scene, Kioto	,,	227
The Inland Sea of Japan	W. S. Caine	229

LIST OF ILLUSTRATIONS.

	DRAWN BY	PAGE
Pappenburg Island, Nagasaki Harbour	W. S. Caine	230
The Kowloong Hills, Hong Kong Harbour	,,	233
Chinese Town, Hong Kong	J. Pedder	237
Singapore: a Mango Breakfast in July	Geo. Bickham	260
Adam's Peak, Ceylon	W. S. Caine	262
The Dekanda Valley, Ceylon	H. S. Dale	265
On the Kandy Railway—Sensation Rock	,,	266
The India-rubber Tree, Kandy	,,	269
The Giant Bamboo, Peradenia Gardens, Kandy	,,	272
Sir John Coode's Breakwater, Colombo	,,	281
Devil-dancer and Tom-tom, Ceylon	J. Pedder	285
A Cingalese Workman	H. S. Dale	297
A Village Shop, Ceylon	J. Pedder	303
In the Bay of Bengal	,,	306
The Bathing Ghats, Benares	,,	315
Nothing is Sacred to a Snake!	Geo. Bickham	320
The Jasmine Tower, Agra Fort	H. S. Dale	327
The Taj Mahal, from the Summit of the Great Gateway	J. Pedder	331
View from the Terrace of the Fort, Agra	,,	333
The Tomb of Akbar, Sikandra	,,	336
The Palace of Fattehpur Sikri	H. S. Dale	337
Birbul's House, Fattehpur Sikri	,,	341
The Mausoleum of Prince Etmad Dowlat	,,	343
The Kutab Minar, Delhi	J. Pedder	352
The Ruined City of Indrapat, Delhi	,,	354
The Jumma Musjid, Delhi	H. S. Dale	355
The Pearl Mosque, Delhi Fort	,,	357
Street Scene at Jeypore	J. Pedder	362
The Ruined City of Amber	,,	367
The Great Well of the Dargah, Ajmere	,,	369
Carved Window of the Mosque of Rani Sipri, Ahmedabad	H. S. Dale	371
Pierced Marble Window of Sidi's Said Mosque, Ahmedabad	,,	372
The Tomb of Rani Sipri, Ahmedabad	,,	374
Cave Temple of Elephanta	J. Pedder	378
Aden Harbour	,,	392

A TRIP ROUND THE WORLD.

CHAPTER I.

FROM LIVERPOOL TO QUEBEC.

ON Thursday afternoon, the 18th of August, I embarked with my eldest daughter on board the Allan liner "Sarmatian," on my voyage round the world.

Our first care on coming on board was to find our cabins, and get the luggage for the voyage safely stowed in them. I had wisely left the choice of the cabins to my old friends, Messrs. Allan Bros. & Co., and found they had provided for our accommodation the first officer's and purser's cabins, on the spar deck, so situated as to secure the minimum of motion with the maximum of fresh air. Compared with the accommodation furnished on an Atlantic liner for the ordinary passenger, which is humorously termed a "state-room," our cabins are little palaces, replete with every comfort. The officers turn a nimble ninepence during the summer months by letting their cabins for the voyage to passengers who like the extra accommodation, but find their luxury acceptable enough in the terrible voyages which they have often to endure in the winter. I write this letter in a room about 12 feet square, with four windows, a hot-water apparatus, a fine mahogany desk, a wardrobe, a chest of drawers, a wash-stand which disappears into a recess when not required, a large and comfortable sofa, and a bed. When the cabin passengers are sent to bed at ten o'clock, wakeful or sleepy, and their lights arbitrarily extinguished, I lie on my sofa reading by the light of a handsome duplex lamp till sleep comes without effort; then I turn in. I know no more fearful punishment for an unhappy Member of Parliament, trained by sad experience to sit up and keep awake till three in the morning, than to be sent to bed at ten, with his light, dim and unsatisfactory at the best, ruthlessly put out at half past, leaving him tumbling in bed at his very wakefullest moments.

We settled down in our comfortable cabins, put our clothes neatly away in the drawers, thankfully remembering other voyages when we have had to get to the bottom of portmanteaux while the ship was standing on her head, and then sallied forth for a tour of inspection round the ship which is to be our floating home for the next ten days.

The "Sarmatian" is a fine steamer of the second class. She has a speed of 13 to 14 knots, as her five full-day Atlantic runs on this voyage show, viz. 314, 318, 320, 322, 320 knots each day, giving a shade over 13 knots an hour. She carries a goodly family to provide for on the voyage. There are 631 souls on board—105 cabin, 85 intermediate, 325 steerage passengers, and a crew of 116.

The anchor is weighed at five o'clock, and soon New Brighton fort and lighthouse, the various lightships and the foaming sandy bar of the Mersey, drop astern one by one, and we take our last look of England for six months, going to bed to dream of home and friends, mingled with intermittent visions of the Rocky Mountains, the Flowery Land, the Mikado, "the spicy breezes that blow o'er Ceylon's isle," and the horrors of sea-sickness.

August 19th.—We wake up to find ourselves running close in

along the Antrim coast, which gives us some of the finest scenery in the kingdom. I am glad to view from the sea points of interest I had previously enjoyed on shore. Garron Head and Fair Head were well in sight, then, passing through the strait between Rathlin Island and the mainland, Carrick-a-Rede, with its terrible rope bridge 120 feet in the air, the organ rock of the Giant's Causeway, the rising watering-place of Portrush follow in rapid succession, and at eleven o'clock we steam into Lough Foyle, and drop anchor off Moville to wait for the mails

A magnificent Atlantic steamer is already there, and my thoughts fly off to my constituency as I recognise the good work of the Barrow Shipbuilding Company in the Anchor liner "Devonia."

The mails come on board by four o'clock, and away we go. By nine the light of Tory Island disappears, and we are rocked upon the bosom of the treacherous Atlantic, with a breeze fresh enough to send us to bed with mingled fears and hopes for the morrow's breakfast.

August 20th.—The hopes have it! It is fairly calm, and but few passengers are absent from table. The glass has fallen a trifle during the night, and the bill of fare is scanned carefully with a view to wholesome dishes. The choice is varied: you may have tea or coffee, rolls, toast, potato scones, brown and white bread, corn-meal bread, oat cake and porridge, beefsteak and onions, savoury omelette, fried fish, Finnan haddie, sausages, bacon, grilled bones, cold ham, tongue and beef, eggs and marmalade. The morning keeps fine, and the saloon deck presents the usual aspect. Ladies are grouped about in pleasant corners in easy deck-chairs, reading (yellow-back novels mostly), chatting, and working. Shuffle-board, a sort of deck bagatelle, and rope quoits, are in full swing, and we all go about making acquaintance with one another. The bright keen-looking gentleman, with white hair and a clean shaved face, is Sir Alexander Galt, a well-known Canadian politician, who was at one time Finance Minister. He has spent four years of a long and useful life on board Atlantic steamers, having crossed and recrossed from Canada to England more than 100 times. He is in conversation with Mr. Gibbs, Q.C., one of the leaders of the Northern Circuit, who is spending a well-earned long vacation in Canada and the United States. That active cleverfaced lady, who seems almost ubiquitous, is Miss Macpherson, who is taking 47 orphan lads from London slums to Canada. The breezy fellow in a yachting cap, whom every one says is the purser, is J. P. Sheldon, Professor of Agriculture at Downton College, near Salisbury, and a defeated aspirant for Parliamentary honours, who is going to Canada to report on the farming resources of the North-West Provinces on behalf of the Dominion Government, the Canadian Pacific Railway, and the Allan Line, all of which august bodies are jointly interested in the commission. The Japanese gentleman, who leans against the smoke-room door puffing his cigarette, is the head of a firm of engineers and shipbuilders in Tokio employing 400 hands, and I have already made an appointment to go over his works with him in October. The bright jolly-looking young lady watching the gulls astern is a teacher in the Girls' Collegiate Institute at Toronto. The eager pale face, whose earnest grey eyes look out of gold-rimmed spectacles, belongs to a young missionary, who, years ago, was taken from the London gutter by Miss Macpherson, and is going to join the China inland mission. The sturdy young fellow who walks the deck with him is another of Miss Macpherson's lambs, also destined for China, but who in the meantime is to have a winter's colportage work at Toronto. . . . But there goes the luncheon bell, and the deck clears like magic.

For this meal we have excellent hot soup, cold meats of all kinds, cold fresh salmon, salad, sardines, stewed fruit, pastry, and cheese. It is a light and trivial meal compared with breakfast and dinner.

The afternoon is mostly spent in slumber, induced by the strong, fresh Atlantic breeze, through which we are bowling along at the rate of 14 miles an hour; but every one wakes up at the sound of the dinner bell, the event of the day to those who are able for it. This is indeed a meal. Here is the bill of fare :—

Soup.

Mulligatawny.   Vermicelli.

Fish.

Boiled salmon.   Parsley sauce.

Entrées.

Grilled pigeons and mushrooms.   Veal and ham pie.
Fillet of beef à la Francaise.   Vol au vent of lobster.

Roast.

Beef and Yorkshire pudding.   Lamb and mint sauce.
Sucking pig and currant sauce.   Gosling and apple sauce.

Boiled.

Fowls and lemon sauce.   Mutton and caper sauce.
Ham.   Tongue.   Beef.

Vegetables.

Plain and mashed potatoes.   Broad beans.

Puddings and pastry.

Jam rolls.   Rice puddings.   Rhubarb pie.
Plum pie.   Italian cream.   Apple charlotte.
Lemon cheese cakes.   Marmalade tartlets.

Dessert.

Apples, oranges, plums, raisins, figs, nuts, tea, and coffee.

There is a slight roll getting up, and I notice with interest that boiled fowl and rice pudding are in great demand, and that sucking pig, gosling, vol au vent, jam rolls, and lemon cheese cakes are not much sought after.

The lavish profusion of the bills of fare in Atlantic liners always seems to me very unnecessary; but as there are 116 in the crew, and sometimes 500 to 800 steerage passengers, I suppose the enormous surplus gets eaten up somewhere.

The intermediate passengers fare quite as well as the saloon, but with a simpler list of viands. The steerage passengers have for breakfast fresh bread and butter, porridge, Irish stew, tea and coffee; for dinner, soup, hot joints, potatoes, and bread; for tea, bread and butter and tea; for supper, oatmeal porridge. When the weather is decent their capacity for innocent enjoyment in the way of food is astounding. There are biscuits *ad libitum* at eleven, so that I was not surprised to hear a fat German emigrant say, "Himmel! vot a ship! Five square meals a day, and noding extra to pay!"

To-night we run into the tail-end of a gale, and soon find out how utterly miserable 500 people can be at sea. The ship is largely laden with steel rails—as a member of the iron trade, I was glad to hear this at starting, but before night was over I was fain to wish they were at the bottom of the mine instead of the bottom of the "Sarmatian." Their dead-weight caused the ship to roll like a pendulum, and it was impossible to sleep. I sat up reading all night, and at breakfast next morning it was found that quite two-thirds of the passengers were badly under the weather, my daughter among the rest. This roll continued more or less during the 21st, 22nd, and 23rd, to the vast discomfort of everybody; but on the 24th we entered the great Labrador current, and all were happy. The temperature, however, fell to about 42 degrees, and everybody was glad to rummage up their warm clothes. The wind was fresh and keen, blowing straight "from Greenland's icy mountains." This great current flows continuously at the rate of about two miles an hour direct from the Arctic sea, and every one was on the lookout for the icebergs which it brings down into the Atlantic. None appeared, however, though the captain told me next morning that he had passed three large ones during the night in Belle Isle Strait.

We have now got away from the Atlantic and are bowling across the Gulf of St. Lawrence. The air blows fresh and bracing off Labrador, but the sun is bright, and all on board are happy and joyous. We see whales blowing for the first time on the voyage, and much excitement is caused by a hawk settling in the rigging, completely spent by its flight, for we are far out of sight of land. The sailors tried to catch it, but it hopped feebly from spar to spar, and they failed. During the afternoon, after three or four hours' rest, it suddenly sped landwards, and we saw it no more. Sometime afterwards a small finch paid us a similar visit, but we were then much nearer land.

This evening I had sat up rather late reading, and going on deck for a little fresh air at midnight before turning in, I found the whole northern sky ablaze with Aurora Borealis. Of course I have often seen at home what we call "Northern lights," but now I beheld the real thing of which I had often read in books of Arctic travel, and its weird beauty is beyond all description. Even here it is only seen in perfection at rare intervals. The light sprang in a great arch, like a low rainbow, from horizon to horizon. The sky beneath the arch was black as ink, but with one star bright enough to show that it was as clear below as it was above. The arch was a wide band of strong well-defined light, out of which sprang curling clouds of vapoury-looking flames, and sharp spears of light flying up almost into the zenith. The light given by this beautiful phenomenon was as strong as the full moon, and I do not think I ever saw a more beautiful sky, by day or night.

AURORA BOREALIS.
From a sketch by the Author.

The 26th finds us in bad weather again. Rain all day, with a heavy sea rolling up into the Gulf direct from the Atlantic. At night thick fog, half-speed, and the steam whistle murdering sleep; but the morning of the 27th brings us into calm water and fine weather, the ship running within three or four miles of the coast of Gaspé, well into the mouth of the St. Lawrence.

At the request of a number of the passengers, a large proportion of whom are teetotallers, I gave an address on the Temperance Movement on deck this afternoon. This vessel affords fresh proof of the rapid strides with which the Temperance Reformation has advanced of late years. In conversation with Mr. Heaton, the pleasant and courteous gentleman who acts as chief steward, he tells me that the change which has come over the drinking habits of the saloon passengers during the last ten years is very remarkable. Turning up his books for 1878, he showed me entries of over £120 paid in a single voyage for strong liquors by forty-five cabin passengers. This voyage 105 passengers will not spend £30. Nearly half the Canadians on board are abstainers, and of those who are not, few drink at their meals. Only thirteen passengers take wine or beer at dinner, and these are English. I am within the mark in saying that fully half the intermediate and steerage passengers are teetotallers.

This evening a concert was given on behalf of that most valuable charity, the Liverpool Seamen's Orphanage, and a handsome collection was taken. A large number of the 750 children cared for by this institution have lost their fathers by the perils of the sea crossing the Atlantic, incurred while conveying passengers and cargo to and from America. There is no class of the community needing an orphanage to the same extent as seamen. Since this institution was founded sixteen years ago, more than 40,000 British seamen have been drowned at sea, and 27,000 more have died in foreign ports. It is a disgrace to us as a maritime nation that 2,500 of our seamen should thus find a watery grave every year, and only such legislation as that which Mr. Joseph Chamberlain vainly endeavoured to make law will cope with this terrible loss of life. A large amount of money is secured for the orphanage by means of concerts and other entertainments, and the collection on Sundays on board all Atlantic liners is devoted to this object.

I have been much interested in the children who are being taken out by Miss Macpherson for adoption by Canadian farmers. Miss Macpherson does not emigrate pauper children, but rather seeks those children who are on the edge of the workhouse schools, and who, but for her interference, would quickly find themselves there. Let me give the stories of two or three of these on board as a sample of the whole.

A. B. is a lad who was found ten years ago by a city missionary in an underground cellar; he was then about four years old, and nothing could be discovered as to his belongings. He was taken to the Islington Boys' Home, and has been recommended as a good willing boy suitable for emigration to Canada.

C. D. was a gutter arab, motherless, son of a drunken father who beat and starved him. He drifted into a boys' home at Winchester, and now, at fifteen years of age, is off "to reap and mow, to plough and sow, and be a farmer's boy" in Canada. He is a bright, sharp lad, full of expectation and hope, and will do well. There are a dozen such lads among the forty-seven on board, but sometimes the facts are reversed by the father being dead and the mother gone to the bad, while others have lost both parents, the loss being the lad's gain.

E. F. is a bright, sharp little girl of ten, delighted with the ship and all on board, the pet of the steerage. When I asked her how she liked her cabin, she said, "Jolly! I've got a whole soap-box all to myself for a bed." This was the realisation of her wildest notion of luxury. Hitherto, if she had had a soap-box at all, she shared it with other children. Her father was drowned at sea, and she has been half starved by an unsatisfactory mother all her life. She is about half the size she ought to be.

G. H. is a lad who has been deserted by his parents, who fell at once into kind hands. A lady in his neighbourhood pays the cost of his emigration.

Many of the children have been rescued from horrible ill-treatment at the hands of step-fathers and step-mothers, others have been adopted by Miss Macpherson out of large poor families, whose parents seem glad enough to let them go, and others are orphans from various boys' homes.

All these children are purged as far as possible from the evil influences of their past lives by the kind and judicious treatment they receive in Miss Macpherson's homes in England and Canada. Their excellent behaviour on board ship, under the relaxed discipline which is inevitable from the sea-sickness of their superintendents, speaks volumes for their brief training, and they live in the continual praise of all the passengers.

Miss Macpherson has taken out to Canada altogether four thousand four hundred of these waifs and strays, every one of whom would otherwise have gone to swell the ranks of the dangerous or pauper classes. The results fully justify her action. Two thousand five hundred are now comfortably settled on Canadian farms, the adopted children rather than the servants of the farmers. Five hundred have been formally adopted by childless people, another five hundred have been put out in trades, over two hundred are married and doing well; some, of course, have died, but of the whole lot only seven have turned out hopelessly bad, and are now in reformatories with whatever poor chance those institutions afford for a fresh start in life.

All wonder at this happy result vanishes before an hour's chat with the gracious Christian lady who is the life and soul of it all. This emigration of poor children is but an incident in the noble life of Miss Macpherson, and is her solution of one aspect of the sorrow and suffering passing under her notice in her work among the densely-crowded districts of East London. These poor children, taken away from their horrible surroundings in time, grow up useful God-fearing citizens of Canada, and often rise to good positions. More than a score are in professions, and one of the brightest and most intelligent men I ever met, now going out on this ship, destined for a missionary's life, is one of Miss Macpherson's rescued boys.

Probably no man is better acquainted with the inner social life of Canada than Sir Alexander Galt. He has fully confirmed me in the deeply favourable impression I have formed of Miss Macpherson and her work, and assures me that in his judgment no one person is at this time promoting to the same extent the real interests of the Dominion of Canada.

I was not surprised to hear from Miss Macpherson that she utterly refused to emigrate children who had once entered the doors of a workhouse school. My own experience as a Guardian of one of the largest unions in London confirms her wisdom. I wish every one of these detestable and costly institutions were abolished and the boarding-out system made universal; but this is a domestic issue that pertains not to the story of a voyage round the world.

I do not wonder that Dr. Barnardo, and others who have the care of orphan children of the very poor, are following Miss Macpherson's noble example. May God bless her and her patriotic work! It is, indeed, "something accomplished, something done," to have turned 5,000 street arabs from probable thieves and lost women into prosperous Canadian farmers and happy wives and mothers.

We are now running up the St. Lawrence, and an amusing incident has just occurred. The Dominion Government have a law that no one shall enter Canada who has not been vaccinated during the last seven years. Yesterday the ship's doctor went through all the intermediate and steerage passengers, examined their arms, and informed those who had not recently been vaccinated that they would not be let ashore without a fortnight's quarantine on an island unless they submitted to his lancet. About four dozen were operated upon; but a Wesleyan minister and another flatly refused even to show their arms. A medical officer of health came on board at Rimouski at one o'clock this morning, and the two recalcitrants were roused out of bed to face him. They continued obstinate, and were in consequence reported by telegraph to the Quarantine Station, whose officer has just stopped the ship. The martyrs have broken down at last, on seeing their luggage placed upon the quarantine launch, and, with much indignation, have submitted to vaccination. They do not seem to have had scruples about vaccination itself, but refused on what seems to me the very just ground that the saloon passengers have been entirely exempt from the operation of the law. There were no exemptions in the original Act, until it was found that saloon passengers were exempted from a similar law in the United States, and that in consequence saloon passenger traffic was being diverted from Quebec to New York.

Shortly after lunch the picturesque city of Quebec hove in sight, and the "Sarmatian" steamed alongside the wharf at Point Levis, the terminus of the Grand Trunk Railway, on the opposite side of the great river.

We have had a delightful and prosperous voyage, the pleasantest of all the five journeys I have made across the Atlantic; but we are all glad to see land again, and to rush off to the telegraph office to send word to those at home that we have arrived safe and well.

CHAPTER II.

QUEBEC TO MONTREAL.

As soon as the medical officer had issued his fiat permitting the passengers to go ashore, my daughter and I started off for the ferry, determined to see all we could of Quebec in the three hours before the steamer once more started off up the river to Montreal.

It seemed ridiculous on British territory to be hailed in French by a car-driver, to read the shop-signs in French and English, with even such simple directions as were needed to point the road to the steam ferry, being given in both languages, thus—

THIS WAY!
PAR ICI!

And yet I am told that if any public institution such as a steam ferry omitted the "Par ici" it would bring about an immediate revolution. Quebec is as French as Boulogne—yet as loyal to the British Crown as Folkestone. The ancient province of Lower Canada has maintained unimpaired the language and religion of its original settlers. Three-fourths of its population are French-speaking Roman Catholics. French customs, language, and laws remain intact, though the British flag waves from its citadel. Champlain, the famous navigator, who discovered and settled Quebec, established a fort, a trading station, and a chapel. The Quebec of to-day is simply an enlargement

QUEBEC, FROM POINT LEVIS.

of all three. The town lies on a tongue of land under the shelter of a bold cliff 350 feet above the water, with the Charles River protecting it on the landward side. The citadel crowns the hill, and all round are forts and bastions commanding every point of the river. The whole forms a fortress that would be impregnable if armed with modern guns, and which would hold the gates of Canada against any navy that could be sent to force them. The armaments, however, are of an ancient and obsolete character, with the exception of three Armstrong guns of about six or seven tons weight, which escaped the fire of last year. There is, however, a brass howitzer, on which is engraved, "This gun was captured at the battle of Bunkers Hill"—a bit of British swagger which greatly amuses Yankee visitors, who are apt to remark, "Wal, if you have the gun, I guess we've got the hill!"

There are few more picturesque towns in the world than Quebec. As we steamed away up the St. Lawrence, the lofty citadel and its satellite forts, with the quaint old French town nestling under its protection, were all one dark purple mass against a glorious sunset sky, relieved only by the twinkling lights of the houses and streets, just blinking into notice as the day darkened and closed—a scene of beauty not easily to be forgotten. Quebec is going down hill. It was a melancholy place for a business man to visit ten years ago, when I was there seeking custom for English iron, but it seemed to me sadder than ever in the walk we took through the business streets. It still maintains its supremacy as the great seat of the timber trade; but as that trade finds its way to the sea more and more by the great network of railways which centre in Montreal, lumber will follow wheat and locate itself in the up-river port, to the neglect of poor old Quebec.

Sunday morning, August 28th, found us 50 miles above

Quebec, on the broad bosom of the St. Lawrence, the great highway of the Dominion of Canada, and the outlet of the greatest body of fresh water in the world. The vast inland seas of Superior, Huron, Erie, Michigan, Ontario, Nepigon, and Champlain, besides a thousand lakes of less degree, pour out to the Atlantic past the citadel of Quebec. This noble river drains an area of over 400,000 square miles of territory, and contains more than half the fresh water of the globe. The total length of its course is over 2,000 miles, and its principal port, Montreal, is 150 miles distant from salt water. By the aid of the Welland Canal three-masted vessels with 1,500 or 2,000 tons of wheat in their holds can load at Port Arthur on Lake Superior, 1,200 miles from the sea, and after traversing the St. Lawrence, cross the Atlantic and discharge their cargoes at Liverpool or Barrow.

The St. Lawrence from Quebec to Montreal is from one to three miles wide. Its banks are thickly populated by the descendants of the early French Settlers, every village clustering round a fine Roman Catholic Church, whose tin roofs and spires glitter in the morning sun. The people are very poor, and have been rendered so by a bad system of sub-division of land similar to that which prevails in many parts of Ireland. The *habitants*, as these French Canadians are called, are a hardy, thrifty race; their young men form the great strength of the lumber trade, and a backwoodsman would move Mr. Gladstone to amazement and envy by the way in which he can wield the axe.

About three o'clock in the afternoon the wooded heights of Mount Royal appear above the low river banks, and the passengers throng into the bows of the ship for the first view of that city of churches, Montreal. As we round the last bend of the river, the fine stone quays, flanked by a long mile of noble warehouses, overtopped by a hundred spires and domes, the whole set in the olive-green of Mount Royal, form a fine panorama. In less than an hour we are fast to the Allan Wharf. A polite customs officer declines to suspect a British M.P. of smuggling. Our luggage is placed in the hotel waggon, and we jolt through the disgracefully paved streets to the Windsor Hotel, a marble palace of 800 rooms, which condescends to board and lodge its visitors handsomely for 17s. 6d. a day. We certainly had no reason to complain of the treatment we received. The head clerk, on seeing my name, asked me if I was not a British Member of Parliament. I owned the soft impeachment, and, knowing what a mixed lot we are, waited with trepidation the effect. Should I be refused admission, or be huddled away in some garret? To my great delight we were ushered into a gorgeous apartment, consisting of a large drawing-room and two spacious bedrooms, with fine bath-rooms attached. I protested that this splendour was quite beyond my means, but was at once politely assured that I was, so far as these handsome rooms were concerned, the guest of the landlords of the "Windsor."

Monday, August 29th.—We rose betimes to catch the 7.45 train for Lachine, a pretty village which stands at the head of the chain of locks which raises the water traffic of the St. Lawrence over the far-famed Lachine Rapids, which it was our intention presently to descend in a steamer. It was a glorious morning, the hot sun tempered with a touch of autumn frost, which threw a thin veil of mist over the river, and its beautiful wooded banks and islands. The steamer left the moorings under the care of an ancient half-breed Indian pilot, who steers her into the broad expanse of river which spreads out above the fall. The old explorer Jacques Cartier took it for a fresh ocean, that would, if he dared venture to cross it, lead him on to

China; standing on its shores, exclaiming "*La Chine! La Chine!*" he little thought that 350 years later the Canadian Pacific Railway would cross the point on which he stood, carrying passengers and mails from Europe to China in the short space of five weeks. Soon the broad river narrows into a width of about two miles, and the increased speed of the vessel lets us know that we are nearing the great Lachine Rapids. The pace becomes tremendous as she leaps into the roaring cataract. Standing in the bows, it seems as if nothing could save the steamer from being dashed to pieces on the mighty rocks which split the stream; but the skilful pilot drives her down between the two biggest, which almost brush the vessel's sides, and in another minute we are paddling down a gentle ripple, and Montreal, glistening in the morning sun, comes into view.

The interest of this delightful little trip, which hardly lasts two hours, has been greatly enhanced by the magnificent cantilever bridge by which the Canadian Pacific Railway crosses the St. Lawrence at the head of the Lachine Rapids, seeking an outlet for its western traffic through St. John and Halifax and the New England States. This bridge is built on the same lines and plan as the well-known Tay Bridge in Scotland. The steamer swept under it with such speed that all detail was lost, leaving only on the memory the impression of the lightest and most beautiful iron structure I had ever seen.

Montreal can boast the possession of two of the finest bridges in the world, for the great rival of the Canadian Pacific, the older Grand Trunk, owns the famous Victoria Tubular Bridge, which was designed by Robert Stephenson, built by Peto, Brassey, and Betts, and formally opened by the Prince of Wales in 1860. This bridge connects lower Canada with the United States, and carries off all the Montreal traffic during the six months of winter when the St. Lawrence is blocked with ice. This stupendous work cost £1,200,000. It stands upon 26 piers, and the centre is about 60 feet above the level of the river. It is over 3,000 yards long, and contains three million cubic feet of masonry, and over 8,000 tons of iron. It links together the system of the Grand Trunk Railway, which on both sides of the St. Lawrence embraces some 2,200 miles of road.

After breakfast I called at the offices of the Canadian Pacific Railway, and made the acquaintance of its president, Sir George Stephen, Bart., and Mr. Van Horne, its vice-president and general-manager. They were good enough to give me nearly three hours of their valuable time, and allowed me to see their rate-books, and classification-books, and gave me much information of great interest to a Member of Parliament who had served for two years on "The Select Committee on Railway Rates."

The rest of the afternoon I spent in calling upon the many old friends in the iron trade who, before I became absorbed in politics, were valued customers, and to whom I used to export iron and other metals. Much of our conversation naturally turned on the recent heavy increase of the import duties on iron and steel, which has so much excited the indignation of our iron trade at home. I found an almost universal opinion, in which I fully share, that these protective duties will not be sufficient to call into existence any important rolling-mills within the Dominion, though it may do something for iron and steel manufactured goods. The duty on finished iron is raised from 17s. 6d. per ton to £3. The first result of this will be to drive the iron trade into the hands of great capitalist merchants, and to squeeze out small dealers and importers. A dealer could, under the old duty, buy a stock of 500 tons of merchant iron from England and put it duty paid into his warehouse for about £3,200, and as he could obtain four to six months' credit from English merchants for £2,500 of that amount, he only required £700 in cash capital to pay freight and duties. By the increase in the tariff he finds this amount suddenly raised upon him to some £1,700, and unless he can immediately bring an extra £1,000 in hard cash into his business he must either reduce his stock or be otherwise crippled. In all my business experience, I have always found these sudden changes in tariff rates the most disturbing element I have had to cope with.

The strong protests which were made, at the time the tariff was changed, by the English iron trade, were successful in inducing the Canadian Government to make some important alterations in favour of Great Britain, so far as it affects the interests of the mother country and the rival interests of foreign countries. A memorandum has been recently issued by the Canadian Minister of Finance, which endeavours to show how far the tariff changes are actually beneficial to British manufactures. An analysis of the imports into Canada of iron and steel and manufactures thereof exhibits the remarkable fact that while five years ago Great Britain contributed 55 per cent. of the dutiable and 94 per cent. of the free imports of these goods, last year the proportion from that country had declined to 50 per cent. and 86 per cent. These figures are put forward with some justice, as showing a drift of trade from British to foreign iron producers, and the Finance Minister contends that if the old tariff had remained in operation the Canadian market must in time have passed under the control of the manufacturers of the United States, Belgium, and Germany. I do not believe this myself; but if the conviction has come home to the Finance Minister, and induced him to vary the tariff with a view to preventing it, we need not complain.

I never could understand the infatuation of new countries

for Protection. For years past Canada has been paying 50 per cent. more for every article of clothing than we pay in England, with a view to creating textile industries of her own Yesterday I went through the largest retail drapery store in Canada, containing every kind of textile fabrics for both sexes. The owner admitted to me that he had not in his store, from cellar to attic, five shillings' worth of Canadian manufactures. The one great pleasure of Canada is fishing. Yesterday I bought a green heart trout rod; in England it would have cost me 21*s*.—I paid 32*s*.; two dozen trout flies, 8*s*. per dozen—the same flies in England would cost 2*s*.; gut casting lines, 4*s*. each instead of 1*s*. 3*d*.—and all imported from England. I asked specially for a Canadian-made rod, but the dealer hadn't got one fit for fly-fishing; all his stock had come from England or the States in spite of 30 per cent. protective duty.

The duties on foreign iron in the United States practically double the price of iron all over that country, yet fail to keep out foreign competition. The total importations of manufactured iron and steel productions into the States last fiscal year were 100,000 tons in excess of the two previous years combined. During the fiscal year just ended the States imported 1,524,000 tons, against a total in the two years of 1885-1886 of 1,445,000. The same appears in iron ore, last year showing 1,142,000 tons imported, against a total of 1,127,000 in the two years previous. There seems to be no signs of any diminution of this great import. I do not wonder to read this week in a leading New York commercial paper that "indications warrant the belief that the heavy importations of manufactured iron and steel production to this country are a very serious menace to the industrial prosperity of America. The pertinent inquiry arises—"How much longer can this country keep on importing foreign iron and steel in such enormous quantities without precipitating a first-class collapse in the iron and steel industries?"

I have no fear whatever of any disastrous result to the English iron trade from Canadian Protective tariffs. Canada will continue to buy from us in increasing quantities; and if any capitalist is fool enough to start extensive iron-works in the Dominion, they will end in what the Yankees call a "first-class collapse."

CHAPTER III.

NIAGARA.

On Tuesday morning, August 31st, we left Montreal for Toronto by the new route of the Canadian Pacific Railway, which passes through a thinly-settled district of some beauty abounding in lakes and streams. In 380 miles we only passed two towns of any size—Perth, the centre of a good farming district, in which many Irish have located themselves, and Peterborough, placed on the Otonabee River, which here falls about 150 feet in nine miles, furnishing water-power for many corn and lumber mills. At the end of 12 hours we reached the great capital of the province of Ontorio—Toronto. Our journey was made pleasant by the magnificent parlour-car in which we rode, furnished with large arm-chairs, movable tables, and that best of all luxuries when travelling in hot weather, a sumptuous lavatory. We had an excellent lunch and tea served to us, and I noted with satisfaction that no alcoholic liquors appeared in the bill of fare which was presented to us, the Canadian Pacific refreshment-rooms on this section being apparently conducted on strictly temperance principles.

Toronto is at once the most English and the most prosperous town in Canada. Its citizens are justly proud of it, and take no pains to conceal their pride. I noticed on the voyage that, if any passenger walked the deck with an air of being Somebody, if any lady sat in her deck-chair with a cold and repellent air towards strangers, they were sure to hail from Toronto. It is the Boston of Canada. All culture and refinement begins and ends there so far as the Dominion is concerned. Europe may furnish interesting relics of the past, but there is no real progress outside Toronto. I never converse with a Toronto citizen without being reminded of the old Peebles anecdote. "I've seen London and Paris, but for downright pleesure gie me Peebles!"

However, with all the "side" taken off, Toronto is a very fine city of over 100,000 inhabitants, to which it has grown from a tenth of that number in about 50 years. It has plenty of fine buildings, broad and handsome streets, electric lights, and the usual detestable pavement, which seems inevitable in every American town. It has a noble frontage to Lake Ontario of several miles in extent; viewed from the lake on a fine evening, it has almost the appearance of Venice from the Lido, and is quite the most picturesque town in all Canada, except Quebec.

The University is a large Norman building, situated in the public park, in which is a monument to the students of the University who were killed in resisting the iniquitous Fenian invasion of 1866, one of the unpunished villainies of the Irish scoundrels who abuse the hospitality of the freest country in the world. The new Parliament House—in which, when finished, the Ontario Parliament will exercise its carefully-guarded functions—is only just above the ground, and we could not judge of its merits. We visited the Normal School, in which the elementary teachers of the province are trained, and found every possible advantage to the students, well arranged in a stately building.

In different quarters of the city we saw various colleges, denominational and otherwise, which are affiliated to the University, for the Ontario system of university education has been successful in including within its teaching influence, both

Roman Catholic as well as all Protestant denominational colleges—an example I should like to see followed by our ancient seats of learning at Oxford and Cambridge. The University has an endowment of £200,000 and an income of £16,000 a year, with 1,800 graduates and about 400 students. It contains excellent museums of natural history, mineralogy, geology, and ethnology.

The churches of Toronto are one of its chief glories. It boasts the tallest spire, and the handsomest church clock on the Continent of America. We went over the leading Methodist Church; it will seat nearly 3,000 people, and has, besides a handsomely-fitted lecture-hall to accommodate 600, the finest series of Sunday-school class-rooms I ever saw, and a noble suite of drawing-rooms, in which are held that peculiarly American institution—the "Church Sociable"—at which the minister receives the whole of his congregation at evening parties, on terms of absolute social equality.

From Toronto we crossed the lake to Niagara, where we spent three delightful days. I will not add to the thousand and one failures to describe the indescribable. I have seen pictures of Niagara. I have read poems on Niagara. They are about as like what they try to describe as Martin's "Plains of Heaven." The only honest attempt to describe Niagara was made by a poet who was specially commissioned by the *New York Herald* to produce a description in verse that should for all time stand in the forefront of every other. The poet went, stayed three months, and then sat down to write. He began—

> "Niagara! Niagara!
> You are indeed a staggerer!"

He could get no further, and his body was found three days after in the whirlpool.

But without attempting to emulate the poet, I will try to give to those of my readers who have never seen, and may never see this wonder of the world, some faint idea of what it really is.

Niagara Falls are formed by the sudden descent of the Niagara River down a ledge of perpendicular rocks half a mile wide and more than 160 feet in height, into a huge foaming caldron over 400 feet in depth. The river flows out of this caldron in smooth circling eddies for a mile or so, and then rushes through a mighty gorge only 300 feet wide at the rate of 30 miles an hour, piling its roaring and foaming waves 30 feet higher in the centre than at the margin, sweeping at its outlet into a vast circular basin surrounded by high precipitous cliffs, forming a huge whirlpool in which the river circles previous to its final rush into Lake Ontario. To state the bare fact that, according to Sir Charles Lyell, the water passing the Niagara falls, travels at the rate of 1,500,000,000 cubic feet per minute, may convey to the minds of my readers a dim notion of the terrific force and sublimity of this stupendous cataract.

When I was last at Niagara, some ten years ago, both banks were in the hands of speculators, who charged a dollar for every coign of vantage, and before the unhappy tourist could see his Niagara he had to pay out £4 or £5 for admission fees. But these fiends had other methods of making money. As you stood on the table rock, the finest point from which to view the Horse Shoe Falls, a huge board, which you could not possibly evade, informed you all the time that " Jennings' liver pills were sure, quiet, but searching." The fine trees which frame every lovely picture on Goat Island had been let out to a wretch who had painted on every trunk the startling fact that " Gargling oil was good for man and beast," and the lovely rocks of Luna Island

HORSE SHOE FALL, NIAGARA.

resounded with the cry that "Lovell's worm powder was never known to fail"! But two or three years ago the enlightened Governments of the United States and Canada purchased both sides of the river, and swept out speculators and quacks with the besom of destruction. Every approach of the falls is now free as air, the land being cleared of every building, and turned into two national parks. Niagara appears to have irresistible charms

WHIRLPOOL RAPIDS, NIAGARA.

for the fools who enjoy seeing performances in which the main attraction is danger to human life. We saw a number of people respectfully surrounding a big but very stupid-looking young man. Asking who this was, we were told that he was a hero from Buffalo who had shot the Whirlpool Rapids last week, boxed up in the small hold of a canoe decked over for the purpose. There was no skill displayed in this foolhardy performance, as the hero of it was simply cargo and nothing more, yet scores of people were turning their backs on the grandest scene in the world to gape and stare at this foolish youth.

In the height of the season, multitudes of people come in from Buffalo, Detroit, Toronto, and even Chicago and New York, not to admire the wondrous beauty of Niagara, but to see a female named Signorina Maria Spelterina dance on a tight-rope over the Whirlpool Rapids.

We were fortunate in visiting Niagara at the full moon, which added greatly to its charm. This was my third visit to this scene of wonder, and each visit deepens the impression that so far as I have seen Nature, Niagara is the sublimest and most beautiful sight on earth. In the winter of 1872 I saw the falls in the grasp of the severest frost ever known to living Canadians. The caldron beneath the falls was frozen over, and it was possible to walk into the very face of the cataract, whose dark green waters contrasted with the pure white snow and massive icicles which hung about the edges. The spray which rises always like a lovely veil from the base of the falls, had frozen as it rose and encrusted everything on the banks—trees, shrubs, railings—with a delicate frost-work that glistened like pure silver in the bright winter sunshine of Canada, and, falling on the frozen surface in front, had formed enormous cones of ice, one of which, 120 feet high, I mounted, gaining an unusual familiarity with the inner recesses of the falls, that was deeply impressive. But I do not venture to express any opinion on the rival charms of Niagara in winter, spring, or autumn, in each of which seasons I have seen and wondered at its strange beauty and terrible sublimity.

We managed to snatch half a day from Niagara to visit the locks on the Welland Canal, which connect the navigation between Ontario and Erie, and make it possible for vessels to surmount the obstacle presented by Niagara. Erie is on a higher level than Ontario by 300 feet, and this level is reached by a chain of locks on the Welland Canal 26 in number. Each lock is over 300 feet long and 45 feet wide, and vessels of 2,000 tons burden, drawing 14 feet, can pass them. It takes a ship about 14 hours to get through the complete chain of locks, and they pay dues amounting to 9d. a ton if loaded, 8d. if in ballast. It was a wonderful sight to stand on the upper lock and see the vast steps of masonry sweeping round the hillside for miles, with large three-masted ships mounting to Erie or dropping to Ontario all along the great curve, undoubtedly one of the finest public works in the world.

The Canadian Government, with a view to divert the great grain trade of the lakes to Montreal, have reduced the tolls on grain coming to that port through the Welland Canal to 1d. per ton; but although the old rate of 9d. is charged to American vessels the quantity of grain passing down the Welland Canal from United States ports to United States ports increased from 47,000 tons in 1880 to 151,000 tons in 1886, while the carrying of grain from lake ports of both nations to Montreal has rather decreased than increased. This is owing to the great development of railways in the Dominion of Canada, which seem destined here, as at home, slowly to press water-carriage out of existence.

The quantity of cereals arriving at Montreal *viâ* the two great railway systems of Canada, the Grand Trunk and the Canadian Pacific, has steadily increased during recent years as follows:—

1882	1883	1884	1885	1886
Tons.	Tons.	Tons.	Tons.	Tons.
75,000	99,000	142,000	161,000	166,000

The quantity passing down the St. Lawrence system of canals to Montreal for the same period was—

1882 Tons.	1883 Tons.	1884 Tons.	1885 Tons.	1886 Tons.
230,000	263,000	174,000	134,000	272,000

American experience also goes to prove the growing ascendancy of railways over canals. The New York canals last year brought to that port 1,490,000 tons of cereals, while the New York railways in the same year carried over 3,800,000. I think a careful study of canal and railway statistics in Canada and the United States would be profitable to the venturesome capitalists who are taking shares in the Manchester Ship Canal.

The road from Niagara to Welland and back led us through many fine farms, the yards and orchards of which gave evidence of much prosperity. This is a famous fruit district, and produces the Newtown pippin, the American apple that is such a favourite in England.

On Saturday, September 3rd, we bid a reluctant farewell to Niagara and its beauties, and started off to spend Sunday with a relative who had settled on a farm near St. Thomas, in the best agricultural district of Canada. Shortly after the train started, which was the express from New York to Chicago, we were amused by the conductor calling out in the car—"The next station is Falls View—five minutes allowed to see Niagara Falls!" And there are quite a number of Americans who are happy and content to have seen their greatest wonder in this hasty fashion.

It may perhaps interest some of my readers to know what is the life of the average Canadian farmer. My relative, Mr. Emery, has a small farm of about 70 acres of very good land. His house is built of wood entirely, consists of one storey, and contains a kitchen, dining-room, parlour, and five bedrooms. The farm, with the exception of groceries, furnishes food for the family throughout the year, the produce consisting of wheat, Indian corn, peas, hay, vegetables, and fruit. There is abundance of milk and cream, eggs, poultry occasionally, and the meat of three pigs each year, in the shape of pickled pork and bacon. During the three hot months very little meat is eaten by the average Canadian farmer, but when the frost fairly sets in he supplements his pig-meat with a sheep and half a bullock,

EMERY HALL.
From a sketch by the Author.

which he hangs up in the frosty air in some place where vermin cannot reach it, and saws off the meat as he wants it. It keeps perfectly fresh as long as the frost lasts, which is four or five months. He sells his surplus produce, after feeding his family and his stock out of it, and as he has no rent to pay, his wants are confined to clothing, groceries, and a few minor sundries. He educates his children free. He has great opportunities for putting out his family in the world. My relative has five sons and two daughters. Two of his sons are well placed in the employ of a great railway company in the Western States, one of his daughters being a shorthand type-writer in the same employ with a good salary. Another son went off platelaying on the Canadian Pacific while it was being made, saved the bulk of his wages, chose his location as he went along, and is now farming 600 acres of his own near Calgary, in the North-West Province. He has one daughter at home to help her mother, and one son who manages the farm. His youngest lad is 16, and goes to a high school at a neighbouring town of 2,000 population, where he obtains, entirely free, an education equal to any of our great public schools, with four University men to teach him. He lodges in a single room, for which he pays six shillings a month, and on Monday morning drives over to his school, taking with him a basket of provisions to last him till Friday evening, when he comes home for the week end. He will probably become a school teacher for a few years, save money, and eventually educate himself for the medical or legal profession. The more I see of Canada, the more convinced I am of the incalculable benefits of a system of free education, which enables any lad of brains to work himself up from humble circumstances to any position in the Dominion. I wish we had it in the old country.

I never tasted such delicious apples as were ripening in my cousin's orchard. His farm is in the very primest part of the great fruit-growing district that lies on both shores of Lakes Ontario and Erie. Apples, pears, quinces, melons, chestnuts and grapes grow in great abundance, and as we travelled from Niagara to London, the country-side was gilded with the rich fruit of the farm-orchards. Splendid apples can be bought for 1s. 6d. per bushel, and many of the farmers make a special trade of apple-packing for the English market, and have houses specially built for the purpose. The growth of the trade is shown by the returns of exports, which have increased from 50,000 barrels in 1874, to nearly 300,000 last year. In England we do not know what luscious fruit Canada can produce, as the best varieties will not carry without decay. It is, however, proposed to construct cold chambers on the ocean steamers by which these short-keeping and delicate varieties may be brought to England in perfect preservation.

On Monday, September 5th, we left our relative's hospitable roof for London, a town of 30,000 inhabitants. An old friend met us at the station, and drove us round before dinner. "New" London imitates old London as closely as possible. The streets are called Cornhill, Regent Street, Piccadilly, Bond Street, &c., &c. Our friend lives in Westminster, on the other side of the Thames; and there is even a Westminster Abbey, though that, alas! in New London, is a tavern.

Westminster is under the Scott Act, and the Westminster Abbey is, *nolens volens*, a temperance tavern. I was struck with one singular result of the Scott Act. Both my friends, the farmer and my London friend, live under the Scott Act. Neither of them are teetotallers, yet in deference to public opinion, as expressed by the adoption of the Act, neither of them place intoxicating liquors before their guests, or keep them in their houses. I hope to write at some length on the operations of the Scott Act and the prohibitory laws of the North-West when I have seen more of the country.

Tuesday, September 6th, we spent at Toronto, chiefly in visiting old friends. The town was all astir from the opening of a provincial exhibition, to which his Excellency the Governor-General had come. I had an interesting conversation with Lord Lansdowne, who asked me to come and see him to discuss some of the political questions which are coming to the front in the Dominion. In the evening we dined with my old acquaintance

Professor **Goldwin** Smith, who is taking the **lead** in the agitation for commercial union with the States, the most burning question of the hour in Canada.

Wednesday, September 7th.—We left Toronto at 10.30 for Winnipeg. The train took us through a beautiful country to Owen Sound, situated on Georgian Bay, Lake Huron. Here we got on board the "Alberta," a magnificent Clyde-built steamer of 1,800 tons burden, specially designed for the Canadian Pacific Railway to carry the passenger-traffic between Owen Sound and Port Arthur, their station on the north shores of Lake Superior. She and her sister ship, the "Athabasca," steamed across the Atlantic, were cut in two at Montreal, towed through the lakes and the Welland Canal, and joined together again on the shores of Huron. It was blowing a gale of wind, and it was soon made evident that it is quite as easy for people to be sea-sick on fresh water as on salt. We ran up Georgian Bay under shelter of a long peninsula, but about ten o'clock at night we felt the full brunt of the storm blowing up Lake Huron, and were tumbled about quite as much as if we had been on the North Atlantic. Early in the morning the wind abated, and we breakfasted in peace and plenty under the shelter of Manitoulin Island. Soon we entered the St. Marie River, which flows for about 40 miles connecting Lakes Superior and Erie. The shores are low, and covered with forest, the changing tints of which warned us that summer was departing. The river channel is very crooked, but is carefully buoyed, though the passage is even then so difficult that it is never attempted at night. By noon we reached the Sault St. Marie, a pretty cataract rippling over a rocky bed, falling about eighteen feet in a quarter of a mile. This cataract is surmounted by a fine lock. We had to wait while a big four-masted steamer, bound from Duluth on Superior to Buffalo on Erie, and laden with 2,300 tons of wheat, was taken through. Then we entered, and in fifteen minutes were raised to the level of Lake Superior. The lock is 515 feet long, 80 feet wide, 60 feet at the gates, 39 feet 6 inches deep, and will pass vessels drawing 14 feet. The banks of the lock are laid out as a pretty little park, which is the favourite resort of the population of Sault St. Marie, many of whom "saw us through."

Half an hour brought us to Lake Superior, the afternoon

SAULT ST. MARIE LOCK.

being bright, sunny, and calm as a mill-pond. Some wonderful effects of mirage, distant islands and vessels being raised into the sky just above the horizon, were watched with much interest by all the passengers. Presently the masts of a large screw-steamer are seen sticking up out of the water—no mirage, unhappily, for we are told that she foundered in the gale of last night, and that seventeen lives were lost. At ten o'clock this evening, as we were all going to bed, a sudden storm of thunder and heavy rain burst upon us, followed by a smart blow and tumbling sea; but this morning breaks fine and cold, and we pass Silver Island and Thunder Cape glistening in the morning sun.

THUNDER CAPE, LAKE SUPERIOR.
From a sketch by the Author.

CHAPTER IV.

WINNIPEG.

On Friday, September 9th, at ten o'clock in the morning, the good ship "Alberta" moored alongside the pier at Port Arthur, and at two o'clock the same afternoon we joined the Pacific express on our way westward.

Port Arthur was our first experience of the rapidity with which quite large towns spring up like mushrooms in the wake of the Pacific Railway. Ten years ago there was only a landing-place and one or two shanties, the trade of the north shore of Lake Superior being centred eight miles away at the old trading port of Fort William, at the mouth of the Kaministiquia River, which affords a good harbour, and which place is still used by the Canadian Pacific as their chief coal depot and distributing point for timber, rails, and other heavy supplies. Port Arthur, however, attracts the general trade of the district, and if a twentieth part of the hopes entertained by the sanguine mining speculators who are exploring Thunder Bay and the islands are realised, it will not be long before the present agglomeration of wooden stores and houses give way to a second Swansea and Barrow-in-Furness rolled into one. There is undoubtedly great mineral wealth, copper, silver, manganese, and magnetic iron ore, that some day will be developed and make Port Arthur populous and thriving. A hard-working and enterprising population of about 4,000 souls have settled here during the last four or five years, and the country round is being rapidly taken up and farmed. Its own natural resources, added to its position at the juncture of the railway with the head of the St. Lawrence navigation, make the prospects of the place unusually promising.

The scenery at the head of Lake Superior, of which we had heard much exaggerated praise, was disappointing. Thunder Cape is a fine range of cliffs, about 800 or 1000 feet high, but the rest of the country is flat and dull. We did not see the Nepigon region, lying some distance from Port Arthur, which is the paradise of the Canadian sportsman. We met some fishermen returning from a month's camping out, and mistook them for negroes recovering from a bad attack of confluent small-pox. Their remarkable complexion, however, was due to elaborate precautions against mosquitoes and sand-flies. Immediately on arrival at the shores of Nepigon, each sportsman coats himself over with a gruesome mixture of which coal tar, raw petroleum, and peppermint are the leading ingredients. This is renewed from time to time, and never washed off till he departs; on getting home, he undergoes a detergent process of many hours. This precautionary measure is only partly successful, for if it cracks, every mosquito and sand-fly within a mile "goes" for that crack.

The country between Port Arthur and Winnipeg contains little of interest. It is poor, thin, stony soil, covered with poplar and shabby little spruce trees, and the only point of attraction to the traveller is the beautiful clear-flowing Kaministiquia, a river which makes an angler's heart ache with envy as he views from the train its almost virgin stream. At one of our lonely stopping-places, at which the small gang of men who looked after that section of the line were the only living souls for twenty miles round, I asked the station-master if he ever fished the river. "Occasionally," was the reply. "What," I asked, "would you expect to catch in an afternoon's fishing?" The reply was, "I could catch as many trout as I could catch grasshoppers for bait. I suppose I could bring home 150 or 200 in a good day's fishing, weighing about 120 lbs."! The general appearance of the stream makes this statement quite credible.

A night in the sleeping-car of the train, made more or less hideous by the presence of thirteen weary and unchecked babies and small children, brought us to the capital of Manitoba, the new and thriving City of Winnipeg. The wonderful change in travel which the Canadian Pacific has brought about in the North-West of the Dominion of Canada is well shown in a comparison between our journey from Toronto to Winnipeg in 1887, and Lord Wolseley's journey over exactly the same ground with his little army in 1870. He took ninety-five days to complete a journey which we accomplished in forty-five hours.

After settling down at the Leland House, the principal hotel in Winnipeg, we called on our only acquaintance in the city, Mr. R. A. Barker, a son of Mr. T. H. Barker, the well-known secretary of the United Kingdom Alliance. Mr. Barker holds a responsible position in the Government offices of Manitoba. He called for us after lunch with a carriage and pair, and drove us all round the city and its suburbs. In 1870 Winnipeg was only a few small wooden shanties clustering round the old Hudson Bay Company's trading port of Fort Garry, with 200 inhabitants, rendered memorable in modern history from having been the centre of the French half-breed rebellion under Louis Riel in 1870. In 1875 it had grown to 5,000 inhabitants, in 1879 the railway reached it and raised its population to 8,000, in 1880 it was 12,000, and now it is a handsome well-paved city of nearly

30,000 in population, which will probably reach 100,000 before the end of the century. Winnipeg is, and must always be, the capital and trading focus of the whole North-West, a fertile region reaching from the Red River to the Rocky Mountains, and from the United States frontier to the North Saskatchewan River, a tract of over a million square miles. It is impossible to forecast the future of the focus of such an area, but Winnipeg land-jobbers tell me that Chicago must take a back seat in much less than twenty years.

Winnipeg is well situated on the tongue of land formed by the meeting of the Red River and the Assiniboine, about 90 miles from the United States frontier, and 50 miles south of the great Winnipeg Lake, into which the Red River runs, and which opens up by water all the vast and fertile region of the Saskatchewan River, which is 550 miles long and drains an area of 250,000 square miles. The main street of Winnipeg is one of the finest in the world. It is about two miles long, 132 feet in width, perfectly paved with blocks of wood, with wide side-walks, and is bordered by a long succession of fine buildings in brick, stone, and timber, the City Hall, the Hudson Bay Company's stores, the Bank of Montreal, the post office, and others being lofty and imposing structures of which any town in England might well be proud. The shops are as fine as those in Regent Street in London, and the Hudson Bay stores alone turn over about a quarter of a million sterling every year. One of the finest buildings in Canada is the new grocery store of Messrs. Galt, son and nephew of Sir Alexander Galt, who trade over the whole country of which Winnipeg is the centre. The stir, bustle, and business activity of the people are such as one sees in an American town like Buffalo, Cleveland, or Chicago, and the whole place is brilliantly lighted at night by electricity.

I took some pains to inquire into the prospects afforded

by Manitoba and Winnipeg to intending emigrants from the old country. We partook of the hospitality of the Lieutenant-Governor of Manitoba, Mr. Aikens, with whom I had a long conversation, and I also spent an evening with Mr. John Galt, who was one of the earliest pioneers of trade in the North-West country. Mr. Barker, to whom I have already referred, has exceptional opportunities of knowledge, and I also got much help from a very clever and capable young accountant, Mr. J. W. Rigby, who has been all over Manitoba in half a dozen different capacities, with his eyes open all the time, so that I think my authorities are as good as I could find.

With regard to the city itself, it is at present a trading and not a manufacturing community. There is no opening at all for commercial men from the old country. The ground is taken up not only in Winnipeg, but all over Manitoba, by men who have had ripe experience in the stores of Montreal and Toronto; any commercial man or shopkeeper coming over from England would be doomed to certain failure. I put a hypothetical case to a dozen of the best authorities. I asked what were the chances of success for a smart Englishman of five-and-thirty who had had a 15 years' training in some good merchant's office in Liverpool or London, and had saved £2,000? The replies were all the same—Manitoba wants neither him nor his money. All the trade of the country is plucked before it is ripe by Canadians from Ontario and Quebec.

The ordinary clerk or book-keeper is a drug in the market; he can only get labourers' wages. The town is full of them, sent out by friends in England. They go by the name of "Remittance men," because their chief occupation is borrowing dollars "till they get their remittance from home."

There is, however, a real demand for agricultural labourers, who need not remain at the Emigration Depot at Winnipeg for a week, and there is also a fair demand for first-class artisans. The town is manned at present by second-rate hands from Canada and the States, and if a good English artisan, who is really capable and sober, comes along, he quickly displaces the inferior Canadian. If he comes out with a few pounds in his pocket, and is a thrifty, saving fellow, he becomes a master very quickly in Manitoba, and can go right ahead without a check. It was pleasant to find that with every tradesman I interviewed teetotallers are in great demand as workmen, and get an early chance of showing what they are good for. The time to arrive in Manitoba, for all classes of emigrants, is March or April.

I made careful inquiries among different tradespeople and others as to the rates of wages actually being paid to-day in Winnipeg. Carpenters in regular work get two dollars, or 8s. 4d. a day; cabinetmakers, 8s. 4d. a day; upholsterers (by piecework), 12s. to 14s.; smiths, 12s. 6d.; foundrymen (limited demand), 8s. 4d.; wood-turners, 12s. 6d.; bakers, 10s. 6d.; tin-smiths, 10s. 6d.; labourers, 6s. in summer, 3s. to 4s. in winter; a first-rate printer can earn 15s. a day; and good tailors (at piecework) can make 15s. to 17s. 6d. a day.

There is also plenty of good employment for women. Hotel servants get £4 a month with board; domestic servants, £3 to £3 10s. a month with board, and they are rushed for the moment they arrive in the town. Seamstresses get 3s. to 4s. a day with meals for plain sewing. A lady showed me a plain stuff walking-dress for the making of which she had paid 33s., and an ordinary print house-dress cost her 16s. to get made; she of course finding all materials. Telegraph and shop girls get 4s. a day. Agricultural labourers of good quality can get places by the year for about £50 to £60 in money and good board. Mr. Barker told me that a Member of the Provincial Parliament, who lives in his constituency 80 miles

WINNIPEG.

from Winnipeg, is constantly writing to him to send along agricultural labourers at these rates of pay, but that the men are always being snapped up by farmers at intermediate stations who waylay them on the road, and bid higher. There is no doubt that a good steady unmarried agricultural labourer can come out to Manitoba, save £30 or £40 a year for three or four years, and then take up land of his own and become a prosperous farmer on his own account.

But to all those pleasant pictures there is a reverse side. The cost of living in Winnipeg is undoubtedly higher in almost all respects than it is in England, largely in consequence of the heavy protective tariff of the Dominion. The single man gets off best in the way of food and lodging, as he can board well, with meat three times a day if he wants it, at 16s. a week. The married man with a family will, however, find that he cannot make his high wages go much further than his lower wages in England. Free trade enables him at home to buy everything that Manitoba produces in his own markets for less money than he would pay in the capital of Manitoba. Winnipeg market prices last week were: Beef and mutton, very inferior to English, 7½d. per lb.; fresh pork, 5½d.; bacon and ham, 7½d.; sugar, 4½d.; bread, 6d. for 4-lb. loaf; butter, salt, 10d.; cheese, 7d.; tea, 2s. 6d.; coffee, 1s. 8d.; tobacco is cheap, 4s. per lb.; a ready-made slop suit of cheap tweed costs £4; a good cloth suit, £8; an overcoat, £5; white calico shirts, 9s. each; ready-made boots, 24s. per pair; made to measure, 30s.; very bad coal, 40s. per ton; wood dear and scarce. The fuel is a serious item in a climate with nearly six months of winter in which the thermometer is seldom higher than 15 or 20 degrees below zero. I went through the fuel-bills for a four-room cottage, and they reached a total of over £15 for the year. House-rent is very exorbitant. A four-roomed cottage cannot be got for less than £2 a month, and a small six-roomed house fetches £3 easily. On the whole, however, the high wage more than makes up for the extra cost of living, and a thrifty artisan who gets steady work is, on the whole, much better off in Winnipeg than in the old country. He gets his children's education free, which must also be taken into account.

The emigrant who is really wanted in Manitoba is the clever agricultural labourer who is a single man. He can get employment at once, and can easily save £30 or £35 a year. In three years, having £100 of capital and a knowledge of the country, he can take up his 160 acres of good land, and become a yeoman farmer on his own account. I had the curiosity to trace the success or otherwise of such men as these when they take up land, and I will give a few specimens.

A. B. took up 160 acres in the autumn of 1881, with £40 of capital, with which, and a little credit, he purchased a yoke of oxen for £30, a cow for £10, a heifer £6, and a horse. To-day he has cleared himself from debt, has 40 of 160 acres broken up for crops, and has the following possessions :—

	£
10 head of cattle . . . . . worth	74
1 horse . . . . . . „	40
100 head of poultry . . . . „	10
1 pair harrows, a good waggon, a plough, a reaper, a mower, and a rake, half paid for „	36
A good, well-built house of hewn logs, three stables, a barn, and a granary . . . „	300
	£460

And if you add to this the improved value of his land, it is greatly understating the case to say that his £40 of capital has grown in six years to fully £700. I have no doubt he could get more than that to clear out. This man never hired any help; he had a big family of growing lads, and his eldest, 22 years of age, has just taken up his own 160 acres. His arable land crops 25 bushels of wheat, 50 bushels of oats, and 45 of barley to the acre, on average years.

C. D. bought some good land in 1883 for £150, paying half cash, and getting credit for the rest. He broke up 20 acres in 1883, and 40 more in 1884, in which year he cropped

MANITOBA HOMESTEAD.

35 bushels of wheat to each of his 60 acres. His position to-day is as follows (capital to begin, £75):—

	£
Debt paid off	75
11 head of cattle	50
Good log house	40
Mower, rake, and reaper	55
Set of binders	50
Plough	5
Yoke of oxen	30
Team of horses	60
Waggons	15
Value of land	450
	£830

So that his capital has been increased, in four years, fully ten-fold.

E. F. took up land in 1877, the usual 160 acres. He started with £320 of capital. His position to-day is—houses, implements, waggons, stock, &c., £550; value of land in open market, £600; total, £1,150.

G. H. took up land in 1881, with a capital of £160, just 20s. for each acre. First year he broke 30 acres, and cropped 34¼ bushels per acre the year following. He has now 140 acres under plough, and gets an average of about 2,200 bushels a year off 100 acres of wheat, and about 1,200 bushels of oats off 40 acres. He owns 21 head of cattle, three span of mules, 29 hogs, poultry, a complete set of good implements, an excellent house, a large granary and stable, and 100 tons of hay stacked. This stock and plant is worth £920, and for the whole farm, land, and stock, he could get £1,500 at least.

I. J. began with £100 in 1879, and is now worth £900.

K. L. started in 1878 with £160, and is now worth £750, and I should not exaggerate if I said that more than half the farmers in Manitoba can tell similar stories.

The bulk of these prosperous men are the sons of Ontario and Quebec farmers, but there are hundreds of them who have come out from the old country. A man *must* be a farmer to succeed. The broken-down tradesmen who are helped out by friends, the young scapegraces who are shipped by their relatives with a draft for £100 on a Winnipeg bank, are doomed to certain failure, and even an English or Scottish farmer is the better of a year or two of service with an older settler before taking up land for himself, if only to help him the better to choose his location. "Glenbeigh" and "Bodyke" tenants, if they were generously helped out to this magnificent country, and lent £100 per family to stock their 160 acres of granted land, would thrive and do well. If the British Government, instead of embarking on the doubtful policy of Irish Land Purchase, would spend 20 millions in settling gradually in Manitoba 200,000 families of Irish tenant farmers from the congested districts, there would be no difficulty in getting back the money in easy instalments from the prosperous yeomen they would thus create, and by easing the undue competition for farms in Ireland, they would bring the landlords to fair rents, by the simple laws of supply and demand. But as long as Ireland is the shuttlecock of political party, while Irish agitators hold the battledore, common sense has but a poor chance.

CHAPTER V.

CALGARY AND THE RANCHING COUNTRY.

THE country between Winnipeg and Calgary traverses the great Canadian prairie for over 1,000 miles, and we did not leave the train between the two points. The Canadian Pacific Railway run restaurant cars with each train, and provide a capital breakfast, lunch, and dinner, for a uniform charge of 3s. each. Of course the Pullman sleeping-car is also part of the train, and by these two conveniences the fatigue of the long journey is greatly reduced.

The first part of the journey follows the course of the Assiniboine River, a pretty undulating country, covered with fields of stubble, with great stacks of wheat in the centre waiting for the threshing machine. The homesteads are the usual Canadian frame-house, built of sawn planks nailed to a strong wooden frame. They are as ugly as it is possible to make them. The first important station is Portage la Prairie, the market town of the richest district of Manitoba, and the junction of the railway, a considerable portion of which is opened for traffic, which is to bring down the produce of the great Saskatchewan district. This is a busy place, with paper-mills, biscuit-factory, and flour-mills, and enjoys a considerable grain trade. Another 80 miles of rich wheat lands brought us to Brandon, a flourishing market town of 4,000 inhabitants, with extensive grain elevators or

THRESHING OUT WHEAT STACKS ON THE PRAIRIE.

warehouses at the station. We ran all afternoon through a district very thinly settled, and it was dark before we reached Indian Head, where the famous Bell Farm is situated, the train running through it. If there had been any hotel accommodation within reach I would have stayed over to see this farm, one of the most interesting agricultural experiments on the Continent of America, but I was obliged to pass it by. The Bell Farm is the property of a limited company, managed for

RAILWAY DEPOT, BRANDON.

the shareholders by Major W. R. Bell. Its area is about 64,000 acres, or about 100 square miles, and is the largest arable farm in the world. Of course it is not yet all under cultivation. The farm was started in 1882, and was acquired by the company under a special Act of Parliament. The land is the famous black soil of the prairie, and is well watered by streams. The contract with the Dominion Government was a purchase at

5s. per acre, the company undertaking to bring the land under cultivation at the rate of 5,000 acres a year for the first five years. The scheme of the company is first to bring the land under cultivation by the use of the best machinery and then divide it into 250 farms, each provided with house and buildings, to be sold to the men in their employ at a valuation price, payable by instalments over a term of years.

No steam plough is used. There are 200 horses employed on the farm, and they would stand idle for want of work in ploughing time if steam were used. The ploughman sits on his plough, and can generally turn 20 miles of furrows in a day's work. The furrows are often two miles long. Forty-five ploughs are on the ground each day till the work is finished. £90,000 of capital has been sunk in the farm, and employment is given to about 200 men. If the ploughing had to be done with a single team it would have to travel 140,000 miles, nearly six times round the world. The value of the 10,000 acres now under cultivation is about £4 per acre, and is increasing rapidly every year. The produce is, on an average, about 20 bushels per acre. The great wheat belt of Manitoba of which this is a portion, is about 500 miles long and 250 miles wide, and is capable of producing sixteen hundred million bushels of wheat, if it were all under good cultivation. The more I see of this wonderful stretch of land, with soil often 200 or 300 feet deep, the more I wonder why a wealthy country like England endures the misery of the congested Irish counties, when a few millions would remove and settle their starving populations in the midst of plenty and content, with the certainty of the repayment of every farthing expended.

We passed Regina, the capital of the province of Assinaboia, at midnight. This is the head-quarters of the Indian service, and of the North-West mounted police, a magnificent body of men, 1,000 strong, whose business it is to keep the Indians in order, and to enforce the rigorous prohibitory liquor law which exists in the North-West territories. These officers board the trains, searching passengers and luggage at will, to guard against the importation of strong liquors. The morning of September 13th found us out on the boundless prairie, travelling through a desolate and entirely unsettled country. For over 200 miles no sign of human life was visible, except that every 10 miles or so a cottage was placed at a railroad siding, in which lived the three or four men whose duty it is to patrol the line daily. The prairie appeared very fertile, covered with an abundance of grass. The only life visible was an occasional flock of ducks or wild geese on the small lakes, now and then a large species of hawk, and the universal "gopher," a comical little burrowing animal, which is found all over the North-West. At noon we reached Maple Creek, a post of the mounted police, and a station for a large ranching district some 15 miles to the southward. Near this place there is a reserve of the Black Feet Indians, and the noble savages crowded round the platform offering polished buffalo horns for sale. The days of wampum and buffalo robes have passed away, and these braves were attired in remarkable costumes of bright coloured blankets, cut into home-made jackets and trousers by the squaw. One of them had wide peg-top breeches and loose jacket of white blanket, covered with huge circles of red, blue, and green about the size of a cheese-plate, the whole surmounted with a veritable clown's white jelly-bag hat; as his face was picked out with a devious vermilion pattern on a rich ground of yellow ochre, he felt justified in maintaining a dignified and superior demeanour, leaving dirty trade to his squaw, who was 30 years of age, and looked about 300.

At Dunmore a narrow-gauge railway runs 109 miles across the prairie to Lethbridge, where an English company, under the management of one of the many clever sons of Sir Alexander Galt, are working a valuable coal mine capable of producing 2,000 tons a day if a market were available. At Langevin, a single house station, the man who was located there as line inspector sunk an artesian well for water, but found it undrinkable. A chance light explained the cause, for he had struck a well of natural gas. I went into his cottage, and saw a large stove lighted and heated by this gas, without any other fuel, brought up from the well by a pipe. He can warm his whole house to 70 degrees with this gas alone when the temperature is down to 35 or 40 below zero. Perhaps some day a valuable deposit of mineral oil will be discovered at Langevin.

At one o'clock on Wednesday morning, the 14th September, we alighted at Calgary, well content to be at last at the end of our 37 hours' confinement in the railway train. Calgary is a thriving infant of two years old. It is a place of much vigour and bustle, with a population of nearly 2,000. Building is going on everywhere, and, with three or four exceptions, everything is of wood. The place looks exactly like a great international exhibition a week or two before the opening day. It is laid out or "graded," as they say here, in the usual ambitious fashion, in wide streets, covering an area of about two miles each way. The bulk of these noble streets are at present prairie, but a brisk trade goes on in "town lots," which seems the favourite form of gambling in these new western towns. Last year Calgary was incorporated, and a Mayor and Council elected. There was, however, some informality in the election, and the town proceeded to elect a fresh lot. The first Corporation, however, declined to resign, and both of them proceeded to govern the town. After a good deal of ill-feeling the matter was settled by litigation, and "now there is one." Calgary is beautifully situated at the junction of the Bow and Elbow Rivers, fine clear streams of pure water, fresh and cool from the Rocky Mountains, whose snow-clad outlines were visible on the horizon 60 miles away.

Calgary is the capital of the magnificent grazing country which lies along the foot hills of the Rocky Mountains, between the South Saskatchewan River and Montana. This is probably the finest ranching country on the Continent. For some years the Dominion Government admitted cattle free of duty into this

CALGARY.
From a sketch by the Author.

district from the States; but the rush of cattle from Montana and Oregon, whose ranchers threw up their holdings to secure this superior grazing, was so great that last year an import duty of 20 per cent. was levied, and is still maintained. The area of this fine grazing country is about four million acres, well watered throughout by streams from the Rocky Mountains. I drove over three or four of the smaller ranches lying round Calgary, and also had the pleasure of a long interview with

Mr. Stimson, the largest rancher in Canada, who has taken up 100,000 acres about 50 miles south of Calgary, on the foot hills. This gentleman settled on his present holding in 1881. He pays the Dominion Government one halfpenny per acre rent; he has the option of buying 5,000 acres at 5s. per acre, and got his usual 160 acres free for homestead purposes. At that time he was ranching in Idaho, and he drove his head of 3,600 cattle and 200 horses over the frontier to his new tract in Canada. In five years he has increased his stock to 9,000 head of cattle, 1,000 calves, 500 horses, and 150 colts. This is natural increment only, as he has not only bought nothing, but during the five years he has sold 1,500 beasts and 100 horses, the sale of which has enabled him to pay working expenses and invest £1,200 in plant and building. He employs ten men, eight cowboys, a man for the horses, and a cook. A smart cowboy can earn £10 a month and his board, so that if he doesn't care to spend his money, he can save £100 a year, and soon become a rancher on his own account. Two of Mr. Stimson's cowboys are worth £800 and £1,200 respectively, well invested in cattle, which run with Mr. Stimson's herd. Presently they will have enough to form a small herd of their own, when they will wish him good-bye and start for themselves. Mr. Stimson told me that three years ago he took a smart young English lad of 18 on a month's trial. He was the son of an officer in the army, well educated, and a strong lithe fellow, who could ride well. At the end of the trial he engaged him permanently. The lad saved a year's pay, took up a homestead of 160 acres, took cattle on shares, he looking after them, his partner finding the money, and in three years he has made £1,000 out of nothing but a good seat in the saddle, a clear head, and a strong constitution. Any young fellow with these three qualifications, who can stand a rough life in a country where he cannot get a drop of strong drink (except on the sly in a town 50 miles away from his work) can easily become a rich man in 10 or 20 years. But he must serve his apprenticeship as a cowboy first, for ranching, like every other trade, must be learnt.

While at Calgary we drove out with Mr. Springett, one of the Indian agents, to visit the reserves of the Sarcee Indians, a fighting tribe which, under the lead of their chief, Bull's Head, at one time gave a good deal of trouble to the Govern-

BULL'S HEAD.

ment, but are now peaceable enough under the generous treatment they receive on their reserves. Each Canadian Indian who settles on a reserve is paid five dollars a year per head of his family, including the papoose of a week old. For each person in his family he gets daily one pound of beef and half a pound of flour, with a good allowance of tobacco and tea. For his protection against the Indian's curse—strong drink —the sale and manufacture of drink is prohibited throughout the whole North-West territory, and any person, white or brown, found with liquor in his possession without a special permit from the Governor, is fined heavily, and may be severely imprisoned as well. The week before I reached Calgary a raid had been made on some illicit dealers in whisky, and fines amounting to £260 inflicted. The interpreter who accompanied my daughter and myself in our visit to the "wigwams" or "topees," as their tents are called, translated for me the high-sounding names by which the braves of the Sarcees are called. I will quote a few:—Big Crow, Big Bear, Big Knife, Prairie Head, Badger, Bear's Cap, Going to War, Fire Long Ago, Eagle Rib, Flint, Holy, Dog Skin, Hit First, Hit Twice, Lazy Boy, Little Calf, Many Horses, Lodge Pole, Many Swans, Old Man Spotted, Starlight, Splashing Water, Stops Outside the Lodge, Heavy Behind! Walking in the Water, Weazel Head, Went to Slaughter, Wolf Carrier, White Knife, Rolling Hills, &c.

Bull's Head, the monarch of the Sarcees, has a Civil list of ten dollars a head per annum for himself and family, and two pounds of beef and one of flour daily, with tobacco and tea.

In the middle of the camp was a comfortable two-storied house, surrounded by a few good fields and a garden, the residence of Major de Bellenhard, the Government agent, whose excellent wife teaches the Indian children the three R's in a smart little school-house. The Indians live in tents in the summer, and small one-roomed log huts in the winter. They were busy getting these huts ready for occupation. Their tents were about 12 feet in diameter at the base, and the whole family ate, slept, and cooked their rations inside it. They sleep on the floor, rolled up in blankets. The squaws are hideous and over-worked. They catch and harness the pony, cut the wood, dig the potato patch, smack the children, cook the food, and do everything but spend the Government grant, which is all the work a brave will condescend to do, except smoke his pipe and shoot an occasional duck. The Cree and Sarcee Indian has no religion. He has a few superstitions, but the missionary can make nothing of him.

The Indian's vices are drunkenness and gambling. The mounted police make the first practically impossible. The second still prevails, and an Indian will gamble away everything he possesses, to the shirt off his back and his next issue of rations. Those who know most about them despair of ever

SARCEE SQUAW AND PONY-CART.

bringing them into harmony with Anglo-Saxon civilization, and say the reserve system must go on indefinitely.

The great feature of Calgary society is the overwhelming predominance of the male sex. Hardly a woman is to be seen in the streets. The men have not yet had time to think about matrimony; that will follow in a year or two, when the many adventurers settle down to whatever they are fit for. Neither did I see any old men. The whole population appeared to be under thirty years of age, and almost entirely English. The hotel at which we stayed was full to overflowing, many sleeping two in a bed, and all young men; my daughter was the only lady in the house. If the Leland Hotel had possessed a liquor bar it would have been impossible for decent, quiet people to stay there, and a similar town to Calgary across the frontier, in

EAGLE RIB, A SARCEE CHIEF.

Idaho, Montana, or Dakota, would have been one long avenue of liquor saloons and low dancing and music halls. The same class of population frequent Calgary—cowboys, farmers, idlers waiting their chance, swarm everywhere—yet the town is as quiet as an English country village. The popular amusement is the Salvation Army, conducted by a captain and three comely young women, who were treated everywhere with marked respect. We went to their meeting in the evening. They marched round the town in their usual fashion, passing through crowds of cowboys and similar young fellows, without encountering a jeer or a coarse word. When they entered their barracks all the

"BRAVO, TED!"

men in the place swarmed in after them, to the tune of 500 or 600, took their seats quietly, joined heartily in the choruses of the hymns, which they seemed to know by heart, and evidently enjoyed themselves thoroughly. The Salvation Army young ladies were cordially welcomed with clapping of hands. The meetings seemed to have been successful, for there were arranged in a row on the platform a dozen young fellows of the cowboy pattern, who had been converted at previous meetings, and who

F

gave their experience in simple, and sometimes very touching sentences. One of them was received by the whole audience with several rounds of warm applause, and cries of "Bravo, Ted!" I was informed that Ted was the champion rowdy of Calgary, and the population were evidently much pleased that "he had got religion, and was going right ahead into better ways," as my next neighbour said to me.

Ted made a rattling speech, in which he appealed very pointedly to some old pals in the hall to come up to the penitent form, and was launching out into somewhat minute details of his past life, when the captain put both hands on his shoulders, wheeled him round into his seat, and told him his was "an experience that had better be taken in sections, and they would have some more to-morrow night." I conversed with several of the audience coming out, and they all spoke in the warmest terms of the officers of the army in Calgary, and it would evidently fare ill with any cowboy or idler who ventured to say a rude word to any of the hallelujah lasses. My evening at the Calgary barracks strengthened the high opinion I hold with regard to the Salvation Army. I think nothing has impressed me on my journey so much as the moral tone and great respectability of this crude population, composed almost entirely of young men whose occupation is rough, who had many of them come in to the town after months of hard life on the prairie, and who might naturally unbend for a little fun. If liquor were sold, Calgary would be the rowdiest place in the Dominion. Prohibition makes it one of the quietest, most respectable, and law-abiding places, with the Salvation Army barracks as its most popular place of entertainment. Of course the existence of a small amount of secret drinking raises in some quarters a cry for a license law; but I am quite sure that if a license law were passed for the North-West territory it would become a dead letter from the universal adoption of the prohibitory clauses of the Scott Act.

Calgary has a fine volunteer fire brigade, and needs it, for a fire to windward in a gale would lay it in ashes in about an hour. There is no gas in the town, and the streets are pitch-dark at night, but in a week or two the electric light will change all that. It is a curious sign of the entire newness of the line of country opened up by the Canadian Pacific Railway that there are many towns in which gas never has been and never will be known, and where the first illuminant used in the public streets has been electricity.

Calgary will be a big town very soon, the centre of that great cattle, horse, and sheep trade that is rapidly taking up all the suitable land in the district. There are now about 120,000 head of cattle and 12,000 horses breeding upon the ranches, and there is every reason to believe that this number will be more than doubled during the next eight or ten years.

I left Calgary with regret, for I should have liked to stay on and see more of the striking characteristics of a region that will eventually become one of the wealthiest and most prosperous provinces of the Dominion of Canada.

I would like to note that every soul in Calgary is Free Trader to the backbone, for duty, sea and land freight, and the profits thereon, make the cost of everything sold in the stores fully double that of English stores.

CHAPTER VI.

THE CANADIAN NATURAL PARK.

AT one o'clock in the morning, on the 16th of September, we got on board the Western train at Calgary Station bound for Banff. The train soon reaches the Gap, the gateway of the Rocky Mountains, through which the Bow River flows on its 1,500 miles journey to Hudson's Bay. As we were to reach Banff in less than four hours, we did not get much sleep, but were on the look out for the dawn to see all we could of the magnificent scenery we were entering. We had just light enough to see the weird rocks at Canmore, before we were turned out at Banff Station in the grey of the morning. We drove at once some three miles to Dr. Brett's Sanitarium, the only accommodation at present available in the great natural park of Canada. The Canadian Pacific Railway are building a gigantic hotel which will accommodate 300 guests, but it will not be open till next year. We sat down to an early breakfast, and then set to work to see as much as possible of the beautiful, and in many respects unique scenery by which we were surrounded.

Dr. Brett took us up to the top of the house that we might take in the general prospect. We saw stretching out before us a broad, flat valley, about two miles wide, filled with primeval forest. The sombre green of pine and spruce contrasted with the brilliant yellow of the fading poplar and the vermilion of dying

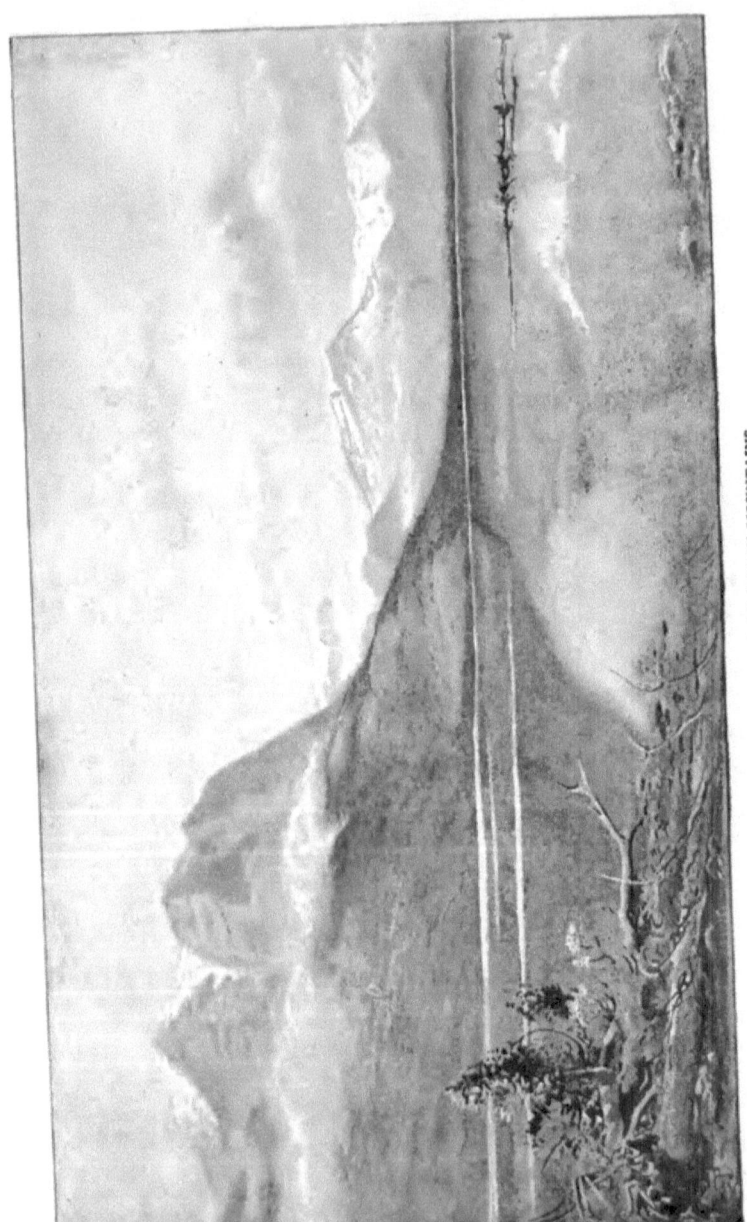

THE GAP: ENTRANCE TO ROCKY MOUNTAINS.

maple leaf; while the Bow River—the loveliest on earth—winds through the whole in a bright blue ribbon. Right in front towers the snow-capped Cascade Mountain, so called from a small stream which leaps 1,000 feet from its flanks. On the left the Castle Mountain range—a magnificent panorama of

CANMORE ROCKS.

eternal snow, reminding me somewhat of the Jungfrau group as seen from Lauterbrunnen; on the right the Devil's Head group, with the singular rock towering above the whole mass, justifying by its remarkable outline the Indian name of which this is the translation, while behind are the pine-clad Sulphur

Mountains, and a terrific row of lofty crags known as "The Twins." The whole forms a panorama of mountains from 10,000 to 11,000 feet high, which for beauty and grandeur can only be equalled by the Cortina dolomites in the Austrian Tyrol.

Dr. Brett's Sanitarium is intended mainly for the reception of those invalids who require the treatment which the hot sulphur spring furnishes, and we took our first walk to see the caves from which these healing fountains issue. The two principal

CASTLE MOUNTAIN.
(*From a sketch by the Author.*)

springs, which are now being utilised, flow from the central spur of Sulphur Mountain, 800 feet above the level of the Bow River. The main spring issues at the rate of a million and a half gallons daily, and has a temperature of 115 degrees. At a short distance another spring is found, of a heat about 85 degrees, which is used for a plunge-bath. On the other flank of the mountain is a cave, with a narrow entrance up which a wooden ladder leads into a spacious chamber, lighted by a hole in the stalactite roof. In this chamber is a large pool about 30 feet wide and from 3 to 6 feet deep, in which hot

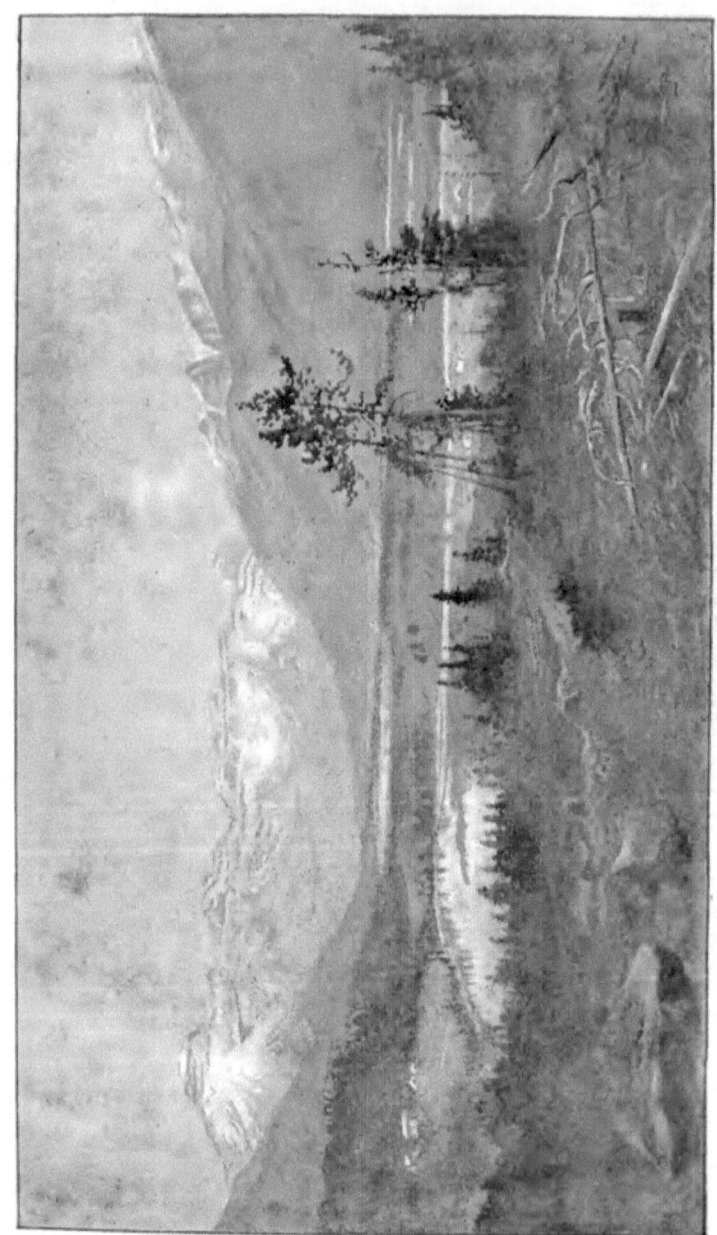

VIEW OF BANFF FROM ABOVE THE SANITARIUM.
(*From a sketch by the Author.*)

springs bubble which fill the cave with steam, and make the atmosphere almost unbearable with the sulphur fumes which are thrown off. Persons suffering from rheumatism bathe in this cave, and some wonderful cures have been performed. A crutch hangs on the wall with this dubious label on it, " Owner has gone home ! "

I do not pretend to know anything about the curative properties of these springs, but as the leading medical men of the United States and Canada seem all agreed about recommending them for various diseases, it is probable that Banff will become a place of great resort for invalids troubled with rheumatism and affections of the skin and blood. There is a nice plunge-bath in the open air near the bath-house, in which the water stands at about 85 degrees, and in which I had a pleasant swim. Without the springs, the bracing and pure air and the delightful scenery will always be sufficient to attract thousands of visitors every year.

Just below the sanitarium is a new iron bridge, almost completed, which is to take the place of the bridge of boats which is now the only means of communication between the hotel and springs and the railway station. On a bit of cleared forest at one end of the bridge, a handsome, aristocratic Englishman lives in a small tent, looking after half-a-dozen canoes belonging to one of the small inns. He is reputed to be the Honourable Somebody Something, and looks the part well enough. The Twin Peaks, the great feature of Banff, are best seen from this bridge.

The Bow River presents a most attractive appearance to the angler, but does not, in experience, come up to his expectations. There are trout, and large ones too, but they are hard to catch, and have an aggravating way of inspecting your fly, which they follow to the bank, and then refuse with slow scorn. I tried every fly in my book, from a " Dusty miller " to a black gnat, but could catch nothing at all. A youth who came along informed me that "it was no use trying with them things, guv'nor—you try a bit of beef liver!" Later on in the day I met an angler who had come down to "beef," and he caught one small and pallid trout. On rare occasions they take fly in the spring and early summer, but they have a bad character for capriciousness generally. I heard of wonderful fish being caught in the Devil's Head Lake, a piece of water about 10 miles from Banff. I saw a man who had been there and had caught 77 trout, weighing 220 lbs., in a single day, trolling with a couple of hand-lines and spoon-bait, and one trout weighing 43 lbs. was caught there last year with a piece of beef. The place was too distant for me to reach, as it is uphill, and the only path an old Indian trail, but an active young Englishman rode over during our visit and did his best, but never saw a fish of any kind. The following day we explored one of the small streams tributary to the Bow, with a view to learning how to manage an Indian birch-bark canoe. These canoes are so light that a boy can lift them out of the water and carry them on his back. The paddler sits or kneels in the stern and propels the canoe with a broad, single-bladed paddle, steering with a sort of back stroke that takes a good deal of learning. However, I managed to canoe my daughter up two or three miles of a swift running brook, and across a very beautiful lake from which it flowed called the Vermilion Lake. Probably no white man had ever seen that lake till two or three years ago, and it was a most perfect bit of wild and untouched nature. The day before, we had vainly endeavoured to reach this lake by land, but the forest was so dense with fallen trees piled one over the other that it was quite impassable. I cannot find words adequately to describe the unique charms of the primitive and unspoiled scenery. The lake was as smooth as glass, its banks were a wild tangle of brushwood, poplar and

BRIDGE OF BOATS AND TWIN PEAKS, BANFF.

maple, a perfect blaze of autumn red and gold, out of which sprang tall and sombre cedars and pine trees. Behind these were the snow-clad mountains, the whole perfectly repeated on the surface of the water.

We spent a quiet and pleasant Sunday at Banff. This rising watering-place cannot yet boast a place of worship, though a wooden Wesleyan chapel is nearly finished, and a site has been selected on which to build an Episcopal church. Service is held in the Town Hall, a humble edifice of logs and shingles. The only regular service is on Sunday evening, conducted by Mr. Williams, the Wesleyan minister, an energetic young Welshman, who for many years had been doing a fine pioneer work amongst these new western villages and towns. His service is largely attended by the workpeople engaged in building the new hotel, by whom he is greatly esteemed. He also holds a morning service at Anthracite, a colony of coal miners, about eight miles from Banff. The Episcopalians hold a morning service when they can catch a clergyman, and this Sunday they caught a real live bishop, the Bishop of Saskatchewan, who is a good father to his own children, whatever he may be to his scattered diocese, as any one could tell who saw him feeding his baby most tenderly with spoon-meat at breakfast in the hotel. He was accompanied by the archdeacon, a jolly young Irish-Canadian, who occupied a front seat at the Wesleyan service in the evening, a not unusual occurrence in Canada, where the absence of a State Church leads the Episcopalian clergy into more cordial intercourse with their brethren of other denominations than seems possible in the old country.

The whole of the Banff valley and adjacent mountains, to the extent of 100,000 acres, have been set apart by the Dominion Government as a national park for ever. They have voted various sums of money, in all about £16,000, for the making of roads and footpaths through the dense forests to various points of attraction, and will continue to vote further sums until the work is satisfactorily completed. I had two conversations with Mr. G. A Stewart, the National Park Ranger, who explained to me all that he intends doing, and the work could not be in better or wiser hands. He will let nature alone as much as possible; he will strictly preserve all the wild beasts and birds, carefully regulate the fisheries, and content himself with making good roads and pathways through and through the Reserve to all

CASCADE MOUNTAIN.
(*From a sketch by the Author.*)

points of interest. He will also endeavour to acclimatise forest trees not indigenous to the soil. No land speculator can smirch the beauty of the place, as no land will be sold, only leased under strict terms and for specific purposes. When Mr. Stewart has completed his labours, the Canadian National Park will be one of the most attractive holiday resorts on the globe.

The park will be 24 miles long and 9 wide. Within its area will be found 15 miles of the Bow River (of which 9 are deep water, capable of navigation by a small steamer), 6 miles

ON THE BOW RIVER, BANFF.

BOW FALLS.

of the Spray River, a clear crystal mountain stream with a fall of 100 feet within the limits of the park, flowing through a forest which just now is one blaze of orange, vermilion, and gold. The Ghost River and the Cascade River, the Forty Mile Creek, and half a dozen other brooks, combine altogether a great wealth of the finest river scenery, in infinite variety. The area of the park also contains the Devil's Lake, 12 miles long and 2 wide, and the Vermilion Lakes. The water of these fine sheets is deep and clear, and mountain ranges on each side rising thousands of feet above their surface, present scenery of the greatest beauty. The Vermilion Lakes are linked together by short streams navigable by light canoes, and are the resort of a great variety of wild fowl.

The junction of the Bow and Spray River is extremely beautiful. The Bow falls over a leap of rock about 70 feet high, in a succession of cascades, into a fine pool about 200 feet across, into which the Spray rushes. The Tunnel Mountain breaks just over this pool into a frowning precipice 700 or 800 feet high, the broken base of which is covered with a wealth of maple, poplar, and undergrowth, the autumn colour of which beggars all description.

Large game as well as fish are becoming very scarce in the neighbourhood of the National Park. It has long been a favourite hunting ground of the Indians resident in a large surrounding area. Skin hunters, Indian fishers, who net the streams, and lately have added other resources of civilisation in the shape of dynamite, have made sad havoc. Mr. Stewart fully realises the importance of preserving the animals and fish, which add so many wild attractions to the scenic beauty of the National Park. Among the four-footed game still to be met with in its area is the Wapiti deer, or blue elk, admirably adapted by form and habit to the park-like woodlands which fringe the small prairies and cover the green slopes of the surrounding mountains, while the gullies which extend far up the mountain sides afford ample shelter during the winter. The lesser deer are more numerous, and are often to be seen in the glades. Among these are the black-tail, the white-tail or jumping deer, the red deer, and the prong-horn antelope. In the mountain tops are bands of big-horns, a huge wild sheep familiar by name to all boys who love Mayne Reid and Fennimore Cooper, as well as goats with long silky hair, much hunted by Indians for their handsome skins.

There are three kinds of bears—grizzly, cinnamon, and black.

VERMILION LAKE, NATIONAL PARK.

The grizzly is almost extinct except in remote and unexplored parts of the Rocky Mountains; and the cinnamon and black bear are vegetarian feeders, harmless unless wantonly attacked. There are many other beautiful animals pursued by Indian and other hunters for their fur, such as beavers, otter, musk, fishers, muskrats, martens, badgers, marmots, squirrels, and such-like, as well as many varieties of plumage and song birds.

All these Mr. Stewart proposes strictly to preserve and encourage, while at the same time he will endeavour to exterminate all those animals which prey upon others, such as wolves, coyotes, foxes, lynxes, skunks, wild cats, catamounts, panthers, and porcupines, together with such birds of prey as feed upon fish.

Feathered game consists chiefly of migratory or water-fowl. Wild swans, geese, and ducks breed freely in the lakes, swamps, and woodland streams, the Bow River being one of the great migration waters from the valley of the Columbia River. Besides these, herons, bitterns, gulls, grebes, pelicans, cormorants, landrails, coots, partridge, blue grouse, ptarmigan, sage-cock, and prairie fowl all nest and hatch in spring and summer time, an added charm to the wanderer who loves nature in all its forms. These also will be strictly preserved.

The fish in the various streams comprise white fish, which takes no bait or fly, having a small mouth and living on suction—a fine fish for the pan, however; several varieties of trout, one of which, *salmo irideus*, I had never seen before I caught one with a small phantom minnow—it is so called from its brilliant rainbow-like tints when first caught; grayling, which take the fly well, mountain herring, a bright silvery little fish, very like the Welsh "gwyniad"; gold eyes, a sort of carp cat-fish, small chub, and suckers. The trout spawn in April and May, but get into good condition in September.

I had a breakfast of the *salmo irideus*, which was excellent eating, with firm white flesh.

Mr. Stewart wisely intends to confine all fishing to fair rod and line only, solely for sport and private use, and to increase the stock, now sadly worn down by the improvident destructiveness of Indian fishing, by artificial hatching and rearing. He will also plant the lakes and marshes with wild rice, which is very attractive to wild fowl of every kind, both for food and shelter.

Mr. Stewart also proposes, by damming up some portions of the many streams which run through the park to fill up a chain of old marshes, and turn them into lakes. I rather protested against this interference with nature, for I found a special beauty in these marshes such as I had never seen before. But he explained that his chief object was not so much to create lakes as to act as a fire-break from the many conflagrations which rage through the Rocky Mountains during the summer, and which might at any time sweep through the National Park. There was some dread of this during the late very dry summer, when forest fires have been frequent and extensive. I have myself seen areas of 15 or 20 square miles of burnt forest, with every vestige of green life burnt up, and only the thicker trees standing up, the gaunt charred ghosts of their former grandeur.

Mr. Stewart also talks of importing pheasants and quails from Vancouver Island, where they were introduced some years ago, and have thriven.

It is proposed to give the Indians who have hitherto hunted, trapped, and fished over the area of the National Park some compensation in the shape of increased rations or other allowance, and then absolutely prohibit them from further operations of the kind. It is thought that with an efficient staff of police at Banff to maintain order, enforce regulations, and

A FOREST FIRE, NATIONAL PARK.

uphold the special measures necessary, composed of forest rangers qualified by mountain experience and familiarity with the haunts and habits of the wild animals of the country, of which force selected Indians would form a part, there would be no difficulty in gaining the objects in view, and in securing the strictest protection for the game and fish still inhabiting the park.

The Government have been urged to establish at Banff a museum of Natural history and an aquarium, so that the efforts of Mr. Stewart may be made of service to science, and no doubt this recommendation will be carried out.

CANADIAN PACIFIC RAILWAY HOTEL, BANFF.

Such then are, briefly, the particulars of one of the most interesting experiments of modern times, and I venture to predict that in a few years, when it has been thus cared for and opened out by roads and pathways, there will be few more delightful holiday resorts in the world than the National Park of the Dominion of Canada.

The magnificent hotel which is being built by the Canadian Pacific Railway will furnish that foreground to the marvellous landscape which always won the special admiration of Dr. Johnson.

VIEW IN THE SELKIRKS.
(*From a sketch by the Author.*)

CHAPTER VII.

THE SELKIRKS.

ON Monday, September 19th, we were roused from our beds at 4 o'clock A.M., as the westward bound daily train passed through Banff at five o'clock. At the station we met with the only instance of neglect of duty on the perfectly-ordered Canadian Pacific Railway. The station-master did not condescend to leave his warm bed to see the train off, and we had to carry our luggage ourselves from the omnibus to the luggage car, and let them go on unchecked to Field, our next stopping place. It was a cold, sleety morning, and the magnificent scenery through which we passed was not seen to the best advantage, as the tops of the mountains were enveloped in snow clouds. At seven we passed a

SUMMIT LAKE.

station called Silver City. Three or four years ago there was a "boom" in silver mines in the Rocky Mountains; a good deal of exploration went on, and a considerable wooden village was built. But there was no "silver," and now there is no "city." Its glory has departed, and only the empty and deserted log-houses remain to tell of its butterfly existence. Shortly after, Mount Lefroy, a commanding snowy peak 11,658 feet above sea-level, comes into view, and presently the birthplace of the noble Bow River is discerned in a small glacier wedged in between Mount Hector and Goat Mountain, both over 10,000 feet. Then the highest point of the railway is reached, 5,300 feet above the sea, at the summit lake, marshy and shallow, from which trickles a stream at each end, one of which travels 2,000 miles to the Atlantic, and the other 1,500 to the Pacific Ocean. We now bid good-bye to the beautiful Bow River, which has been our genial companion for so many pleasant days, and under the shadow of Mount Stephen, the monarch of the Rocky Mountains, said to be over 12,000 feet, and named after the president of the Canadian Pacific Railway, we enter Kicking Horse Pass. This pass received its ridiculous name from an incident connected with some obstreperous horse ridden by one of the surveyors of the line, which will stick to it for ever. A magnificent view meets the gaze. A huge valley, filled from side to side with magnificent pines and cedars, their dark green intensified by the red-brown of huge areas burnt up by forest fires, in which the enormous trunks stand up like black masts 200 feet high, and 10 or 12 feet thick, is flanked by peak and pinnacle, the Kicking Horse River meandering through the bottom like a silver ribbon. The train, with two powerful engines reversed, and every brake screwed to its tightest, slides down a gradient of 1,250 feet in less than 10 miles. The road is cut out of the sides of great cliffs, hundreds of feet above the roaring torrent, and every now and then we crawl over a trestle bridge two or three hundred feet

KICKING HORSE PASS.

above some gorge torn out of the mountain side by a rushing torrent. At nine o'clock we draw up at Field Station, a lonely

FIELD STATION.

post in the heart of the Rocky Mountains, where the Canadian Pacific Railway Company have built a comfortable little hotel, at which we decide to stay for 24 hours. It was a great comfort to know, as we came down this terrible descent, that we were travelling on rails made from good honest Cumberland Hæmatite. I have noted, with interest, but without surprise, that the word "Barrow" always appeared on the rails which the Canadian Pacific Railway have laid down in dangerous places, or where there is specially heavy wear and tear.

We found the hotel at Field one of the most comfortable and well-ordered hotels in Canada, and the manager at once claimed acquaintance with me as having "voted for me when I stood for Liverpool." Our party, consisting of four officers from the Fleet at Esquimault, Mr. F. W. Gibbs, Q.C., a most delightful and charming travelling companion, a young friend of his, my daughter, and myself, very nearly filled the little hostelry, which we had to ourselves. After an excellent breakfast, the materials for which were brought from Calgary, 130 miles away, the nearest town where a shop exists, we sallied forth to view the magnificent scenery. The landlord informed us that he had the day before set a snare for mountain goats, and invited us to go up the mountain for a mile or so, to see if any had been caught. All went except my daughter and myself, and we started off for a walk down the line, the railway being actually the only path of any kind for 30 miles each way through the dense forest which everywhere clothes the mountain sides, and which is practically impassable. About a mile from the station the valley narrowed to a very small space, with the Kicking Horse River running quietly between two gravelly banks. Here we saw a very fine bear on the other side of the river, coming in and out of the woods, seemingly hunting for something on the gravel beds. Just at that moment three or four men from Field, line inspectors, came up on a hand trolly, and

Cathedral Peak.   Mount Stephen.
THE MONARCHS OF THE ROCKY MOUNTAINS.

we called their attention to the bear. They at once turned back to the Field Station, begging us to follow down the line keeping Mr. Bear in sight, as he showed himself every now and then out of the wood, while they fetched a miner who owned a Winchester rifle, and who was a crack shot. In about half-an-hour he arrived. We had seen the bear frequently, and pointed out the spot where we had last noticed him. The owner of the rifle at once plunged up to the middle in the icy river, waded across, and entered the wood stealthily. In a few minutes the bear trotted out on the gravel, much perturbed in his mind. Presently he seemed reassured, and began to grub in the ground with his nose. Then the hunter crept out of the bushes till he was well within range. Taking aim, he gave a shrill whistle; the startled bear threw up his head, and in a moment he was shot through the heart, and all was over. The others then rushed through the river, dragged him back through the water, and presently he was laid on the trolly in triumph. He was a fine "silver-tip" bear, about as big as a large calf, with very formidable teeth and claws. I have his skin, which I shall get dressed into a hearthrug when I reach Victoria.

On Tuesday morning, the 20th, we again took train, and journeyed as far as "Glacier House," another comfortable little hotel erected by the Canadian Pacific Railway at the foot of the great glacier which comes down from the eternal snowfields of Mount Sir Donald, the highest peak of the Selkirk Range, about 11,000 feet above the sea, named after one of the directors and first promoters of the railway, Sir Donald Smith. We reached it at noon, and after lunch started off to explore the glacier, to the foot of which a trail has been cleared. It is a fine and imposing glacier, half-a-mile wide, and seven or eight miles long, but bearing no comparison whatever with such vast ice fields as the Gorner or Aletsch glaciers in Switzerland. It was covered with fresh snow, and looked very beautiful in the bright sunlight. Mount Sir Donald has never yet been climbed, and there is a legend at the hotel that the first man to reach the summit will receive a thousand dollars and a free pass over the line for his life, from the directors of the Canadian Pacific Railway. In the opinion of my friend Mr. Gibbs, Q.C., who is a member of the Alpine Club, the thousand dollars may be pocketed by the first smart Alpine Clubbist who comes along, and certainly to my comparatively inexperienced eye it did not seem impossible to an active Cumberland shepherd. It is however a superb mountain.

The scenery of the Selkirk Range is finer in all respects than the Rocky Mountains, which are devoid of glaciers, and also of any extent of snow fields. From the railway platform at Glacier House there is a view which rivals any of the notable Swiss cycloramas, and I counted at least a dozen fine peaks, all of which appeared to be at least 10,000 feet high, and whose flanks bore miles of snow fields and many picturesque, though comparatively small glaciers. The Hermit Range, so named from its fancied resemblance to a Monk of St. Bernard followed by his dog, is as fine a group of snow mountains as the world can furnish.

Next morning we walked up the line to see the great snow sheds, and some of the trestle bridges which span the cataracts rushing down the sides of these magnificent mountains. One of these bridges is 176 feet high and 600 feet long, and another crossing the Canyon of Stoney Creek is 296 feet high and 450 feet long. These structures are truss bridges supported upon great timber towers, built up from the bottom of the valley far below, and Stoney Creek Bridge is the highest

THE BEAR HUNT.

timber railway bridge in the world. The whole structure is of wood, cut from the forests through which the railway travels.

The snow sheds are solid buildings of crib work and piling,

SNOW SHEDS.

with very strong roofs of two courses, one of logs and another of planks, strongly backed with heavy stone work. These sheds are placed along the line wherever the devastated track of a "snow slide" or avalanche appears on the mountain side. It is impossible to describe adequately the tremendous power of these Selkirk avalanches. Enormous volumes of snow gather during the winter in some hollow high up the mountain side, and in spring rush down with a force which nothing can resist into the valley below. Everything is swept before them—trees of the largest size, boulders, soil, brushwood, are torn up and tumbled into a confused mass at the bottom of the valley. The wind caused by the avalanche is almost as resistless as the slide itself, and the trees on each side of its track for a wide area are broken into matchwood. These slides have been a great difficulty and danger to the line, and have caused stoppage of the traffic for weeks at a time, besides much loss of life. But now the trains run through the snow sheds, and their powerful roofs, inclined to the angle of the slide, enables the snow and debris to shoot harmlessly over. There are still some 3,000 men at work along the line at these various snow sheds, some of which are over half a mile long, and their many canvas encampments form picturesque incidents in the scenery through which the line passes. The Canadian Pacific Railway Company engage to feed and lodge them for four dollars a week, and right well these fellows live, with three good meat meals a day, and the finest air in the world for sauce.

During the morning we walked back up the line to Rogers Pass, the highest point reached by the railway in crossing the Selkirk Range. Here is a collection of wooden shanties, used as liquor-saloons, music and dancing-houses, and places of worse resort still, to which the more loose-living of these workmen resort. I found, however, that the bulk of them were steady, sober men, intent on saving their surplus wages, and on the look-out for favourable chances in this new country. There was a good deal of snow at Rogers Pass, which is a narrow gorge closely hemmed in by lofty snow-clad mountains.

MOUNT SIR DONALD AND THE GREAT GLACIER.
(From a sketch by the Author.)

Leaving Glacier House on Wednesday, 21st, we found attached to the train one of the handsome private travelling carriages which are used by directors and officials on the long lines which cross the American Continent, and which are travelling homes of both comfort and luxury. Shortly after starting, a coloured servant brought me a card bearing the name of Mr. Baker, the General Superintendent of the Manitoba and North-Western Railway, a line which opens up a fine agricultural district north of the Canadian Pacific Railway. Mr. Baker wished my daughter and me to ride through the beautiful scenery of the Selkirk range in his carriage, which, being at the tail of the train, commanded a clear view, and he also asked us to dine with him afterwards. He first showed us over his car, in which he lives all the year round for nine days out of fourteen travelling up and down his line. It was a carriage somewhat longer than a North-Western first-class coach. It was divided into a dining-room, large drawing-room, kitchen, pantry, and two comfortable bedrooms, all handsomely furnished, with a small platform or terrace at each end, on one of which was kept the stores in ice-lined boxes, and the other was a sort of balcony on which to sit and view the passing scenery. An admirable dinner was served, consisting of soup, oysters, roast beef, two vegetables, pudding, and dessert, with a cup of excellent coffee. Mr. Baker was taking a holiday with some English friends. The car was shunted at any station along the line which they wished to visit, and the party were enjoying excellent opportunities for sport on the many lakes along the prairie, the resorts of a great variety of wild-fowl, as well as being able to see the whole scenery of the Rockies and the Selkirks by daylight, by hooking on to freight and ballast trains. We left them behind about ten o'clock, p.m. on an arm of the great Shuswap Lake, where they had good duck shooting next day, while Mr. Baker killed six trout over

2 lbs. each. Soon after quitting Glacier House Station, the railway descends 600 feet in two miles of actual distance. This is done by utilizing two ravines which meet at right angles, and is a triumph of engineering skill. The line runs along one side of the first gorge for about a mile, then crosses a high bridge, and comes back along the other side close to where it started, but on a much lower level; thence it runs into the

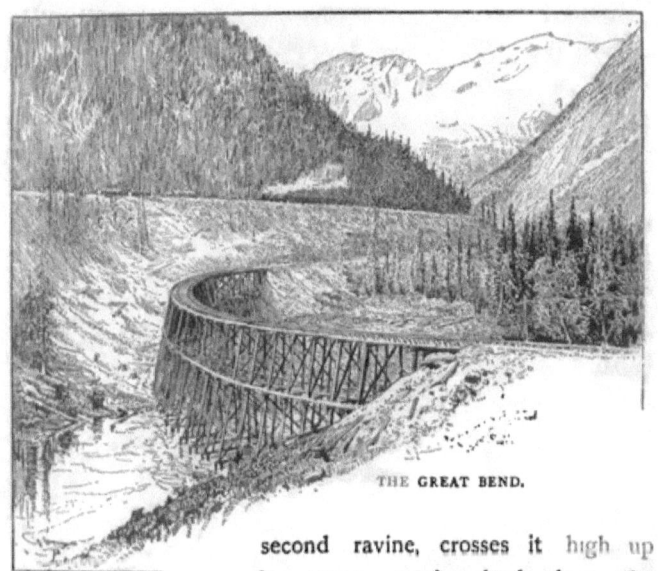

THE GREAT BEND.

second ravine, crosses it high up its course, coming back down the opposite side 120 feet below its entrance, yet only 130 feet further down the pass; then it doubles upon itself in the main valley, crosses the river, and presently recrosses. From the top of these loops one can view six almost parallel lines of railway, each at a lower level than the others, and the whole largely composed of trestle bridges and elaborate timber cribbing. It is a wonderful sight to stand at the top and watch a train

ROGER'S PASS; THE SUMMIT OF THE SELKIRKS.

twist in and out of this succession of loops like some hissing snake. The whole forms a remarkable feat of engineering skill.

Morning found us in the Gold Range, running down the valley of the Thompson River, a tributary of the great Fraser River, into which it flowed at Lytton, a colony of gold miners. The Gold Range is not so lofty as either the Selkirks or the Rockies. There are no glaciers at all, but many of the peaks are snow-capped, and the sides of the mountains have a much greater variety of timber, giving a richness and depth of colour which is more beautiful than the dark greens of the loftier ranges. As we descend the slopes, and get into the valley of the great Fraser River, we reach the better settled parts of British Columbia, and the landscape is brightened by farmsteads, Indian villages, and Chinese camps, engaged in the three leading industries of the country — farming,

INDIAN SALMON CACHE,

salmon preserving, and mining. Every now and then a group of Indians would be seen, ingeniously hanging dried salmon on trees in such fashion that bears or other climbing animals cannot reach them. This is the country of big trees and endless forest, which must eventually become the main timber supply of the whole American Continent, as the vast and increasing population of the States consumes its own limited and rapidly decreasing lumber districts. All through British Columbia the summer is warm and rainless, and its forests are scourged by continual fires, mainly the result of careless Indians and other dwellers in tents. We saw many of these forest fires, for which, when near the line, probably sparks from Canadian Pacific Railway engines are mainly responsible. In ordinary pine woods they rage through the brushwood and undergrowth, the big trees escaping with a scorching, which does not seem greatly to injure them, except in appearance. But wherever there are big cedars the flames burn merrily, and everything is destroyed. The trunks of these trees become hollow and decayed, and when they are reached by the fire they draw like a factory chimney, and the trunk falling, with its 200 feet long in blaze, gives the fire a fresh start. It is surprising with what speed this genial climate fills up the blackened spaces with fresh vegetation, and ten or twelve years replaces the fallen giants with thriving children which an English park might feel very proud to raise in thirty years of growth.

Sometimes these fires are disagreeably hot to the passengers on board the train, as they rush through them at the rate of 25 miles an hour. On one occasion a whole train, except one carriage, was entirely destroyed. The engine driver was running through as usual, when he ran quietly off the rails into the middle of the track. The heat of the fire had expanded the rails and warped them. The passengers were all got out easily enough, as it is possible to walk from one end of an American train to the other, and no one was seriously injured except the conductor, who was badly burned in trying to get out the mails. They managed to get away the end car, a Pullman sleeping car, but the rest of the train added itself to the ashes of the forest fire.

It is, however, after all but a small percentage of these vast forests which fall under this scourge, and every station affords proof, by the quantity of logs, dressed timber, and firewood waiting despatch, that the new railway is laying the foundation for one of the biggest lumber trades in the world.

Up the valley of the Fraser, and afterwards up the Thompson, runs the only waggon road in British Columbia, from New Westminster to Cariboo, the centre of the gold-mining district, round which there are also several flourishing settlements of farmers. This road was made by the Government of British Columbia at very great cost, and the lower portion of it is now superseded, so far as through traffic is concerned, by the Canadian Pacific Railway. The traffic on this road is carried on by waggons drawn by teams of oxen, ten or twelve yoked together, and it is also used by Indians moving their camps from point to point after salmon and game of various kinds.

The Fraser River is the chief watercourse of British Columbia, rising in the far north of the Rocky Mountains, and is navigable for about 120 miles from the sea. The railway follows it for 250 miles, giving an infinite variety of beautiful scenery. Now it flows through some deep and rocky ravine, foaming and tumbling in a series of rapids and falls, then flowing in rippling stream and placid pool, forming sand bars which are being washed over for gold by the industrious heathen Chinee, and other "placer" miners, and presently broadening into a noble river, navigable by steamboats, dotted

by Indian canoes salmon fishing, and bordered by variegated
timber ablaze with autumn gold and copper, with every now
and then a comfortable homestead farm and herds of fine
cattle. At New Westminster, 15 miles from the mouth, it
widens into a stream two miles across, from whence it distributes
its wealth in ocean ships and steamers all over the world. I saw
a vessel leave New Westminster for London with 2,200 tons of
tinned salmon on board.

SALMON CANNERY ON THE FRASER.

We got out on the morning of the 22nd, at the little roadside
station of Agassiz, that we might spend 24 hours on Harrison
Lake, a sheet of water 50 miles long, in the heart of the best
district of British Columbia. We drove in a waggon some six
miles over the very worst road I ever saw in my life, to a new
hotel which has just been built on the edge of the lake, the
only house upon its beautiful shores, but which we found very
comfortable and scrupulously clean. The lake is surrounded
by two ranges of mountains, the first densely wooded to the

summit, the second bare and snowcapped. The scenery is about half way between Windermere and Como. With the exception of the rough track from the station, there is not a footpath which does not end 100 yards from the hotel in dense impenetrable forest. We spent the day on the lake, exploring its beauties, and occasionally trying for a big trout, but only catching one very small one of remarkable beauty.

The next day we went on to Vancouver, the Pacific terminus of the Canadian Pacific Railway, and brought to a close a

HARRISON LAKE.
(*From a sketch by the Author.*)

railway journey of over 3,000 miles, which, whether for human interest or natural beauty, far exceeds any previous journey of my life.

Vancouver is the youngest town in Canada. It was commenced less than three years ago, when it was a forest of Douglas pines, cedars, and spruce, of enormous size. I measured one stump which had been sawn off about 6 feet from the ground, and it was 11 feet 8 inches across. In June last year, after it had reached a respectable infancy, Vancouver was completely burnt down, not a house escaping, so that the present "city," as the Vancouverites insist on calling it, is just fifteen months' old. It is of course still a wooden town, but several fine brick and stone buildings are already erected, and many are rapidly reaching completion. The Canadian Pacific Railway Hotel is a handsome building, almost ready for opening, which will accommodate some 200 guests. Extensive wharves and warehouses line the shore, and ocean-going steamers of 3,000 or 4,000 tons can load and discharge there. The main street is full of handsome shops, and there is a busy, hardworking population of 4,000 souls, mostly men. Vancouver will be a town of 20,000 or 30,000 population before it is ten years old.

THE "YOSEMITE" LEAVING VANCOUVER.

CHAPTER VIII.

BRITISH COLUMBIA.

On Saturday, the 25th, we left Vancouver in the steamer "Yosemite" for Victoria, the capital of British Columbia, where we were to spend a fortnight previous to sailing for Japan. I have long been anxious to see this colony, so remote and inaccessible until it has been brought near by the Canadian Pacific Railway. Five years ago the only direct communication between British Columbia and the mother-country was by sea round the Horn, a voyage of six or seven months for the smart barques which have so long carried on the trade, and which show no signs of being displaced by the railway. Now the two countries are within 14 or 15 days of each other, and the ease with which emigrants can reach this land of infinite capacity and resources will quickly develop it into one of the most important portions of our Colonial Empire. I propose to give a brief account of the impressions I have formed of British Columbia, based upon careful investigations made during the three weeks I have travelled over it—investigations in which I have had the guidance and help of the Lieut.-Governor, Mayor Fell, Senator Macdonald, and many other old colonists.

The sail from Vancouver to Victoria gives one a very good idea of the general characteristics of the country, which has been compared to a sea of mountains and valleys. These valleys as they approach the sea become long inlets often 100 miles in length, which large ocean-going steamers can navigate to the very top, while at the same time the long chain of islands of which Vancouver, 300 miles long, is the chief, lying between these inlets and the Pacific, render their smooth waters equally navigable to the Indian's birch canoe and the unwieldy stern-wheel trading steamer. There is no country in the world whose area is so wonderfully opened up by water carriage as British Columbia. These bays, inlets, and rivers swarm with fish of excellent quality, valuable for food and oil. I priced the stock of a fishmonger in the leading street of Victoria. He was selling fresh salmon at 2d. per lb.; cod, 2½d.; halibut, 4d.; fine plaice, 3½d.; fresh sardines, a delicious dish, ½d.; herrings, 1½d.; smelts, 4d.; whiting, 3½d.; trout, 4d.—all per lb. Fine crabs, 3s. per dozen. I suppose the fisheries of British Columbia must be practically inexhaustible. Although salmon is the great staple food of the people, they exported in 1885 7,324,000 lbs. of canned salmon. This means a catch of about two millions of salmon at 7 lbs. each, which appears almost incredible; yet the take this year is larger than ever, and is virtually confined to the Fraser River and its tributaries.

There are three separate runs of salmon every year. They run for fresh water in the spawning season, ascending as far inland as possible, after the manner of salmon at home. Those entering the Fraser River work their way to a point 800 miles from salt water. The main seat of the salmon fishing is New Westminster, and for miles above the town the river swarms with boats, manned chiefly by Indians, who scoop the fish out of the water with nets like the ordinary landing net, but much larger. There are other canneries on Burrard's Inlet, Aleet Bay, Skeena River, and others north of the Fraser, altogether thirty in number, affording employment in one way and another to

INDIANS SALMON FISHING ON THE FRASER RIVER.

5,000 or 6,000 hands. A fresh development of the salmon fishery has sprung up in the last two years, in the shipment of fresh salmon to the markets of Winnipeg, Toronto, Montreal and Chicago, packed in refrigerator cars, that will become an important feature of this trade. There seems to me to be no limit to the expansion of an industry that can send such wholesome and nutritious food to be sold retail in England and the Continent at 4*d*. per lb., for there is certainly no limit to the supply. In some rivers the run is so great that the fish literally shoulder one another out of the water, and die by thousands on the banks. Within three miles of Victoria this sometimes happens in a small creek leading out of the harbour, and the fish are used by farmers for manure. It is a curious fact for anglers that the Pacific salmon takes no bait or fly in fresh water, but may be taken readily in salt water. My daughter caught a fine, silvery fish last week in Esquimalt Harbour with a spoon-bait, though the run is not on at present. When it is, the officers of the fleet tell me they turn out with rod and line, and consider a dozen fish, from 7 to 20 lbs., a very ordinary catch for each person.

After salmon, the most important fishing is that of the oolachan, or candle fish as it is called, because it is so oily that when dried it will burn like a candle, and is so used by the Indians. The oolachan is about the size of a sardine. They are a delicious fish when fresh, salted, or smoked. The oil of this fish is considered far superior to cod-liver, or indeed any other fish oil. The oolachans begin running in March, chiefly on the Nass River, and great numbers of Indians assemble on its banks to wait for them. They are caught in purse nets, and often a canoe load is the result of a single haul. They are then boiled in iron tanks for several hours, and the oil is squeezed out through willow baskets in cedar boxes. When cold it is like thin lard, and is used by the Indians, as Mr. Keiller says of his marmalade, "as an excellent substitute for butter." Like the salmon, the supply of this useful fish is practically inexhaustible.

Herrings are very plentiful. They are smaller than those of our seas, but are quite equal in quality. The Indians catch these with a primitive weapon, like a large hay rake, with nails driven through as teeth. They paddle their canoe into a shoal of herrings, and, sweeping this rake through the water, bring up half a dozen or so each time, and soon fill the boat with fish.

Halibut, cod, haddock, sturgeon, large flounders, crabs, prawns, cockles, and mussels are abundant everywhere along the coast, and in every bay and inlet. The native oysters are not larger than cockles, but very delicious, and in such profusion as to make it certain that cultivation would produce as many of the finest varieties of Atlantic oysters as could be marketed. Experiments in that direction have been commenced.

As usual, where fish of the herring and oolachan sort is plentiful, the seas swarm with every kind of dog-fish, and a large factory, employing hundreds of Indians, is engaged in extracting oil from dog-fish livers. Some 400,000 fish are caught yearly, yielding 40,000 gallons of oil, the finest lubricant in the world.

The seal fishing is also an important industry, checked for the present by the arbitrary seizure, by the American Navy in the Behring Straits, of several sealers hailing from Victoria—a matter which will form a considerable portion of the work of the International Court of Arbitration, of which Mr. Chamberlain has recently been appointed a member, to the great satisfaction of all Canadians. About 15 schooners and steamers are engaged in this trade, employing 400 or 500 sailors and hunters. The annual catch is about 13,000.

It is supposed by those qualified to judge that in the deeper waters of the Pacific there are banks where cod will be taken in quantities equal to those found on the great bank of Newfoundland.

I have given very much thought to questions relating to fisheries during the last few years, and nothing has impressed me more deeply in considering the natural wealth of British

Columbia than the limitless profusion of the fish supply. The time cannot be far distant when, with the new and speedy way to market opened up by the Canadian Pacific Railway, such a profitable field for the use of capital will be much more largely cultivated.

One of the largest markets for tinned fish and other provisions of a like nature is our Australian and New Zealand Colonies. At present large quantities of salmon come to London round the Horn, and are transhipped to Australia by the Suez Canal, going round the world to a market in the same ocean as that in which the fish are caught. It will not be long, I expect, before some enterprising firm from Lowestoft, Yarmouth, or Aberdeen, will have a branch establishment at Victoria, and will send every description of canned and dried fish to the many markets of the Pacific, north and south.

Salmon forms at present the largest item of export from British Columbia, being about 900,000 dollars. Next on the list comes coal, which reaches some 800,000 dollars, mostly to the United States and the Sandwich Islands. Coal has been found all over British Columbia, but is only worked seriously at Nanaimo, on Vancouver Island, where large quantities of good quality are being raised. This is an excellent steam coal, used by H.M. ships of war stationed at Esquimault, and by the line of steamers plying between Vancouver and China. There are five mines employing about 2,000 miners, whose earnings are 8s. to 12s. per day. Close to these mines, on the neighbouring island of Texada, are large deposits of magnetic iron ore, assaying 68 per cent. of metallic iron, with a very low percentage of phosphorus. This ore is being profitably shipped to iron-works in Washington Territory, in the States, where it is mixed with brown hematite. It cannot be long before this juxtaposition of coal and iron will result in the creation of iron and steel works, which ought to command a share of the Pacific markets, especially if Chinese labour can be made available.

The third item in the list of exports is gold, which amounts to 700,000 dollars, and is all exported to the States. This is produced by placer mining only, the primitive hand-washing of the gravel and sand of the river beds, but capital is now being introduced, and quartz-crushing on a large scale will soon greatly increase the production of gold, as well as give regular employment to a large number of miners. Apart from gold, coal, and iron, no minerals are worked to any extent in British Columbia, but the geological survey now being conducted by the Dominion Government reveals the presence of large deposits of silver.

DOUGLAS PINES, VANCOUVER.

copper, lead, platinum, and other metals, which are fast attracting the notice of prospecters from the States and Canada. Timber is the fourth on the list of exports, about 500,000 dollars, and furs fifth with 250,000, closing the list of important items. I think it will not be long before timber heads the list. Already the markets of Australia, Chili, Peru, China, the United States, and Great Britain have discovered that in British Columbia they can get a class of timber which no other country can supply. Red, yellow, and white cedars, pine, hemlock, spruce, larch, fir, and oak, grow to a size such as no other country in the world can rival. The Douglas fir, a wood in great favour with railroad constructors for bridge work, is the prevailing timber of the country, its height is usually 150 to 200 feet, and from 10 to 20 feet in circumference. I have seen countless trees far larger even than this, and they have been known to reach over 300 feet in height, and 35 in circumference. It will stand a breaking strain of 630 lbs. to the square inch, and is more tough and tenacious than oak, which breaks at 550 lbs. The trees run up 80 to 100 feet without a branch, thus giving an unusual proportion of clear lumber, and I have seen masts ready for shipment over 100 feet long and 42 inches in diameter. The great peculiar value of this timber is that it never warps, and can be used fresh from the saw. In building Vancouver after the fire, trees were felled and the planks sawn up and nailed to the buildings the same day.

No one can estimate the enormous extent of timber in this province. It covers the whole area of the country, which is greater than that of France and the British Isles combined. I have travelled, by rail and horse, over 700 miles through the province, and, except when there have been exceptionally severe forest fires, the timber is uniformly large and abundant. The lumber countries of the United States are becoming rapidly exhausted, and in twenty or thirty years the trade between British Columbia and the Western States will become very considerable, while the Australian, Chinese, and Japanese markets for large timber of all sorts will become the property of this colony much sooner than that. Every saw-mill in the country is working to its full capacity, and new mills are being projected. It is undoubtedly the most profitable industry on the Pacific coast of America.

The soil of British Columbia is prolific, as might be expected from the constant deposit of vegetable matter from ages of successive forests, but it seems to me that agriculture must in the main follow the lumberer, as the cost of clearing the ground of these enormous trees is almost prohibitory unless they can be marketed at once. The land once cleared, however, is of splendid quality, able to produce every fruit, cereal, or vegetable known to the temperate zone. But there are in many parts of the province large valleys and deltas, the bush of which is maple, willow, or poplar of small growth, which can be cleared with ease. Chinamen undertake to clear such land for about £7 or £8 per acre. The surrounding forests furnish excellent pasture for stock, and I have seen fine herds both of oxen and sheep feeding in the densest forest. This week I have driven over 100 miles through Vancouver Island along arable tracts lying between sea and mountain, from two to five miles wide, on which are settled hundreds of prosperous farmers, and where there is room for hundreds more. Some capital, however, is necessary for the settler on Vancouver Island, as the free lands are almost all taken up by speculators, and have to be purchased. But on the mainland there are thousands upon thousands of acres of excellent arable land still unclaimed, in districts where already there are some of the largest and most productive farms in the province; and on the southern boundary there is a large area covered with the nutritious bunch grass, which, left uncut, becomes excellent hay, until it is renewed in the spring, giving the finest grazing for cattle all the year round. I feel sure that for the farmer with some capital British Columbia, from its climatic resemblance to Devonshire and the south coast of England, is a much better settlement than the severe climate of Manitoba. Manitoba, however, gives better chances to the agriculturist who has to make his way without capital, or with only a very little.

The climate of British Columbia is as nearly perfect as possible. It is free from excessive heat in summer and extreme cold in winter, and is healthful and invigorating all the year round. Snow seldom falls, and never lies more than a few days. For a period of three years, on Vancouver Island, the lowest temperature has been eight degrees above zero, and the highest 84 degrees. The mercury has never been known to fall below zero. There is nothing on the Atlantic in the same latitudes that furnishes so excellent a climate as this. The climatic influence which produces it is the great current of warm water which flows in the Pacific Ocean, known as the Japan current, spreading its genial atmosphere from Alaska to Mexico. From this current an almost constant wind blows landward, current and wind combined enabling the Japan and China steamers to make some two days' better time coming east than going west. With all this warmth there is plenty of moisture, the rainfall in Vancouver being 25 inches, and on the mainland 40 to 60 inches. Taken as a whole, British Columbia is one of the most delightful countries in the world, and were I compelled by circumstances to seek a fresh home away from the old country, it would have attractions that would be irresistible to me.

Victoria, the capital of British Columbia, lies on the extreme south of Vancouver Island. It first became a place of any note in 1858, when thousands of miners swarmed into British Columbia after the discovery of gold on Fraser River. The whole trade of the province till lately was entirely dependent on water carriage, as its market centres in Victoria. There is a population of 12,000, a large proportion of which is Chinese and Indian. The harbour is landlocked and capacious, lined with fine wharves presenting a busy scene. The buildings are fully equal to those found in American and Canadian cities of equal importance, and

ESQUIMAULT HARBOUR.
(From a sketch by the Author.)

at night the streets are lighted by electric lamps placed on lofty masts, 200 feet high, giving the appearance of fifteen or twenty moons; the effect is very striking, and the lighting perfect. There is great rivalry between Victoria and its mushroom opponent Vancouver, but I am inclined to think the old capital will retain the general domestic trade of the province, while much of the export business will drift to Vancouver. Probably the old and wealthy firms of Victoria will open branch offices in Vancouver, and thus keep both home and export trade in their own hands. It will be entirely their own fault if they allow

K

upstart Vancouver to shoulder them out. Very large vessels cannot lie alongside the wharves of Victoria, the harbour only taking ships drawing less than eighteen feet; but two miles off is Esquimault, one of the finest harbours in the world, being the station for our Pacific squadron. This is a land-locked harbour three miles long by one to two miles wide, with an average depth of forty-five feet, and excellent anchorage, the bottom being a tenacious blue clay. Here the Canadian Government, helped by a subsidy from the Imperial Government, have built a fine dry dock, which will accommodate vessels of the largest size. It is 450 feet long, 26 feet deep, and 90 feet wide at the entrance. It is a fine piece of work, concrete faced with stone. Here also is a naval hospital, arsenal and stores, with a small repairing shop.

Victoria is not so cheap a place to live in as many other Canadian towns. House rent is dear, a four-roomed working man's house being from 40s. to 50s. a month. Clothing is very expensive, and so is furniture. The long carriage and costly freight from England is a heavy addition to those import duties which make imported goods so dear in a colony where food ought to be cheaper than anywhere else in the world. The following are the prices at which food can be purchased on the retail market in Victoria:—Butter, fresh, 3s. per lb.; salt, 1s. 6d. to 2s.; cheese, 1s. to 1s. 3d.; eggs, 1s. 6d. per dozen; flour, 2½d. per lb.; oatmeal, 3d.; split peas, 6d. Vegetables, all grown by Chinese labour: potatoes, 1s. for 14 lbs.; onions, 2d. per lb.; carrots, ½d. per lb.; cauliflowers, 6d. to 9d. each. Ham and bacon, 9d. per lb.; beef, 6d. to 7d.; mutton, 6d.; pork, 5d. I have already given the price of fish, which is the cheapest food in the market. Sugar is 7d. per lb.; oranges, 4s. per dozen; dried currants, 8d. per lb.; cooking raisins, 1s.; figs, 1s. 8d.; tea, 3s.; coffee, 1s. 8d. Good board for single men, 24s.

a week. Wages, however, are higher than anywhere else I know of, though work is irregular in the winter months. Carpenters, blacksmiths, painters, and tinsmiths get easily 12s. to 14s per day; stonemasons and bricklayers, 16s. to 20s. per day; plasterers, 18s.; common labourers, 6s. to 7s.; fishermen, skilled hands, £10 to £12 per month, with food. The labour market is unsteady—sometimes plenty of work at the highest rates, and then general slackness. But a steady man who means to settle soon gets permanent employ at good wages. Chinamen can be got for 3s. per day, and do nearly the whole domestic services of the towns. Cooking, laundry, gardening, and housemaid's work, is all done admirably and thoroughly by the Chinese, against whom there is a great deal of unjust prejudice, because they are the only cheap labour to be got. A decenter, quieter, or more respectable class of people it would be difficult to find; and I am quite sure the Canadian Pacific Railway would never have been made at all but for Chinese labour. Many of these Chinamen come from Hong Kong, and are as much our fellow-subjects as the British Columbians themselves, and ought to possess equal rights of citizenship. Yet every one of her Majesty's subjects who happens to have been born under the British flag at Hong Kong, has to pay £10 import duty on his own body before he is allowed to land in British Columbia.

CHAPTER IX.

THE TEMPERANCE MOVEMENT IN CANADA.

No intelligent and unbiassed traveller can spend any time in the Dominion of Canada without being forcibly impressed with the sobriety of its population as a whole. I suppose it is a fair assumption that more than half the people of Canada, without being total abstainers, habitually drink nothing stronger than tea or coffee, while the number of abstainers are proportionately larger than perhaps any other Christian nation. The evidences of this state of things are abundant. I have been six weeks in Canada, the whole of which have been spent in hotels—good, bad, and indifferent—in towns like Montreal and Toronto, in country villages, and western mushroom towns. I have never seen a Canadian take intoxicating liquors with his meals. If anyone is drinking wine or beer it is sure to be an Englishman. It is the same in almost every private house. A minister of religion who is not an abstainer hardly exists in all Canada. The medical profession do their utmost to maintain habits of abstinence from strong drink, and members of the Dominion and Provincial Parliaments take the warmest interest in all laws dealing with the liquor trade.

The active temperance movement is healthy and vigorous. The organisations are much the same as those existing in England. Temperance meetings are usually held in connection with church or chapel, and a Band of Hope is attached to every Sunday school.

A strong movement is on foot just now to provide temperance teaching in public schools. The Legislatures of Nova Scotia and New Brunswick have already made provision for the use of a temperance lesson book in public schools, and similar instruction is also given in many districts of Ontario.

The Women's Christian Temperance Union is extending its operations in all the provinces of the Dominion, and is one of the most vigorous societies in Canada. The school movement just referred to is the result of their continual and persistent agitation.

The United Methodist Church, at a recent conference, passed a resolution in favour of introducing temperance text books into schools, urged the Methodist people to do their utmost for the adoption of the Scott Prohibitory Act, and recommended Methodist electors to support only those candidates who were in favour of prohibition. The closing words of their resolution run: "We strongly recommend all to vote as they pray; then "they can pray as they vote. It is a contradiction that "should at once and for ever end, that a Christian man will "pray in one day that God will remove the liquor traffic from "our midst, and the next hour vote to perpetuate it."

The Church of England, especially in Ontario, is very active in the temperance reformation, and has formed parochial and diocesan societies almost everywhere.

The Presbyterian Synod, at its meeting last year, by formal resolution earnestly recommended to office bearers and church members the practice of total abstinence, and also warmly urged the universal adoption of the Scott Act.

Indeed, similar resolutions have been passed at the annual conferences of every religious denomination in Canada, some of them even going so far as to pass resolutions excluding fermented wine from the Communion Table; in fact, throughout the whole of Canada I find a deep and rapidly growing conviction amongst all classes who influence society that the use of intoxicating liquors is morally wrong, and that it is a grave political error to permit their common sale.

The strongest of all expressions of public opinion in countries enjoying a free representative Constitution is to be found in the Acts of Parliament placed on the Statute Book by the elected representatives of the people, and a study of the temperance legislation of Canada brings out very strikingly the rapid development of public sentiment with regard to the liquor trade.

Long before the Confederation of Canada some of the provinces had declared by legislation that a mere licensing system had failed to prevent the liquor trade from becoming a fruitful source of crime, social degradation and misery, and had taken steps, more or less severe, to add the additional check of a popular veto. In Nova Scotia it was enacted that before a licence could be granted the consenting signatures of two-thirds of the surrounding ratepayers must be secured. In many of the counties of this province no licences have been granted for 10, 15, or 20 years, and in the case of Yarmouth County for 40 years. As long ago as 1855 New Brunswick enacted a prohibitory law, but it was in advance of solid public opinion, and was repealed, a very stringent licence law taking its place.

In Ontario and Quebec an Act was passed in 1864 giving power to municipalities to refuse licences by a vote of Council, and many districts, under this Act, declared for the principle of prohibition by large majorities.

After the union of the Provinces, in 1867, the temperance

party began their great crusade in favour of a general prohibitory law for the Dominion of Canada. Meeting after meeting was held in every Province, and in a space of three years petitions, signed by over half a million persons, were presented to Parliament, praying for the enactment of a prohibitory liquor law. The result of this agitation was the appointment by Parliament, in 1874, of two commissioners to make a thorough and complete investigation into the working and results of prohibition in these various states of the United States which had adopted it. I have this report before me as I write, and it is a masterpiece of compiled evidence, altogether in favour of the adoption of prohibitory as compared with license legislation. It was referred to a Select Committee of the Senate and Commons. Their report recommended the enactment of a prohibitory law for the Dominion of Canada, and the report was adopted by both Houses.

Progress was barred for a time by the question as to jurisdiction. It was in doubt whether the Dominion or the Provincial Legislatures had authority to prohibit the sale of intoxicating liquors. This did not, of course, apply to the North-West Provinces of Assiniboine, Saskatchewan, Alberta, and Athabasca, and the Government at once gave effect to the recommendations of the committee in 1875 by passing a law covering the whole of the North-West Territory, prohibiting the sale, manufacture, or possession of intoxicating liquors in the North-West Provinces, except with the written permission of the Lieutenant-Governor of the Territories. I have already referred, in previous chapters, especially the one about Calgary, to the operations of this Act, and their excellent results upon the people. I will only now repeat that in my opinion this Act has done, and will do if maintained, as much to promote the prosperity and rapid development of these valuable territories, as their own natural advantages. The law is rigorously and successfully carried out, and has the sympathy and support of the entire resident population.

In 1878 the Mackenzie Government decided that the benefit of the doubt referred to a few lines back, was in favour of the Dominion, and that it would be within their jurisdiction to pass a prohibitory liquor law for the whole country. They introduced the Canada Temperance Act. It passed its second reading without a division, and became law. The legality of the Act was challenged, but the Supreme Court of Canada confirmed it, one judge dissenting. An appeal was taken to the Privy Council of Great Britain, who gave judgment in June, 1882, fully confirming the constitutionality of the Act.

The Act has since its passing been attacked in Parliament on three different occasions, but as none of these were successful I need not trouble my readers with the details.

The Canada Temperance Act, 1878 (commonly known as the Scott Act) is a local option law, affecting the whole Dominion of Canada, and was enacted for the purpose of enabling a majority of voters to suppress the retail sale of liquor in any city or county.

The Act is divided into three parts. The first part provides the machinery by which the second part may be adopted or rejected. The second part is the Prohibition part, and does not come into force until it has been adopted by a vote of the electors. The third part provides for the enforcement of the law after its adoption.

The following is a synopsis of the provisions of these respective parts:—

PART I.

Petitioning.—One-fourth of the electors in any city or county may petition the Governor-General in Council to have a vote taken upon the Act in such city or county. The Governor-General in Council may then appoint a Returning Officer, fix a day for voting, and make all other needful arrangements for the polling of votes.

Voting.—The vote shall be taken by ballot, and in one day. There shall be a polling place in each polling sub-division of each municipality.

Very severe penalties are provided for any corrupt practices. No treating of voters is allowed, and all places where liquor is sold must be kept closed the whole of the day of voting.

All electors who are entitled to vote at the election of a member for the House of Commons, have a right to vote on the Scott Act.

Coming into Force.—If a majority of the votes polled are in favour of the Act, a proclamation will be issued, bringing it into force; but in counties where licences are in operation, it cannot come into force before at least five months after the voting, nor until all licences in force at the end of these five months have expired. If no licences are in force in a county, the Act may be brought into operation in that county after three months from the day of the vote adopting it.

Repeal.—If the Act be adopted it cannot be repealed for at least three years, nor until the repeal has been voted upon and adopted by the electors. If the Act be rejected or repealed it cannot be again voted upon for three years.

PART II.

Prohibition.—From the day of the coming into force of the Act in any county or city, and as long as it remains in force, no intoxicating liquor shall be sold in any manner or under any pretext except in the cases hereinafter mentioned.

Wholesalers.—Persons who are specially licensed may sell liquor by wholesale; but only in quantities of not less than ten gallons, or in case of ale or beer, eight gallons, and only to licensed druggists, or other wholesalers, or to persons whom they have good reason to believe will carry it to, and have it consumed in, some place where the Scott Act is not in force.

Producers of native wine made from grapes grown by themselves may, when licensed, sell such wine to any persons in quantities of not less than ten gallons, unless it be for medicinal or sacramental purposes, when they may sell as small a quantity as one gallon.

Druggists.—Licensed druggists may sell in quantities of not less than one pint. Not more than one druggist may be licensed in a township, not more than two in a town, and not more than one for every four thousand inhabitants in a city. Druggists are only allowed to sell liquor for medicinal or sacramental use, or for use in some *bonâ fide* art, trade, or manufacture. Liquor can only be sold for sacrament on a certificate signed by a clergyman; for medicine only on a certificate signed by a medical man; and for any other purpose only on a certificate signed by two Justices of the Peace. The licensed druggist must file all these certificates, must keep a full record of all the sales he makes, and report the same to the collector of Inland Revenue.

Part III.

Penalties.—The penalties for illegal sale are:—For the first offence a fine of not less than £10; for the second offence a fine of not less than £20; and for the third and each subsequent offence imprisonment for not more than two months.

The clerk or agent who sells for another person shall be held guilty as well as his employer, and shall be liable to the same punishment.

All liquor and all vessels containing liquor in respect to which offences have been committed shall be forfeited.

Procedure.—Full directions are given as to modes of procedure and instructions as to the powers of all persons who have authority or jurisdiction in regard to offences against the Act.

Enforcement.—Any person may be a prosecutor for a violation of the Act. The collector of Inland Revenue is required to prosecute when he has reason to believe that an offence has been committed.

Provision is made for the appointment of License Commissioners and Inspectors in places where the Scott Act is in force, and provides that it shall be the duty of these officers to see to its enforcement.

Evidence.—In a prosecution it is not necessary that a witness should be able to state the kind or price of liquor unlawfully sold. It is enough to show that unlawful disposal of intoxicating liquor took place. The finding in any place of liquor, and also of appliances for its sale, is *primâ facie* evidence of unlawful keeping for sale, unless the contrary is proved. The husband or wife of a person charged with an offence against the Scott Act is a competent and compellable witness.

Tampering with Witnesses.—Any person attempting to tamper with a witness in any prosecution under the Act shall be liable to a fine of £10.

Compromise.—Any person who is a party to an attempt to compromise or settle any offence against this Act, with a view of saving the violator from prosecution or conviction, shall, on conviction, be imprisoned for not more than three months.

Appeals.—No appeal shall be allowed against any conviction made by any Judge, Stipendiary, or Police Magistrate, Sheriff Recorder, or Parish Court Commissioner.

The first vote was taken on the Act in the town of Frederickton, New Brunswick, in October, 1878. The contest was as keen as a parliamentary election in England. The subject was discussed to the utmost during a long and active campaign. Both the liquor and the temperance party were well organised, and the electors thoroughly canvassed. It was felt on both sides that "first blood" was of great importance in the great fight, of which this was to be the first round. The result was that more electors polled than at the previous parliamentary election, and the Act was adopted by two to one—403 to 203. This victory was quickly followed by others. There are 14 counties and 3 cities in New Brunswick, and the Scott Act is now in force in 10 counties and 2 cities. The leading city, St. John, has not adopted the Act, but in the two elections which have taken place since the Act became law, it was defeated first time by a majority of two only, on a poll of 2,150, and the second time by a majority of 77, on a poll of 3,297. In the three elections which have taken place in Frederickton, it has been found impossible to repeal previous decisions, though the majority in favour of the Acts has been greatly decreased. I have had no opportunity of inquiring into the reason for this.

Nova Scotia has 18 counties and 1 city, of which 13 counties have adopted the Act.

Manitoba has the Act in force in 2 counties out of 5, and the temperance party in Winnepeg, the capital, are about to test it there for the first time.

Prince Edward Island has 3 counties and 1 city, all under the Act.

Ontario has 38 counties and 11 cities; 25 counties and 2 cities have adopted the Act.

Quebec has 56 counties and 4 cities; 5 counties only have adopted the Act, but a considerable portion of Quebec is under prohibition through a provincial Act. British Columbia has 5 Parliamentary constituencies, but the temperance is so feeble, and the liquor interest so rampant, that the Act has never yet been even tested in the province. The sale of liquor to Indians, nearly half the population, is forbidden by the laws of British Columbia under severe penalties, thus giving a protection to Indians withheld from their less fortunate white fellow-citizens.

The enemies of the Act contend that it has not diminished but increased drunkenness in the districts where it has been adopted.

In reply to that I would point out that in all the 63 districts in which the Act has been put into force, it remains in force to-day.* In one instance, in Lambton-Ontario, it has had a chequered experience, being adopted in 1879 by a majority of 215 on a poll of 4,919, rejected in 1881 by a majority of 105 on a poll of 5,819, but once more adopted in 1885 by the tremendous majority of 2,912 on a poll of 6,104; so that in the only case in which a constituency, having once adopted prohibition, has gone back to liquor selling, the experience of the election has been such as to bring forth most emphatic repentance. It is quite clear that those districts who adopt the Act find it to their advantage to maintain it, and it is significant that of the 63 districts where it is in force only 6 have attempted its repeal. The aggregate vote has been 161,000 for and 111,000 against. But after all, the best test of the success or failure of prohibition is to be found in the actual consumption of liquor per

* October, 1887.

head in various districts where prohibition is more or less in force.

The following table shows the number of gallons of liquor consumed per head annually in the 7 provinces of the Dominion of Canada.

Province.	Gallons per head.
Prince Edward's Island	·884
Nova Scotia	1·323
New Brunswick	1·574
Manitoba	2·252
Quebec	3·873
Ontario	4·761
British Columbia	7·779

A comparison of these figures with the extent to which the Scott Act has been adopted in each province, clearly shows that the consumption of liquor decreases in proportion. It is a significant fact that British Columbia, where liquor shops flourish to an extent I have never seen equalled in any town in England, the consumption of liquor is about nine times greater than in Prince Edward's Island, where the Scott Act is in full force in every district.

This year a series of votes were taken in the Dominion House of Commons, which prove clearly enough that the elected representatives of the people support the Scott Act thoroughly. A proposal to repeal the Act altogether was lost by a vote of 145 to 38, and an amendment permitting the sale of wine and beer in prohibited districts was lost by 136 to 47. The vote was in no sense a party one, a majority both of the Liberals and Conservatives being secured for the maintenance of the Act.

The hostile criticisms of opponents have no weight with me in the face of these considerations, viz. :—

1. That districts which once adopt the Scott Act stick to it.

2. That the consumption of liquor decreases in each province in exact proportion to the extent in which the Scott Act is adopted.

3. That Parliament refuses by such overwhelming majorities of *both* political parties to repeal the Act or weaken its provisions.

I have visited a great number of the districts in which this Act is in force. No doubt in some of these the law is administered with great laxity, and the Press is full of complaints of the conduct of the inspectors and police magistrates whose duty it is to bring offenders to justice. But the entire law-abiding population as a rule uphold and defend the Act, and loyally carry out its provisions. I have been a guest at half-a-dozen houses in which my host was not an abstainer himself, yet, in deference to the public opinion, expressed by the adoption of the Acts, had not a drop of liquor of any kind in his house.

But those who speak most warmly in favour of the Acts are tradesmen other than liquor sellers, to whose tills the money goes which before was spent in drinking saloons.

The general opinion is that wherever the Scott Act has been fairly and rigorously enforced it has been a great blessing to the community, and no demand is ever made for its repeal. That where it is badly enforced, it has at any rate destroyed the charm and attractions of the liquor saloon, and has put an end to the system of "treating," which was so common all through Canada.

The sobriety of Canada, as compared with England, is shown by the amount of liquor consumed. Canada consumes one gallon of intoxicating liquor per head, compared with ten in England.

I have not gone into any details concerning the working of the Act. It is enough for the purpose of this chapter to set forth the facts I have enumerated, and I think every temperance reformer in England will agree with my conclusions, which are that it is clear that the people of Canada who have adopted prohibition like it too well to part with it, and that the whole of the Canadian people, speaking through their elected representatives, have no intention of repealing the Act.

The people themselves are the best judges of what is good for them in a matter so closely affecting their interests as this.

The temperance party in Canada look upon the Scott Act as only a stepping-stone to prohibition. I have come to the deliberate opinion that it is only a question of time, and not a very long time either, for Canada to adopt a universal prohibitory liquor law, such as exists in Maine. Public opinion is being educated at great speed by the experiences of the Scott Act, and I find everywhere and in all sections of society an inclination towards prohibition that is very encouraging to the hopes and aspirations of Canadian temperance reformers.

CHAPTER X.

ACROSS THE PACIFIC.

THE Canadian Pacific Railway Company can manage a great railway line to perfection, but they have much to learn before they can claim success as managers of an ocean line of steamers. When I arranged last July to cross the Pacific from Vancouver to Japan, I engaged my passage for a steamer sailing September 23rd. On arriving at Montreal I was informed that the date had been postponed to the 29th. On reaching Winnipeg the sailing was again postponed to October 2nd, and on arrival at Vancouver the date was finally fixed for October 7th. That date found us, with a number of our fellow-passengers, waiting for the "Port Victor," at Victoria; we could see nothing of the "Port Victor," and letters and telegrams to the Canadian Pacific Railway agent in Vancouver elicited no information whatever of any definite character. On the morning of the 8th, however, we were informed that the "Port Victor" was coaling at Nanaimo, would reach Esquimalt about noon, and that we were all to be at the Hudson's Bay Wharf with our luggage at two o'clock, when a tug would take us off. We assembled there at 1.30 to find neither tug nor anyone representing the Canadian Pacific Railway from whom any information could be obtained. We stood about for two or three hours, all grumbling as only Englishmen can, when one of the Canadian Pacific Railway clerks came to say that the tug would be there

L

at five o'clock. This time he was right, and by six o'clock we were alongside the "Port Victor" in the noble harbour of Esquimalt.

Here we found a scene of the wildest confusion. The Canadian Pacific Railway agent that morning had booked an extra sixty Chinese steerage passengers from Victoria, in addition to a hundred or more who had been put on board at Vancouver. He had done this without the knowledge of the captain of the "Port Victor," and the delay in getting us on board was due to the steam-tug having been used to ship these sixty extra Chinamen, for whom there was absolutely no accommodation whatever provided.

THE "PORT VICTOR."

After a hurried scrambling meal the twenty-seven cabin passengers demanded their berths, when it was found that the ship was only designed to carry twelve cabin passengers, and that the Canadian Pacific Railway agent had been obliged to requisition nearly all the officers' cabins, as well as to construct others as makeshifts. We fared better than anyone else, for knowing that the "Port Victor" was only a second-class steamer, I had secured by extra payment two entire cabins for my daughter and myself; these, however, have proved anything but satisfactory on the voyage, as the one I occupy is a bath-room and closet converted for the occasion, and is swarming with cockroaches and such like company, which a week's treatment with Keating's powder and carbolic acid has failed to drive away.

Two ladies who were going out as missionaries were put in a wretched little room converted from a steward's pantry, and twice on the voyage have been drowned out of it by burst pipes, soaking their beds, and the entire contents of their trunks. Two gentlemen found themselves in a temporary structure next to the funnel, with a large stove-pipe enclosed within; the temperature in this dog-kennel has ranged from 85 to 100 degrees, and the tenants have been obliged to sleep on the settees in the saloon. None of the cabins appeared to have been cleaned out after the previous voyage, and when a day or two after starting I insisted on having my daughter's cabin and my own cleaned out, the amount of dirt, dead cockroaches, &c., which had to be removed was terrible.

The saloon accommodates just sixteen persons to table; with officers we are thirty-four, so that two services of each meal are necessary, and the cooks and stewards are certain to be worked beyond their powers.

By seven o'clock we all know our fate for the voyage, and we expect every moment to see the anchor weighed and get away. But presently the steam-tug comes alongside once more with a pile of planks on deck and twenty carpenters, and we are informed that it will be impossible to leave that night, as sleeping accommodation must be provided for the sixty extra Chinamen. We go to bed, but not to sleep. The tramp of workmen, the noise of their hammers, and their drunken blasphemy make night hideous. However, at five o'clock on Sunday morning, October 9th, we get under way, and by noon the beautiful mountains of the Olympian range are fading from view, and we are on the wide Pacific.

In fairness to the Canadian Pacific Railway I must state that they are not directly responsible for this disgraceful management. The line at present is an independent one, run by Sir William

Pearce, M.P., who has a number of old Atlantic liners that he is employing in this service. I suppose, as he is only a stop-gap till the Canadian Pacific Railway can build or purchase fine steamers of their own, he thinks he can afford to treat his passengers with reckless disregard. It is a pity the Canadian Pacific Railway ever allowed their names to be associated with a management not under their own control. I have no doubt that when the line passes into their hands, as it will do in a few months, they will be as careful of the comfort of the passengers at sea as on land. If they are, no one will have anything to complain of.

It is simply dishonest to take double the number of passengers a ship can carry, and when we happen upon stormy weather the discomfort and misery of everyone on board is almost intolerable. I feel it little short of a swindle that I should have been charged a fare and a half for a small cabin which was only fit to sleep in when drenched with carbolic acid, and in which I was generally awakened in the morning by cockroaches making their breakfast on my eyes. I warn any traveller who thinks of coming out to China or Japan to give the Canadian Pacific Railway line of steamers a very wide berth until the management is changed. We have, however, been singularly fortunate in our captain, who has done everything in his power to counteract the disgraceful management of his charterers. Captain Bird is only twenty-six years old, and has been but nine years at sea. He was promoted to the command of the "Port Victor" this voyage, and has fully justified the singular confidence reposed in him by the owners. His whole management of the ship and the comfort of his passengers under the grossly unfair strain which has been put upon him by Sir William Pearce's agents, has earned the gratitude of all on board. I have taken a good many voyages in my day, but never met with a captain whose popularity was so great with his officers, his crew, and his passengers, or whose popularity was so thoroughly well deserved. His conduct of the ship has done much to obliterate the bad impressions formed by all the passengers of the treatment they have received.

A voyage across the Pacific leaves little to be said. We have had good weather on the whole, though we experienced fully ten days of strong head winds, which stretched the voyage out to eighteen days. The Pacific is a melancholy and desolate ocean, with continual fog and rain, and the latter part of the voyage was muggy and intensely hot, in consequence of the warm Japan current which flows up from the tropics at a speed varying from forty to a hundred miles a day. The atmosphere is damp and depressing, and discourages all exertion. The passengers spend their time chiefly in reading novels and books by various authorities on Japan. The most popular book on board has been one I brought with me from England, "East by West," a story of a tour round the world two years ago by H. W. Lucy, the well-known journalist and writer of " Toby's Diary " in *Punch*. I think every passenger on board has either read it or heard it read aloud. At night, when weather permits, we gather under the awning, and amuse ourselves with songs and glees, riddles, recitations, and stories. When the weather is wet or stormy, we go to our stuffy and crowded cabins, and get to sleep as soon as we can.

We get some amusement out of our Chinese fellow-passengers. These are all kept in the forward part of the ship, and, when fine, take their meals on deck. They consume prodigious quantities of rice and meat, and seem inordinately fond of pickled eggs, which they crack and eat with great gusto, giving cries of delight in proportion to the relative " highness " of each egg. When the weather is bad they huddle below, and gamble furiously for "cash," small copper coins, a thousand of which are worth half-a-crown. If the sea is rough they proceed to "Chin Chin Joss." "Joss" is their head deity, and they are quite sure he cannot be aware that there are pious Chinese on board, or he would never tumble "Port Victor" about in such an unceremonious manner. They select a deputation to remonstrate with Joss. They write on sheets of paper the information that though the ship is manned by "Foreign devils," and that the cabin passengers are no better, yet there are hidden from his sight in the lower deck no less than 163 faithful people, who are very sea-sick. They then march round the ship with little paper flags flying, and a plate containing rice and a few copper coins, which with their humble petitions for calm weather they commit to the deep. Joss, however, remained obdurate, and we had nearly a week of head winds and pitching. One of the stewards, a Chinaman, viewed the proceedings with great contempt, as a professing Christian; he informed me, "Me no silly chin-chin Joss, me chin-chin Sky-God, same as English."

At noon on the 26th the observations informed us that we were at last within thirty hours of Yokohama, if the weather remained favourable, and that we might reasonably hope for but one night more on board. But during the night we were kept back by a strong wind and sea, which, early on the morning of the 27th, developed into a hurricane. The captain wisely decided not to attempt to land, as the storm had increased in intensity the nearer we approached it. So at two o'clock the ship was with much difficulty put about, and for twelve hours we steamed slowly with head to wind, and our backs to Yokohama. The seas were tremendous, and at six o'clock were breaking over the ship in great volume, making it impossible to cross the decks without being drenched or washed off one's feet, the wind blowing with full typhoon strength. Under Captain Bird's admirable seamanship, we rode it out without the loss of a spar, with the exception of the Chinamen's galley, a temporary structure on deck, which went by the board as the ship was being laid to. The "Port Victor" behaved as well as a ship could, though we were all considerably rolled about. At two o'clock on the morning of the 28th the storm abated, and after three unsuccessful efforts the ship was at last brought about, and morning found us once more heading for Yokohama.

The passengers were a pallid and limp company. Very few

VRIES VOLCANO.—YOKOHAMA BAY.
(*From a sketch by the Author.*)

of them had slept a wink, and some had sat up all night, too frightened to go to bed ; indeed some who had gone to bed were rolled out so often that they gave it up for a bad job and sat it out on the floor. Our cabins being amidships we slept better than others. I slept from eight at night to six next morning, carefully wedged in between an air-pillow and the mattrass, only awakened by efforts to get the ship about, which would have roused Rip Van Winkle. Some of the passengers had expressed a wish to "see a typhoon." What they did see was near enough to the genuine article to prevent their expressing it any more. The cargo shifted during the night, giving the ship a list to leeward of about three feet. At ten o'clock we were running along the coast of one of the outlying islands of Japan. We passed a good many sampans, or native boats, engaged in fishing, and through our glasses could see quaint villages and wooded hills. One of the islands we passed was a volcano, not a very big affair, but smoking vigorously. At noon Yokohama was in sight, and an hour later we dropped anchor, and bid a glad good-bye to the "Port Victor" from the steam launch of the Grand Hotel.

CHAPTER XI.

YOKOHAMA.

THE passengers by the "Port Victor" were more reconciled to their bad treatment on hearing the fate of the "City of Sydney," the steamer of the rival line from San Francisco, which arrived the day after. She was caught in the same hurricane which delayed us, but fared much worse than we did. Her saloon was waist-deep in water for twelve hours, some of her deck cabins were swept overboard, two of her boats were stove in, and one of her crew drowned.

The passengers came into our hotel at Yokohama in terrible plight. All their luggage was soaked with salt water, and they were much exhausted and worn out. Certainly the Pacific does not deserve its name, so far as our experience has gone.

Yokohama is a modern seaport divided into European and Japanese quarters. The European portion of the town is very handsome, consisting entirely of the offices and residences of merchants, stretching for about a mile in length. There is a fine esplanade called the Bund, on which the principal hotels, a fine club, and handsome houses are to be found. Behind this is Main Street, where the banks, merchants' offices, stores, and other business premises are placed. The town terminates in a fine bluff, on which pretty villas are dotted. The Japanese quarter contains many fine shops and stores, where native products such as rice, silks, embroideries, lacquer-ware, pottery, and fine metal work are exposed for sale.

The trade of Yokohama is considerable. There are no wharves or docks, vessels riding at anchor in a fine bay. This presents a busy and picturesque scene with some twenty or thirty fine steamers of all nations, combined with native junks, sampans, and bustling steam launches.

TEA-HOUSE NEAR THE BLUFF, YOKOHAMA.

I noticed steamers under the flags of the Peninsular and Oriental, the Canadian Pacific, the White Star, and the Holt Lines (all English); the Occidental and Oriental (United States), the Messageries (French), the German Lloyds, the Japanese Mails, with British, American, Japanese, and Russian men-of-war. It is gratifying to know that, as usual all over the world, three-fourths of the carrying trade of Japan is done under the British flag. There are 1,250 European residents in Yokohama, of whom 587 are British, 228 United States, 160 German, and 109 French.

YOKOHAMA HARBOUR.

Yokohama twenty-five years ago was only a small fishing village. It is now a flourishing town of 70,000 inhabitants, the chief port of Japan, a first-class station on the road both from Canada and the United States to China and the East Indies, and is the terminus of the Peninsular and Oriental, Messageries Maritimes, and the German Lloyds in the far East. The entire export and import trade of Yokohama amounts to about six and a half millions sterling.

We took up our quarters at the Grand Hotel, which has the reputation of being the finest hostelry in the East, and I can quite believe it, for I never stayed at a better, East or West. After taking our rooms we started out for a Jin-rickisha ride

A STREET IN YOKOHAMA.

through the town. The Jin-rickisha is the universal conveyance of Japan.* It is impossible to hire a carriage or a horse; every journey, long or short, whether from one point to another in the towns, or for a 200 mile journey across country, except on the two small railways, must be taken in Jin-rickishas. This conveyance is something between a single perambulator and a hansom cab, with a hood that shuts back, and seating one person only. It is very lightly built, with two wheels about 4 feet in diameter, and slender brass-bound shafts, united together by a tie-piece at the end. It is drawn by a man who gets in

* See frontispiece.

between the shafts, pressing against the cross-bar at the end. For long journeys you drive tandem, and a man of weight like myself often engages three. These men trot along at from five to seven miles an hour, and are splendid specimens of muscular development; their calves are a wonder to behold, and would be the envy of a London flunky. The dress of these men consists of a pale-blue cotton shirt with hanging sleeves, and tight-fitting breeches of the same material coming down to the knee. Legs and feet are brown, tanned, and bare, with the exception of the universal straw shoe, tied on by straw twists, with a loop through which they thrust the great toe.

We start off through the European town, admiring the pretty Eastern-looking houses and their lovely gardens, go to the bank for some money, telegraph our safe arrival to friends at home, and then drive on to the Japanese town, eager to see the quaint and interesting people of whom we have heard so much. The shops were odd and strange; they are without fronts, and the floors are raised about two feet from the ground in one high step, some three or four feet back from the threshold. The floor is covered with white fine matting, scrupulously clean, and it is customary to kick off the shoes and enter the shop in your stocking feet. Sometimes, in the case of Europeans, who have an unfortunate habit of ignoring the customs of foreigners, a servant will bring out a large cloth and carefully wipe the dirt off the shoes of customers who decline to take them off.

The goods are displayed on stands and ranged on shelves, the reserve stock being kept at the back or in fire-proof warehouses adjoining, which appear to be built of planished copper sheets fastened on the wood, thick enough to resist flames from *outside* in case the light structures in the neighbourhood take fire.

It matters not at what shop we halt, the proprietor comes

BUYING CHRYSANTHEMUMS, YOKOHAMA.

bowing out and begs us to look at anything we please, never once asking us to buy. At one we see a platform weighing-machine, and our whole party weigh themselves, to the ecstatic delight and amusement of the tradesman and his children, who are summoned out to enjoy the spectacle. Much interest is taken in my portly form, as the diminutive Japanese greatly admire bulk. I am, however, personally gratified to find that the "Port Victor" has taken 15 lbs. off my weight.

Every shop has a pretty china vase standing against the wall, with a few branches of chrysanthemums arranged in it with that singular feeling for colour which seems almost universal in Japan. We bought a great bunch of beautiful blooms from a peripatetic flower-merchant for a few small copper coins.

After a two hours' stroll we were glad to get back to our hotel, enjoy a good dinner and go to bed. No one knows what a priceless blessing is bed, who has not been tumbled about for three stormy nights in the hard bunk of a steamer.

Japan is one of the rainiest countries in the world, and Saturday morning was one of its rainiest days. The annual rainfall at Yokohama is about 160 inches, and, if my memory serves me, I think the only place in the British Islands at all approaching to this is Seathwaite-in-Borrowdale.

Our party for Japan consists of my daughter and myself, with an American gentleman and his wife, named Russell, whose friendship we have formed during the voyage across the Pacific, and who, like ourselves, are travelling round the world. As the rain is so heavy, the ladies go in Jin-rickishas to do some shopping, while Mr. Russell and I go over to Tokio to visit our respective legations, and get passports, without which it is not permitted to travel into the interior.

We had each of us written to our ambassadors the night before, begging that, if possible, we might have our passports next day, as our time was very limited. On arriving at Tokio, we repaired to our respective legations. I not only obtained my passport, but had an excellent lunch and an hour's interesting conversation with Mr. Trench, our *chargé d'affaires*. Mr. Russell, however, when we met, told me to his and my great disappointment that he could not get his passport for two days. I suggested to him that he should go back to his ambassador and express his surprise that America should fail to get passports as quickly as England. He did so, and in consequence got it the next morning.

While in Tokio that afternoon, I called on a lady, an old friend of mine, Miss Dawbarn, of Liverpool, who left England nearly two years ago with a view to engaging in missionary work at her own expense. I found her comfortably settled in a pretty Japanese house, where she teaches English to classes of gentlemen and ladies on alternate days. She makes some charge, and finds she can get as many pupils as she can manage. They are all drawn from the wealthy classes, and she hopes to be able to influence many of them in favour of Christianity. She seemed very happy in her work, and sanguine of success. Many of her pupils are now members of the various missionary churches.

I also saw a native funeral procession, very different from the ugly and depressing institution which prevails in England. The great feature of the procession was abundance of beautiful flowers. I saw at least fifty great garlands of chrysanthemums, five or six feet high and three feet in diameter, each of which must have contained many hundreds of blooms, being borne in the procession, which was headed by a number of priests in bright-coloured picturesque robes.

On the following morning we all left Yokohama early, *en route* for Nikko, a journey of about 110 miles, of which 80 was by railway. Japanese railways are narrow gauge, about three feet wide, laid in double-headed rails on chairs and sleepers, and the train travels about 18 miles an hour. The stations are scrupulously neat and clean, and the rolling stock is very comfortable. The carriages are seated like omnibuses, with the first-class divided into three compartments, all communicating, and it is possible to traverse the train from end to end as in America. There are about 150 miles of railway now open in Japan, and some 450 more are projected, which will be built as soon as funds permit. English engine-drivers are employed, but the passenger and goods traffic is all managed by Japanese.

The line from Yokohama terminates at Tokio, and we had to ride in Jin-rickishas for three or four miles across Tokio to reach the station for Utsunomiya, our next stage sixty miles further on.

This journey was very full of interest, as the line passes through the finest agricultural district in Japan. It is densely populated, and the farms vary in size from half an acre to ten acres. Nearly every house we passed had pretty little gardens full of flowers, mostly chrysanthemums, now in all their glory, with quaintly-trimmed trees four or five feet high, tiny little waterfalls and ponds, with toy bridges and boats. Some of these gardens looked exactly like a willow-pattern plate.

The soil is of magnificent quality and depth, and the whole country is running with clear streams of water, forming a complete system of irrigation. On most of the farms it is quite possible to get three crops in the year off the land. The main crop is rice, the staple food of the Japanese, and the whole country was yellow with the ripe grain, now being harvested. Every inch of the soil is cultivated. There are no hedges or ditches, the farms being divided by a small raised ridge about six inches high, which carries a little crop of its own on joint account for the two farmers whose land it divides. The soil is tilled by hand only. In a journey of eighty miles I only saw two horses, each engaged in drawing a small plough. Most of the cultivation is done by a curious hand plough, which turns up a 3 ft. furrow every blow. The land seems capable of growing any crop that is put into it. Besides rice, I saw patches of tea, onions, daikons (a long white turnip, that seems a great article of diet everywhere), cauliflower, cabbage, beans, cotton, caladiums, buckwheat, ginger, carrots, barley, sweet and common potatoes, peas, beets, pepper, bamboos, tobacco, radishes, lettuce, maize, dhurra, celery, lotus (the seeds of which are a favourite food), artichokes, castor oil, and everywhere small clumps of yellow chrysanthemums, the flowers of which are boiled and eaten with much relish. Besides these ground crops there were orchards of mulberry-trees for silkworm culture, pears, cherries, plums, peaches, and persimmons, weighed down with golden fruit, a great favourite with Japanese of all sorts and conditions. These trees were all hung round with great bunches of rice straw, toughening to be plaited into hats and shoes. Not even in the best parts of Belgium is such perfect cultivation to be found as in this beautiful garden of Japan.

Four hours after leaving Tokio we arrived at Utsunomiya, the capital of a province, with a population of 25,000. We walked up to our quarters for the night, escorted through the streets by an admiring crowd of natives of all ages, who made huge merriment of our various peculiarities of dress, but with a good-natured politeness that took away the smallest trace of offence. I felt quite conceited at the special attention I received personally, due entirely to my six feet of height among a five-foot people. As we walk along, laughing groups run ahead and bring out their biggest men, whom they range alongside of me, driving them away with scorn as they fail to reach my gauge. My beard also receives much attention. One girl came up to me, bowed almost to the ground, and then pulled my beard, and ran away laughing.

M

The children are delightful and quaint beyond all description. The boys have their heads shaved, except odd little tufts on the crown and sometimes behind the ears, the little girls wearing their hair exactly as it appears on the twopenny fans so universal all over England. All the babies are bound on the backs of other children, and it is common to see a baby a year old tied

GROUP OF CHILDREN, UTSUNOMIYA.

on the back of a brother or sister three or four years old. Nothing is seen of the baby but its head, and the combination presents the droll appearance of a two-headed child. The baby is as jolly and laughter-loving as its bearer, and both grin and laugh in happy unison. All the children, great and small, laugh from crown to toe, are fat and well nourished, and are the happiest and jolliest children on the face of the earth. I never tire of the charming groups they make at every street corner. They swarm in every village like rabbits in a warren. Japanese children are the chief delight of their parents. I never saw such happy, well-behaved children. The only time I have ever heard one cry was when I came suddenly round a corner in some country village, when I fear they mistook me for the Red-whiskered Devil. They are never scolded or punished in any

DOLL AND FAN.

way, either at home or at school, and a parent who struck a child would be shunned as a monster. I do not, however, think this treatment would answer in England. I have heard the excellent qualities of Japanese children ascribed to their vegetarian diet, but I must leave wiser dietists than I to settle that question. The Japanese love to turn their children out smartly dressed, with doll and fan, and the bright harmonious colours, the infinite variety of pattern and material, with the quaint cut of the garment added to their absurdly comical heads, plump faces, and beady-black eyes, yield never-failing amusement to us all.

We stayed the night at a Tea-house, as the Japanese hotels are called. We found ourselves, on arrival, in front of a large house, of which the whole ground floor is open to the street; six feet back from the parapet is flush with the street, and the whole of the rest of the floor is raised about two feet. The edge of this floor is used as a seat for Jin-rickisha men, village gossips, &c., and a part of it carries a small counter, on which are arranged little dishes of fish, vegetables, rice, and what not, ready to be cooked at a charcoal fire behind it, for any passer-by who may order a meal. Immediately behind this step the whole of the vast floor is covered with spotless white matting, every one taking off his shoes before stepping upon it. The area is quite bare and empty, divided by black wooden lines, which, on examination, are found to be grooves, in which at night light frames covered with opaque translucent paper partitions slide into position, forming separate rooms for sleeping. At one side is a raised dais, prettily decorated with pictures and choice little works of art, with the usual pot of chrysanthemums in bloom. Every hotel is obliged to have this dais, on which the Mikado, or Emperor of Japan, would sit if he ever visited the village, and selected that particular tea-house as his abode. Every one of the many thousand tea-houses in Japan has one of these dais, all of which are daintily decorated with flowers and household treasures.

At the back of every tea-house is a pretty little garden, with a large bath-house, containing tubs of hot and cold water. The Japanese are as scrupulously clean in their persons as in their houses, and often wash all over two or three times a day. The room in which we had our dinner looked out upon the large open window of the bath-house, in which three men and two women were tubbing, with that absolute disregard of decency which characterised our common parents before the fall, when they were naked and not ashamed. Later on in the evening, as I was passing to my room, one of the waitresses, in the costume of Eve, made me a most profound and grave bow, wishing me good-night. No Japanese has yet become civilized enough, with all their wonderful civilization, to believe it possible under any circumstances that he or she is naked. In summer

INTERIOR OF TEA-HOUSE, BEDROOM FLOOR.

times this condition of things is universal. It is a little embarrassing at first to the modest European, but one soon gets used to it, and accepts it as the primitive innocence of a simple and guileless people.

Europeans cannot eat Japanese food, except eggs and rice; everything else is more or less "high" and pungent in flavour. So all the guides are excellent cooks, and in tea-houses on frequented routes there are nice little kitchens with small charcoal fires, where the guide manages to produce excellent meals, the materials for which have to be brought along from the large towns, as it is only possible in smaller towns and villages to purchase vegetables and rice. Milk is an unknown dainty in Japan, except in large towns where Europeans live. At Nikko, where some 1,500 Europeans go during the year, there are two cows, but I have not seen one since I entered the country.

We have an excellent guide in Mr. Hakodate, of Yokohama, who produced us an admirable dinner of soup, fish, steak, chicken, and pudding. At ten o'clock the servants make up the bed-rooms. They rattle out the sliding paper partitions, and our sitting-room is at once divided into three bed-rooms, on the floor of which our "beds" are laid. These consist of three or four thick quilts, with another rolled up for a bolster. You may have either a thin mattrass with warm covering, or a thick mattrass with light covering. We slept very well on the whole, though the ladies found it a strange and novel experience.

There was no other furniture of any kind or description, and our clothes had to be laid on the floor. In the morning, for our ablution, we had the choice of the bath-house or a tiny basin of water placed on a shelf in the garden, with a tub and dipper by its side. We had brought each a towel and soap, and the whole party took it turn about to wash at the basin, as we have not been long enough in Japan to face the bath-house. After an excellent breakfast we prepared to start off to Nikko, a drive of about twenty-five miles. Eight Jin-rickishas, with a crowd of laughing noisy human horses, were gathered round the door, and soon we were all stowed away in them, rattling through the streets of Utsunomiya to the ecstatic delight of hundreds of jolly children, who pursued us with peals of laughter and cries of "O-hy-o! O-hy-o!" (good-morning). The road to Nikko is all up-hill, rising 800 feet. Each Jin-rickisha had two men in tandem except mine, which had three, I being nearly double the weight of any other member of our party. It is simply astonishing how these vigorous little chaps spin along. Our first stage was 11 miles, which we covered in 1 hour and 35 minutes, our second was 7½ miles in 65 minutes, and our last 6¼ miles in 50 minutes, the whole 25 miles being covered in three hours and a half, or at the rate of nearly eight miles an hour.

They ran their empty vehicles back the same day, delighted to get three shillings each for the job.

We stopped twice at road-side tea-houses, to give the men a quarter hour's rest and breathing. They did not seem to drink anything, although they were streaming with perspiration, but they rinsed out their mouths at the roadside stream, washing their legs and arms as well. At one tea-house they all had dinner.

JIN-RICKISHA MAN IN HIS STRAW RAIN COAT.

This consisted of a bowl of boiled rice, a poached egg, and a mess of stewed vegetables, all served in pretty lacquer vessels on a tray. The cost of this meal, which is their usual dinner daily, was just a penny farthing of our money.

The men put on a new pair of shoes at every stage. They wear a thick plaited straw sole or sandal, bound to the foot by thin swathes, and get three pair for a penny. The horses are shod also with straw shoes, and a main road on which there is much traffic is strewn all the way with old straw shoes.

THE ROAD TO NIKKO.

When the weather is wet the Jin-rickisha men wear cloaks and hats of straw, giving them the appearance of being thatched, like a small walking haystack. The farmers and better sort of folk put on a cloak of yellow oiled paper, perfectly waterproof, similar to that used in a copying-press at home, and all carry gigantic paper umbrellas of gorgeous pattern, oiled to make them waterproof. It can rain in Japan, but it is well worth while to endure two or three wet days for the sake of the odd costumes one meets at every turn.

The road we are travelling on is one of the great highways of Japan, and the whole way is a long avenue of magnificent cryptomerias, a tree something like a fine Scotch fir in appearance. These trees are about 100 feet in height, and this noble avenue runs for fifty miles. These trees were originally planted by a pious Daimio, or prince, and a more imposing preparation for the religious glories of Nikko could not have been conceived. The road itself is an excellent, well-made gravel road, with a stream of crystal water about two feet wide and one deep, running along both sides, conveying water to the populous villages which line the route.

The scenery all along the road is very beautiful. A Shinto shrine, with its odd torii or bird-perches, a quaint roadside tea-house, a farmyard with peasants threshing out rice or millet, charming groups of children playing about some pretty village street, or in its bright gardens, the perfect tillage of the fields, the low ranges of wooded hills gorgeous in autumn tints of vermilion and gold, with the blue mountains of Nikko, 8,000 feet high, for a background, form fresh and delightful pictures at every turn of the road.

The traffic of the country seems all to be done by human beings and a few pack-horses. In the fifty miles to Nikko and back we did not see a dozen carts. There is an omnibus from Utsunomiya to Nikko, holding six people, before which a man runs blowing a furious horn to warn everybody to get out of the way of this terrible and dangerous vehicle.

Men and women alike bear a hand in the transport of goods about the country; the man in the shafts of the handcart, the wife pushing merrily behind, with the inevitable baby on her back bobbing up and down with a broad grin and a nose that wants blowing. The only drawback to Japan is the absence of children's pocket-handkerchiefs.

No animals are to be seen except the pack-horses, which are nasty, vicious, badly-broken ponies; cats with short stumpy tails, an odd dog or two, and some poultry about the size of decent bantams. Cows, sheep, and pigs are no use in a country where nobody eats meat. I have not seen a single butcher's shop, except at Yokohama, during my whole visit.

The only machine of any kind that I saw in my two hundred miles of travel is the rice-pounder, which consists of a long beam of wood swung on a pivot, not unlike a see-saw, at the end of which is a stout peg at right angles; underneath this peg is a stone hollow filled with rice, and a man jumps off and on the other end, which of course makes the peg rise and fall into the hollow, thus pounding the rice into flour.

In large villages this is done by an undershot water-wheel, which revolves a series of tilts, like a tilt hammer in a forge, but the wooden pegs and stone hollows are just the same as in the more primitive farmyard machine.

Every house and cottage in Japan seems to have a stream of bright sparkling water running in front of it. This is used by the whole family or village for promiscuous ablutions, for washing clothes and vessels, for irrigating their gardens and little farms, and is yet always so clear and pure to look at that one could put in a glass and drink it with pleasure, so far as appearance goes. There are, however, few countries where water is so dangerous to drink unless boiled, and I always drink tea, the national beverage, which is a pale, weak infusion, very pleasant and refreshing, when one has got used to its peculiar flavour.

The village graveyard is a small patch of ground surrounded by trees, and each grave is marked by a square, upright stone, with an inscription. It is a puzzle at first to account for the smallness of each grave until one learns that Japanese coffins are square, and the body squeezed in with the knees tucked up to the chin. We passed a funeral on our way, the coffin being about 2½ feet square, the body inside extremely unpleasant, and it was quite time that the ceremony took place.

When a woman marries in Japan, she deliberately destroys her good looks by staining her teeth jet black. I don't know how it is done, but it gives one quite a shock to meet a nice smartly-dressed young woman, with a magnificent chignon of black hair, studded with tortoiseshell pins and combs, and a jaunty rose stuck at the top, and then to have the whole thing destroyed by a black smile, that gives the appearance of the mouth being a vast dark cavern. Strolling through Utsunomiya, I saw the show-case of a dentist filled with "guinea jaws" of shiny black false teeth. I am glad to hear that fashionable people are abandoning this hideous practice, and as fashion is everything in Japan, I hope it will soon disappear. The notion which inspires the custom is, that a girl once married, has only attractions for her husband, and must no longer present a pleasing appearance to the world at large. The success is complete.

Every Japanese man has a pipe-case and tobacco-pouch stuck in his girdle, and these are often beautiful works of art, decorated with raised metal-work or carved ivory. The pipe itself is a straight bronze or bamboo tube with a tiny bowl at the end, in which a pinch of fine tobacco is placed. After three whiffs the ash is thrown out, and the bowl re-filled.

The only intoxicating liquor drunk by the Japanese is saké, a drink made from rice, which has the colour and appearance of pale sherry. This is kept in a barrel and drawn off into long china bottles, which are dipped into hot water and served on lacquer trays with little cups, on which the god of good luck is painted. It does not seem to be largely consumed, and I have only seen one man under its influence. I have, however, seldom seen a more imbecile-looking drunkard, and I am told that its effect makes the drinker more supremely silly than any other known intoxicant. On the whole, I think the Japanese are an unusually sober people.

CHAPTER XII.

NIKKO.

THE hotel at Nikko is a Japanese house, kept in Japanese style, but with generous concessions to European customers. It is true we all have to perform our ablutions in turn on one corner of the verandah, before the gaze of admiring critics in the shape of children, who gather early in the morning on coigns of vantage to see the foreigners wash themselves; but our wash-basin is a marvellously beautiful bit of Japanese workmanship. It is true that the rooms are one vast door, and that you can enter or leave at any point of any wall, by sliding one of the many frames; but we have bedsteads, chairs and tables, a cook who has had lessons from a Frenchman, and our drinking water is placed on the table in a Scotch whisky bottle, and a Bass's beer bottle, with the labels still attached, giving a festive and rakish, though thoroughly English, appearance to the meal, hardly acceptable, however, to good teetotallers like the whole of our party.

Shortly after arrival, the Japanese "chef" served us a very tolerable dinner. When it had been removed, and tea brought in, suddenly every side of the room slid open, and six bowing and smiling Japanese silently entered, each with an enormous bundle on his back. They shut themselves in, placed their burdens on the ground and begun to unfasten them, all the while softly sucking in their breath in a curious faint whistle. We demanded instant explanation, and the ringleader said,

"Mr. Shentlemans! We very good Japanese Number One Curios!" and promptly placed on the table a large pot and a lacquer box. The others followed suit, and soon pandemonium set in. Each of the six pressed his rival wares upon our attention, and the table, chairs, walls, and floor were covered with an assortment of pottery, new and old, lacquer, bronze, old Daimio's robes, swords, knives, embroidery, and what not. Out of a wilderness of modern rubbish, we managed to select some

THE HOTEL AT NIKKO.

really fine specimens of old lacquer, pottery, embroideries, and metal work, which we eventually purchased at about one-half the price demanded. This experience was repeated every night, not only at Nikko, but almost everywhere in Japan, at tea-house or hotel.

Nikko is the great wonder of Japan. Its shrines and temples are celebrated wherever the Buddhist religion exists. "Nikko" means "sunny splendour," and it well deserves the

ROW OF BUDDHAS AT NIKKO; NAN-TAI-SAN MOUNTAINS IN THE DISTANCE.
From a sketch by the Author.

name. The town is small, and is filled with tea-houses for the accommodation of the pilgrims who resort thither at times and seasons of religious festivals. It lies in a lovely valley, through which a clear mountain river rushes, furnishing water for endless streams and leats rippling through street, lane, and garden. It is surrounded by high hills, clad to the summit with magnificent cryptomeria trees, in their turn overtopped by mountains, of which the highest, Nantai-san, about 10,000 feet above the sea, is gorgeous in autumn splendour from base to summit. Here dwells the Wind-god, and pilgrims ascend the mountain in the Spring, to a shrine on the top, where they arrange with his godship for a proper supply of rain and fine weather throughout the year. Nantai-san responds nobly, sending down his generous flanks a dozen ample streams, which irrigate thousands of square miles of fertile land.

The next morning we went up the valley to get a view of the Nikko range, following a path by the banks of a brawling stream full of trout, bordered by luxuriant and varied vegetation glorious in autumn gold and copper. Two miles from Nikko we reach the famous images of Amida Buddha, arranged in a long row of many hundreds by the river-side, contemplating with great serenity of countenance (unless their heads have been knocked off by Shinto blasphemers), the noble range of which Nantai-san is the centre and summit. It is supposed to be impossible to count this long row of images, and while the rest of the party engaged in the attempt to do so, I made a sketch of the beautiful landscape, which is reproduced on the previous page.

Nikko has been a holy place to the Buddhists since the eighth century, when a wise old Buddhist missionary from China visited it, and had a confidential interview with Nantai-san, the Shinto deity of the mountains; instead of declaring him an impostor, as any vulgar reformer might have done, he annexed him as a "manifestation of Buddha," which position he has occupied ever since.

All the glories of Nikko centre in the tomb of the great Shogun Iye-yasu, who drove out the Jesuits and extirpated Christianity. His son buried him with great pomp and splendour in the year 1617, on the top of a hill above Nikko, and the Mikado made a god of him as "the light of the East, the great incarnation of Buddha." Nikko, in all its former magnificence of Buddhist ritual and paraphernalia, with its 200 priests clad in gorgeous robes, must have been a wonderful sight. But its glory has departed with the disestablishment of Buddhism, and now six Shinto priests sell tickets of admission to Christian tourists whom Iye-yasu would have promptly crucified, and the only ritual visible was at one of the large temples, where a melancholy old lady in shining raiment, with a fan and a bunch of small bells, goes through a brief dance for any one who will throw a copper into a bowl. We bought three or four performances for as many farthings.

On leaving the hotel, and walking up the main street of the town, we come to two bridges, one of which is carefully guarded by locked gates. This bridge is made of wood, lacquered a deep red, and has never been repaired since 1638, the year in which it was built. It appeared perfectly sound, and there is no trace of decay from the wear and tear of 250 years of Japanese rain and storm. The blue waters of the river, which is here 40 feet wide only, rush under the bridge between two steep banks, the warm Indian red of the lacquered wood contrasting finely with the dark cool green of the splendid cryptomerias, the whole scene brightened by the torrent beneath. This sacred bridge is only opened once a year, during the great festival week.

Soon after crossing the river, we mount a flight of broad wide steps, leading to the great granite Torii or Shinto archway erected in 1618. It is 27 feet 6 inches high, and the columns are fine monoliths, 3 feet 6 inches in diameter.

Passing under this archway we see a magnificent pagoda of five stories in height, rising 104 feet, the eaves of the roofs being

THE PAGODA, NIKKO.

18 feet in length. The lower story is surrounded by twelve emblematical animals: a rat, bull, tiger, hare, dragon, serpent, horse, goat, ape, cock, dog, and pig; all carved and painted with wonderful resemblance to life. This pagoda is most graceful in form, and its harmonious decorations stand out well against

the dark background of cryptomerias, which everywhere lend such an added charm to the Nikko temples.

Passing on through the Nio-mon, or gate of the two kings, we find ourselves in a spacious courtyard, enclosed by a timber wall lacquered dark red. In this courtyard are three very fine buildings, arranged in the zig-zag so dear to the Japanese, which are used as store-houses for the various "properties" employed

HOLY WATER CISTERN, NIKKO.

at the annual festivals. Here also is a large tree, enclosed by a railing, which is said to have been one that Iye-yasu had planted in a pot shortly before his death, and which was transplanted here. Close to the tree is a handsome stable, in which is a sacred white pony, called "Jimme," kept for the use of the god, opposite to which is the famous holy-water cistern. This is cut from a solid block of granite, and is so carefully set, that the water flows in one even stream from every inch of its four sides. The cistern is covered by a wooden roof, clamped on to twelve square granite pillars, with finely chased bronze plates. The roof is richly carved and painted, and being open, affords a good opportunity of studying the marvellous joinery of these old Japanese carpenters. Just beyond the holy-water

THE KIO-ZO, OR LIBRARY, NIKKO.

basin is a beautiful decorated building, known as the Kio-zo, or library. Inside this building is a complete collection of Buddhist scriptures, mounted in a revolving eight-sided cupboard, with red-lacquered panels, and gold pillars. Round the interior walls are paintings of various subjects on a gold ground. In front of the building are some of the great stone and bronze lanterns, 6 feet in height, which are lighted up on the feast days.

A fresh flight of steps leads us to another courtyard, along the front of which is a stone balustrade, on which is placed a bell tower, a huge bronze candelabrum, presented by the King

KOREAN BRONZE LANTERN, NIKKO.

of Loochoo, a bronze lantern, the gift of a Korean king, and a drum tower. Behind these is a temple decorated with fifteen or sixteen groups of carved birds that well repaid an hour's study.

THE YO-MEI-MON GATE, NIKKO.

Yet another flight of stone steps brings us to the platform on which stands the gem of Nikko, the wondrously beautiful gate called Yo-mei-mon. This is supported by white-lacquered columns, carved with a small regular pattern. On one of the pillars the pattern is carved upside down, lest the perfection of the structure should excite the envy of the gods, and bring misfortune on the architect. This is called the "evil-averting pillar." The gateway has two stories, the lower one being surrounded by a gallery. The side niches to the front contain two ferocious-looking images, armed with bow and arrows; to the back, they contain the sacred dogs of Japan. The entire building is covered with marvellous sculpture. Here we see a tiger and cub, the grain of the wood cleverly used to produce the fur; here a group of flowers or fruit; there, birds, beasts, and fishes disporting themselves like nature itself. The capitals of the columns are the heads of strange, quaint, fabulous beasts. Where the cross-beams of the second story intersect are white-lacquered dragons' heads. The railing of the balcony consists of groups of children at play, and other figure subjects, alternating with birds, and the ends of the supporting beams are carved into the portraits of famous Chinese and Corean sages. The illustration on the previous page is the back view of this marvellous gateway.

Right and left of Yo-mei-mon extends a long cloister, the outer walls of which contain a double row of carved panels, consisting of groups of trees, birds, beasts, flowers and fruit, coloured after nature, all of marvellous beauty and great intricacy of workmanship. The base of the wall consists of great blocks of stone, from which rise uprights about 12 feet apart. These pass through thicker horizontal members. This produces a double row of elongated spaces, one 16 inches high, and the other 5 feet, in which the carved panels are inserted.

The lower range, which is the narrowest, consists altogether of representations of storks, ducks, geese, and other water-fowl, in flight, standing on the banks of streams and lakes, or swimming and diving in the water. The upper range consists of pierced work of floral composition chiefly, treated with great tenderness and beauty, with a masterly decision about the carving such as I have never seen anywhere before—the whole being one rich and harmonious mass of colour, such as only Japan can produce. On the following page is an illustration that gives some faint idea of what I have described so feebly. The cloisters within this wall are decorated with great simplicity.

Passing through Yo-mei-mon, we enter a court enclosed on three sides by the cloister I have just described; on the fourth side rises a great stone wall, built against the face of the hill. In this courtyard are several buildings. One contains a stage for the performance of sacred dances.

In another building is an altar before which worshippers burn sweet-smelling bits of cedar, while the priest recites prayers. A third contains some cars which are used in the annual festivals, in which the spirits of Iye-yasu and other heroes ride invisibly.

Emerging from this court, we enter a quadrangle fifty yards long, which leads to the holy of holies of Nikko, entered by a gateway as beautiful in execution and design as Yo-mei-mon itself. This is called Kara-mon, or Chinese Gate, and is built of precious woods from China, inlaid and carved with marvellous detail and skill. At this door we were met by a bald fat priest, who directed us to take off our shoes. The double doors of this entrance are richly decorated with arabesque work of flowers in gold relief. Dragons which seem almost alive twine themselves round the columns which support the roof. On the door is a mass of varied decoration perfectly distributed, in such beautiful detail and such harmonious completion, as to furnish a perfect

PORTION OF THE YO-MEI-MON CLOISTERS, NIKKO.

example of the thorough mastery of decorative art possessed by the architects and builders of this marvellous series of sacred building.

A few more steps lead into the oratory, a large room 42 feet long by 27 feet wide, covered with matting, in the middle of which is a black table, with a small circular mirror placed upon

NIO-MON GATE, ENTRANCE TO THE TEMPLES OF IYE-MITSU.

it, the sole emblem of the Shinto religion. The walls of this inner sanctuary are decorated with carved oak panels, and the ceiling is also carved and painted.

Returning to the courtyard and passing through a small doorway, over which is a famous carving of a sleeping cat, we mount 200 steep moss-grown steps, which lead to the summit of the hill. Here is the tomb of the mighty Shogun, Iye-yasu, a simple bronze casting, in front of which stands a low stone table on which are placed a huge bronze stork with a candlestick in its mouth, a bronze incense-burner, and a vase with brass lotus-flowers and leaves. Weary with six hours of wandering through these superb temples, we return to our hotel, leaving the minor temples of Iye-mitsu for the next day.

KARA-MON GATE, IYE-MITSU'S TEMPLES.

Passing through the Torii, which forms the entrance to the group of Buddhist temples leading up to the tomb of the second Shogun, Iye-mitsu, we come to two red-lacquered buildings standing together, joined by a covered gallery. One of these is sacred to the Indian goddess Ariti; a demon who had sworn to devour five hundred children in the metropolis of Buddhism, but who, being converted before she could carry out her fell

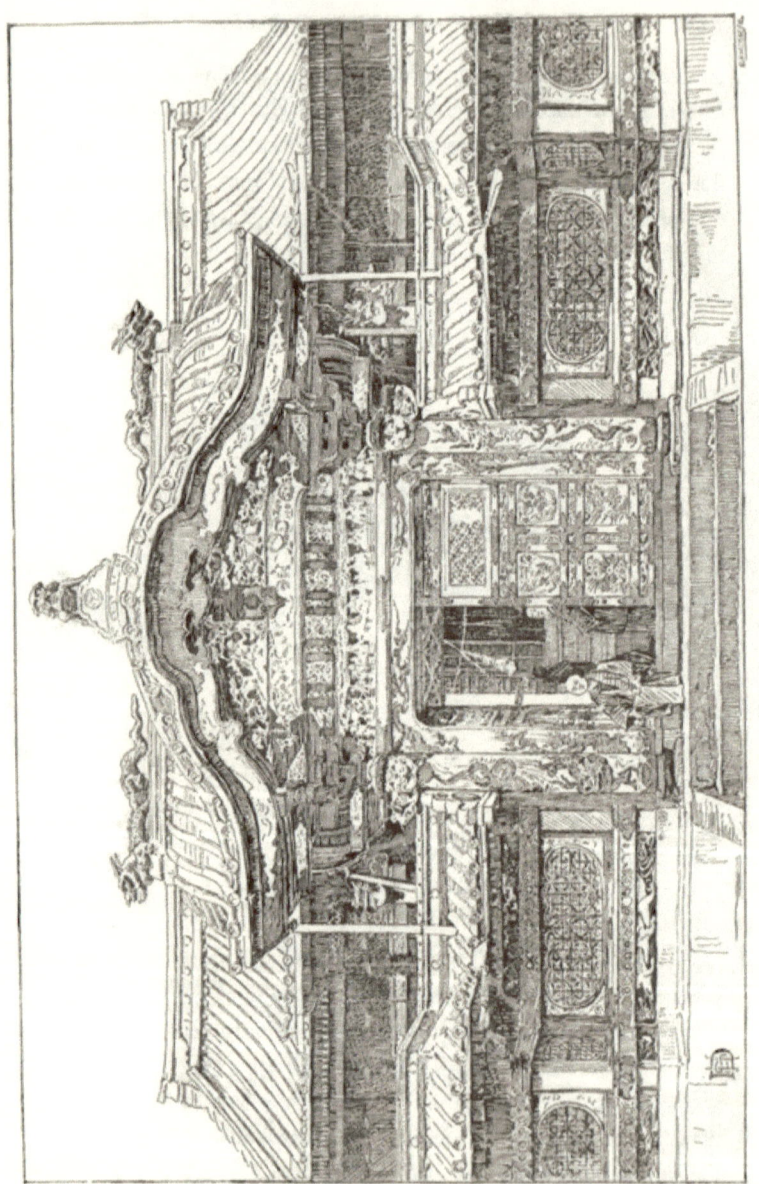

KARA-MON, OR CHINESE GATE, IYE-YASU'S TEMPLES.

purpose, forthwith entered a monastery and became a burning and shining Buddhist light. The other is dedicated to Amida, and in it are preserved the bones of the Shogun Yoritomo.

Beyond these buildings is the Nio-mon, the gate of the two Kings, at the top of a flight of wide steps. The two Kings are a gigantic pair of muscular figures, painted red, with every conceivable expression of warlike ferocity. Another flight of steps leads on to the gate called Ni-ten Mon, with similar statues painted green and red. Inside this gate is an image of the Wind-god, painted green, who carries the winds tied up in a long sack, slung over his shoulder. His companion is the Thunder-god, and both of these are as furious and turbulent-looking as Japanese ingenuity can carve them. The only other gate worth mentioning, in the succession which lead through the many courtyards to the tomb of Iye-mitsu, is the Kara-mon, of which I give an illustration on p. 190. All these courts contain many temples and other buildings fully equal in detail and interest to those of Iye-yasu, surrounded by the same cool green background of cryptomeria trees.

Returning from Iye-mitsu's tomb, we pass a building containing a curious life-like figure of an old man with a long beard, and preternaturally sturdy legs. This is an image of Enno Shokaku, a famous Buddhist saint, who possessed an extraordinary power of working miracles and charming spirits. He had special influence with Hill spirits, and many of the most arduous mountain paths are the result of their joint efforts. There is an unhappy Hill demon, named Hitokotonushi, who dared to disobey him, fast imprisoned in the centre of one of the Nikko mountains, who will not be let out till the Buddhist Messiah appears, 5,670,000,000 years hence. After conferring great benefits on the Japanese people, Enno flew away to China in the year 701, and was never heard of again.

His image is supported by two of his most obedient demons, painted red and green, by name Zenki and Goki. He is still supposed to be able to confer great physical strength, especially in the legs, and is the favourite saint of Jin-rickisha men, who hang up exaggerated straw sandals in all parts of the building as votive offerings.

We spent three days at Nikko, but they were only enough to show us the utter hopelessness of getting even an idea of the wondrously beautiful details of the whole. Nikko remains with me as a beautiful dream; I do not possess much more than a vivid remembrance of its massive temples looming warmly red against the cool green of the dense foliage, and I can only depend on photographs to bring back to my memory the infinite and beautiful details of their superb decoration.

Nikko has a right to stand in equal rank with the finest religious edifices in the world, Pagan or Christian; as a triumph of carpenter's work and of glyptic art, nothing in the world can bear comparison for a moment. It has been an education to have seen them, even in the hasty manner in which it has been possible to me.

During our stay at Nikko we took a day's excursion into the neighbouring mountains, our destination being the lake of Chiu-sen-je, 4,000 feet above the sea, through magnificent mountain and river scenery. The road was quite impassable for Jin-rickishas, so we took the other popular conveyance of Japan, the *Kago*, which consists of a stout basket-chair slung upon two strong bamboo poles, carried by four stout coolies. We were a strange procession to an English spectator. Seven Kagos, containing three Englishmen, three Englishwomen, and Mr. Hakodate, our Japanese guide, borne along by twenty-nine natives (I had an extra man as usual), all stepping in time, and singing weird chants in a minor key. We had eight miles to travel to Chiu-sen-je lake, with a rise of 3,000 feet. They covered the eight miles in just four hours. It was very easy and comfortable travelling, except downhill, which seemed to take it out of our bearers more than going uphill. At the end of the day, however, they did not show the smallest trace of fatigue, and would have been quite willing to run us 20 miles in Jin-rickishas before going to bed.

ON THE ROAD TO CHIU-SEN-JE.
From a sketch by the Author.

Chiu-sen-je is a pretty village, with many fine tea-houses; a place of great resort in summer-time for wealthy Japanese. The lake is a fine expanse of water, about 10 miles in circumference, with lovely surroundings. Nantai-san rises sheer out of the east bank, and both it and the lower hills on the opposite side are clad with variegated forest. The tea-houses all front the lake, and on the other side of the road, under the cliffs of the sacred mountain, are rows of houses inhabited by priests. From one of these houses runs the pathway to the summit of Nantai-san, to ascend which it is necessary to obtain permission from the High-priest at Nikko. The stream which leaves the lake, forms a magnificent waterfall, in two leaps falling some 350 feet.

Count Ito, the Japanese prime minister, had invited us to a great ball in honour of the Mikado's birthday, at which the Emperor and Empress were to be present; but the charms of Nikko were too great a counter-attraction, and we did not go. We left Nikko that morning, and the town, being the Mikado's property, was *en fête*. A bamboo, with the Mikado's flag at the top, was posted in front of every house, and the swarms of children were all running about, making merry with paper flags on little sticks, or flying kites. We returned by the same road by which we came, our Jin-rickisha men running the 25 miles to Utsunomiya in just 2½ hours, or 10 miles an hour. We reached Tokio, the capital, about nine o'clock, and drove 5 or 6 miles through the streets. Although the capital has a population of nearly a million, there is not a single gas-lamp in the streets. This night, however, in honour of the Emperor's birthday, every house had a large brightly-coloured paper lantern hung out, and the thousands of people who thronged the streets carried smaller ones in their hands. It was a veritable feast of lanterns, and the effect was far more beautiful than any illumination I had ever seen before. We went on to Yokohama by a later train.

The next few days were spent at Yokohama, with an occasional excursion to Tokio and the neighbourhood.

One very pleasant day was devoted to a Jin-rickisha ride to Kamakura and its great image of Buddha, called the Daibutz. This colossal figure, of great antiquity, is in a sitting posture, and is forty-seven feet in height. It was cast on the spot in sections of about six feet in height, forming one huge mass of metal, in which the divisions of the several castings are distinctly visible. The figure represents Buddha in meditation, and is full of dignified repose. A large jewel is placed in the middle of the forehead, from which light is supposed to beam, and is significant of Buddha being "the light of the world." The interior is hollow, and is fitted up as a temple with shrines. The curious head-dress is composed of clusters of snails, who, out of

THE GREAT BUDDHA, KAMAKURA.

gratitude to Buddha for his love of animals, shielded thus from the sun the exposed head of their holy friend.

We went to a neighbouring tea-house, of some note with Japanese epicures, where we had previously ordered a real Japanese meal. This nation shines in every fine art except that of cooking. The whole meal was served to us at once in five or six lacquered wooden bowls on a pretty tray, with a huge basin of boiled rice on the floor, in a corner. Three charming young ladies in full native costume served us, and then waited to see us eat, in eager expectation of fun. We first tried the soup. It was hot water, with uncooked giblets of some unknown fowl. No one got beyond the first mouthful. Then we tackled a small fried fish, about the size of a sardine, seasoned with pickled grapes and chestnuts. That we ate. Then we attempted a third dish, which we discovered to be a large piece of absolutely raw fish in pickled daikon, a sort of horse-radish, which is dear to the Japanese stomach, but which has the most horrible smell imaginable. Many times during our stay in Japan we have wondered at the typhoid-suggesting smells we experienced in the dainty and cleanly tea-houses, but on complaint our guide always produced a bowl of daikon, which set our minds at rest. There was also a mess of dubious vegetables and some boiled chrysanthemums, but nothing on the whole tray, except plain boiled rice, which an English palate could stand. We were all hungry, and looked at each other in dismay. The waitresses giggled and wriggled with delight. To our joy, however, one of them left the room, and returned with a huge bowl of fresh bantam's eggs, which, with the rice, furnished a wholesome and abundant meal. As usual, the ladies of our party were subjected to a rigorous investigation by the landlady and her pretty waitresses. Every article of jewellery was passed round and examined; their hats, cloaks, and dresses were scrutinized and discussed, and every sort of curious question put about their families and belongings. We men were treated with indifference and contempt, until the bill was made out, when they all came in smiling, to get their "pocket-money."

We took a boat in the afternoon, intending to visit a small island on which some old Shinto shrines were to be seen, but a fleet of fishing boats attracted our attention, and growing dark as we rowed from boat to boat, examining their tackle and nets, the island was abandoned. Fishing is, after agriculture, the chief industry of Japan. There are about 200,000 fishing boats, giving employment to some two millions of the population. Fish, fresh and salted, is the chief animal food of the people.

We spent a quiet Sunday in Yokohama. In the morning we went to a Union Church, at which all the religious denominations in the European town, except the Episcopalians and Baptists worship together. Nine different missions, American and English, meet together in Christian fellowship, and it is hoped that by-and-by this movement will result in a complete union of all the native churches under the charge of Protestant Nonconformists in one denomination, thus going far to remove what must always be a hindrance to mission work, the appearance of division in the Christian Church. I also saw a native congregation, that of the Dutch Presbyterians. It was crowded to overflowing, as indeed are most of the mission churches. There are now over 20,000 native members of Protestant churches in Japan, and Christianity seems likely before long to crowd out the threadbare superstitions of Shinto and the idol-encrusted religion of Buddha. The strong desire of leading men in Japan for assimilation to European civilization is very likely to take the form of the State adoption of some phase of Christianity. The dread of the missionary is that it will be Romanism. I know of no heathen country where the responsibility of the missionary is so great as in Japan—or where the prospects of success are brighter. The Japanese Christian reaches as high a standard as the English, and the native preachers are quite as intelligent and well taught in the Scriptures as any of our missionaries themselves. Besides this, influential and wealthy Japanese gladly avail themselves of the excellent schools which have been established by American Missionary Societies, where high-school teaching is given, combined with instruction in the Christian religion. Miss Crosbie, an American lady, has 120 Japanese young ladies in her fine boarding-school at Yokohama, many of whom are the daughters of men of high position in the State. Christianity is now more than tolerated in Japan, it is encouraged by some of the most influential people of the country.

Every morning we go out upon the roof of our hotel to get a view of the wonderful mountain which appears so constantly upon the various products of Japanese art and manufacture; painted on paper, woven into textile fabrics, worked upon lacquer and pottery, carved in relief on wooden panels of cabinets, or chased on bronze vases. Fuji-yama, the most sacred mountain in Japan, is a magnificent volcanic snow-clad cone, rising in sublime isolation over 12,000 feet from the plain; its last eruption took place in 1707, and did great mischief. Fuji-yama has rarely been out of our sight during our excursions in the neighbourhood of Yokohama.

On the 9th of November we bid farewell to Yokohama, having taken passage in the Japanese steamer "Yamashiro Maru" for Kobe, 350 miles distant, the treaty port of Kioto, the old capital. This is one of a line of fine boats which carry the Japanese mails from port to port, and sail under the Japanese flag. I have never travelled on a more comfortable steamer. The scrupulous cleanliness of the people was visible everywhere. The state-rooms and saloon were airy and beautifully fitted up, and the cooking admirable. The officers of all the vessels on this line are English, the crews being Japanese. The "Yamashiro Maru" is a ship of about 1,800 tons register, of 14 knots speed, built by Sir William Armstrong and Co. She is fitted for a powerful armament, and could be converted into a first-class cruiser in three days. I inspected every inch of her under the guidance of the captain and chief engineer, and was delighted with everything I saw. During the afternoon we passed Vries

Island, on which is an active volcano, which made a much better show of flame and smoke than I have ever seen from Etna or Vesuvius. We reached Kobe about five o'clock on the afternoon of the 10th, and went up to Kioto by the first train next morning. We put up at the most comfortable Japanese hotel we have yet met with, the Ya-Ami, situated on the slope of a wooded hill, with Kioto spread out before its terrace like a map.

FUJI-YAMA.
From a sketch by the Author.

Kioto covers an area of about 25 square miles, with a population of some 350,000. As every Japanese house is the same height, and all the temples are on the hills behind the hotel, the view is a monotonous stretch of brown roofs, with an expanse beyond of well-cultivated fields, closed in by a fine range of timbered mountains about 10 miles distant. The scenery in these mountains is exceedingly beautiful, fully equal to that at Nikko, but as our main object in coming to Kioto was to see something of the social life and domestic institutions of the Japanese people, we only devoted one day to its enjoyment. We rode in Jin-rickishas some 16 or 17 miles across the range, returning by a magnificent mountain gorge, 7 or 8 miles in extent, with lofty cliffs and wooded hills closing in a fine rapid river, down which we drifted, Jin-rickishas and all, in a large flat-bottomed boat, shooting 24 rapids on the way.

At the foot of the gorge was a charming village, the favourite pic-nic resort of the wealthy inhabitants of Kioto. Here are several very fine tea-houses, and their balconies and open chambers were filled with picturesque groups in all the splendour of Japanese holiday attire. Here and there, alas! were aristocratic parties who have learned to despise the beautiful dresses of their own artistic country, and think it proper to rig themselves out in dreadful flounced imitations of obsolete Paris fashions, of which the predominant colours are mauve, magenta, or solferino. The gentlemen attire themselves in ready-made "reach-me-downs" of black cloth, shiny patent-leather shoes, and round pot-hats. The incongruity with the pretty and charming groups in native dress was complete, and presented a sad and sorrowful spectacle.

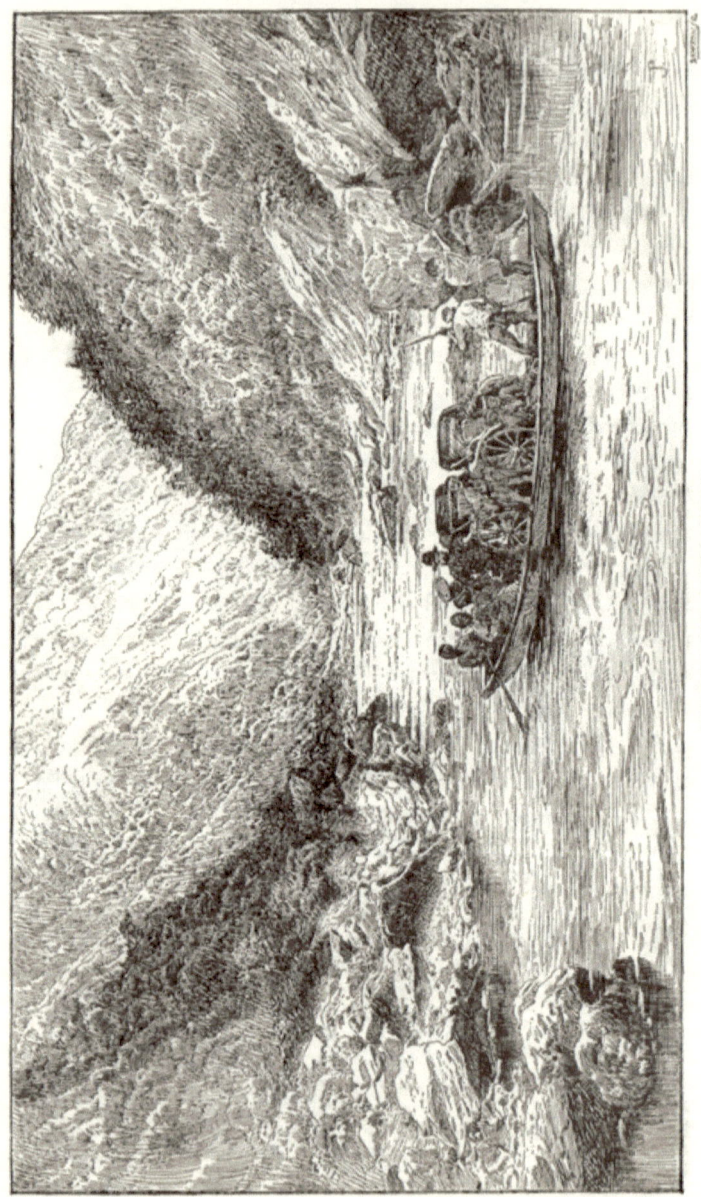

SHOOTING THE RAPIDS, KIOTO.

CHAPTER XIII.

SOCIAL LIFE IN JAPAN.

WE had carefully reserved a full week for Kioto, the ancient capital, and the most intensely Japanese town in all Japan, with a view of seeing all we could of the social condition and habits of the people.

They make a great mistake who think that because Japan is a heathen country it is therefore of necessity low down in the scale of civilization. In everything that makes a country happy, prosperous, and contented, Japan will compare favourably with any nation in Christendom.

The population is composed of four distinct classes, whose difference is sharply defined in Japanese society. It consists of—

1. The Royal Family	30
2. The Nobility	2,000,000
3. Priests: Buddhist and Shinto	320,000
4. Common people	34,000,000

There are very few foreigners resident in Japan, and these are confined to the treaty ports. There are about 2,500 Europeans and 3,000 Chinese. There are also in the treaty ports a considerable number of Eurasians, the illegitimate offspring of European fathers, whose existence goes far to justify the complaints of missionaries that it is the Christian and not the

Buddhist heathen who keep back the spread of Christianity in the East; and also perhaps explains the almost universal contempt with which the merchant class in the East speak about missionaries. The irreligion and open immorality of Europeans in Japan and China, with some honourable exceptions, is very bad indeed.

The working classes in Japan are poor. Wages, from our standard, are exceedingly low. But all the necessaries of life are correspondingly low, and if "he is richest whose wants are fewest," the Japanese are rich enough. The day's work in Japan is ten hours. Labourers get from 8*d*. to 14*d*. a day; carpenters, 2*s*. 6*d*. to 3*s*.; mechanics, 2*s*. to 2*s*. 6*d*.; machinists and blacksmiths, 2*s*. to 3*s*.; farm labourers, 10*d*. to 1*s*., with board; tea firing and packing, 10*d*. to 1*s*. 6*d*.; potters, ordinary hands, 2*s*., skilled hands, 3*s*. to 8*s*., piece work. Painters and decorators of pottery, art metal workers, lacquerers, and the host of artistic workmen who produce the beautiful works which decorate European houses so plentifully, often earn from 10*s*. to 15*s*. a day, and become rich.

The cost of living is very small. It may be judged by the fact that single men in large towns can get good bed and board for 5*d*. a day. Japanese live almost entirely on rice, fish, and vegetables, with eggs as a luxury. I have seen dozens of Japanese meals prepared for the families of working people, and it is invariably the same—three bowls, one of rice, one of mixed vegetables, and one of fish, fresh or salted, and often raw! These meals are sold ready cooked for about three-halfpence, and probably do not cost families half that sum per head. The working people are as well housed as ours at home, and their houses are all scrupulously clean. Taxation, both Imperial and local, is extremely light, and hardly touches the working class. Every town and village has an abundant water supply, the sewage and refuse of every house being collected nightly, and carefully used in agriculture.

Education is cheap to the well to do, and free to the poor. There is a system of Government primary schools professing to be within reach of every child, and this seems probable, as there are over three million of children receiving instruction in 29,000 elementary schools, besides 180 high schools, and 71 normal schools or training colleges, in which are 5,300 persons being trained as teachers. The total annual expenditure on education is £1,500,000.

I visited one of the ordinary elementary schools of Kioto, the Dragon Pond School, at which 500 children are educated. The fees are 8*d.* per month for the lower forms, and 13*d.* for the higher; the poor, as I have already mentioned, being educated free. How the distinction is arrived at I could not find out. The course includes reading, writing, dictation, arithmetic, algebra, and mathematics, the use of the counting machine, a little English, music, and gymnastics. The head-master received us in a large room, on the walls of which were frames containing the rules of the school, the duties of each teacher, and a fine frame containing a testimonial from the Mikado, who once visited the school, and sent this afterwards to the head-master. The inevitable tea was served, and we were then conducted round the buildings, which were a series of one-story class-rooms, grouped round a playground. The first contained a class of girls about ten years old, who went through a series of gymnastic exercises with clubs, dumb-bells, and bar-bells. The second held a class of sixty boys and girls, who were being taught elementary Japanese music, a female teacher marking time with two wooden clappers. The children sang several pieces in a monotonous minor key, which was, to our untutored ears, very dull and disagreeable. The third room

contained a reading class of sixty boys. The master had a
large blackboard, on which he wrote a sentence containing some
moral sentiment. He spelt it over for the class with great
distinctness, and then explained its meaning and application.
Having done so, he asked every boy who thoroughly understood
it to hold up his hand; about half the class did so. The master
then went carefully over the ground again, and asked all who did
not understand to hold up a hand. Three boys responded,
whereupon the master left his desk, visited each of them one
after the other, cleared away the boys' difficulty, and thus got
the whole class instructed. This once secured, each boy, with
Indian ink and paint-brush (the universal Japanese pen), carefully copied the sentence from the blackboard. I went round
the class to see the copies, and at last understood how it is that
the Japanese are the finest draughtsmen in the world. We next
visited the elementary reading class, where the same system of
patiently insisting on every member of the class understanding
his lesson before going on to the next was pursued. The head-
master told me that no boy or girl in the school would dream of
holding up the hand unless they really did understand what the
master was explaining.

The lower forms consist of boys and girls mixed, but in the
upper forms the instruction divides itself, and the sexes with it.
We then went to the classes of the higher standards. Each boy
and girl here has a seat, and a desk arranged to hold writing-
box, books, and slate. There are eight class-rooms in all. In
one I saw the prettiest picture imaginable. It was a large light
room, the walls covered with a cream-coloured paper decorated
with a raised pattern of flying storks, and the floor carpeted with
pale green matting. In the middle of the floor fifteen or twenty
pretty Japanese girls from twelve to fifteen were sitting on their
heels, in the bright-coloured clothes they love so well, each with

a jaunty flower stuck in her chignon, cutting out or stitching men's and women's dresses. Each girl had a nice lacquered work-box full of coloured silks. This charming group of girls, clad in gay but perfectly harmonious colours, surrounded by pale cream-colour and sea-green decorations, formed a tableau not easy to forget. Every girl is turned out of a Japanese school, not only able to make her own clothes, but her husband's also. In another room was a large class of girls singing from European notation. They sang for us some Japanese poetry to the tunes of "Rousseau's Dream" and "Auld lang syne" very sweetly and accurately. In a month or two they will have an organ, and will learn part music.

On the whole, and taking the different social circumstances of the two countries into account, I think the Japanese elementary education is quite equal to our own. I was much impressed both by the excellent discipline of the school and the earnestness of the pupils. No warning was given of our visit; we simply went to the school, and begged admittance. It was to the children the same thing as if six Japanese ladies and gentlemen, in full national costume, suddenly appeared in the class-rooms of a London Board School. Yet not a child whispered to another, and the work went on with the same precision while we were present as when we were absent. The children and teachers seemed at perfect touch with each other, the earnest attention of the one being equalled by the kindness and patience of the other.

The higher schools of Japan are as good in their way as the elementary, and above them all is the University of Tokio, with its five colleges of law and political economy, medicine, engineering, literature, and science. In these colleges are upwards of 1,200 students, taught by 100 professors. Six hundred of the students are taught foreign languages. Among the professors are Japanese who have graduated at Oxford, Cambridge, London,

P

and Victoria Universities in England, Cornell and Michigan in America, Strasburg and Leipsic in Germany. The classics taught are old Chinese and Japanese literature. This University of Tokio is based upon the German standard, and will compare favourably with any of the smaller German universities. German influence is becoming increasingly powerful in Japan.

The Government of Japan appears to be popular and firm. At present it is an absolute monarchy, but a constitution and Parliament is in the air, and will not long be withheld. There is not much political sentiment in the country. Ito, our guide, is a bit of a radical, and took us to a public meeting where some orators were airing a grievance. There was a very small attendance of listless politicians, listening to a fiery speech from a tiny little lawyer, who was as fierce as a dragon. The chair appeared to be taken by two policemen in uniform, who sat at a table making notes of the speech, stopping the speaker with a sounding smack of their staves upon the table when he ran too near the edge of sedition. It was a ludicrous performance, as the little orator was chucked up every two or three minutes.

The Emperor is highly spoken of by every one as an intelligent and progressive monarch. He is thirty-five years old, the direct descendant of the gods, and inherits by primogeniture. The crown has been on the head of his direct line of ancestors for 2,200 years. His advisers are ten cabinet ministers, who are the heads of the great departments of state ; viz.: Foreign and home affairs, finance, law, army, navy, education, agriculture and commerce, public works, and the Imperial household. Below them is a senate of about forty members, chosen by the Emperor for distinguished service to the state. This senate discusses all legislative questions, and their decision becomes law, subject to the approval of cabinet and Emperor. There is also a council of state, appointed by the Emperor, which has administrative

SOCIAL LIFE IN JAPAN. 211

and executive functions. Local government is in the hands of forty-four governors of as many provinces. Local taxation is settled by provincial assemblies elected by men twenty-five years old, who pay not less than 30s. of land tax. There are about 1,800,000 of these electors in the forty-four provinces.

The state religion is the religion of the minority, but it only

A SHINTO PRIEST.

receives about £20,000 of public money. There are two religions in Japan, Shintoism and Buddhism. Their relative strength is 18,000 Shinto priests and 76,000 Buddhist priests. So many of the population belong to both religions, and so many others ridicule both, that one can only estimate their relative strength by the number of priests. I have failed to make head or tail of either religion, having neither time nor inclination for their study.

They seem to me, however, to be fast decaying and ready to perish. They are huge masses of superstition encrusted on a sublime foundation, none of which is now visible.

The national expenditure of the Japanese is the modest sum of £10,000,000. More than half the revenue is obtained from the land tax, which averages about 15s. an acre on rice-fields and about 4s. an acre on other cultivable land. The rest comes from charges on mines, roads, alcohol, tobacco, post-office, stamps, carriages, ships, railways, telegraphs, and import duties.

Justice costs £300,000, police and prisons £400,000, army £1,400,000, navy £450,000, pensions £60,000, and £3,500,000 goes towards the redemption of a national debt of about £50,000,000.

There are about six million landowners with very small holdings, whose tillage I have referred to in previous chapters.

Every man from seventeen to fifty years is liable to military service in case of invasion. The standing army, with reserves, is 110,000 strong.

They have an excellent little navy, well-manned and quite up to modern warfare. It is, I suppose, the most powerful possessed by any nation on the Pacific Ocean.

The area of Japan is 148,000 square miles, with a population of thirty-seven millions.

There is a simple poor law, by which infirm and aged poor receive enough rice to live upon. There are only 10,000 paupers in all Japan. But that is not strange in a nation of tea-drinkers.

The forests mainly belong to the Government, and cover thirteen million acres. I believe there is a law that every tree in Japan over a certain girth belongs to the state. This, however, is not rigorously claimed.

The exports are about six millions sterling, consisting chiefly of tea, silks, porcelain and lacquered ware, bronzes, camphor, ginger, &c.

The imports are about four millions. England has the lion's share of the trade of Japan. At Kobe, when I was there, there were twenty-four large steamers on the berth, of which five were Japanese; of the remaining nineteen, twelve were English, four German, two American, and one Belgian. The tonnage of the English steamers was three times that of all the others combined.

Japan publishes about two hundred newspapers, which have an average circulation of each issue of about four thousand copies.

The country possesses 250 miles of railway, 4,800 miles of telegraph, and 6,000 post offices.

No foreigner is allowed to leave the boundaries of the Treaty Ports without special permission from the Foreign Minister, which must be applied for through his ambassador. The reason of this is that European countries will not consent to submit their citizens to Japanese law, but insist on trying them in the Consular Courts of the Treaty Ports. Whenever European powers are willing to admit Japan to equality as a civilized nation, the Japanese Government will gladly throw the whole country open, and permit Europeans to settle and trade where they please. There is a good deal of soreness on this subject among educated Japanese, and the short experience I have had of their country inclines me to sympathize fully with them in their demand that Europeans shall submit themselves to Japanese law. Their Government is now engaged on a code of criminal and civil law based on the *Code Napoleon*, and when this is completed it will be impossible to refuse them full and equal entry upon the rights of civilized nations. Japan is probably now the safest country in the world for the traveller, either as regards person or property, though twenty years ago it was just the reverse.

The Japanese are a gay and light-hearted people, fond of pleasure and amusement. I spent several evenings in going to their theatres and other places of entertainment, accompanied by Mr. Ito, the clever and intelligent guide who went with Miss Bird in her travels through "unbeaten tracks in Japan," and who had also acted as guide to my friend Mr. H. W. Lucy. He

MUSIC.

is well acquainted with the social customs of the people, and speaks English with great fluency. Women never take part in Japanese theatres; when they come into a play their parts are taken by boys. The Japanese play is a lengthy business, beginning at 10 o'clock in the morning and going on to 11 at night. They are mostly historical romances with tremendous dialogues, reminding me of my schooldays and the dreary pages of "Racine." The company come early and bring their dinners with them, making a day of it.

Other theatres are given up to conjurers, athletes and acrobats, dancing girls, and music, but all are conducted with a decency and propriety very different from similar places at home. There is nothing whatever in Japanese amusements that need call a blush to the cheek of an English school-girl. Intoxicating liquors are never sold at any place of amusement, and very little anywhere else. Tea is the national beverage, and is brought out on every occasion. It is served on a tray with a small pot surrounded by delicate little porcelain cups, and drunk hot without sugar or milk. Saké, or rice beer, is the only intoxicant used in Japan, but the majority of the population are absolute teetotallers, and a drunken man is a rare spectacle.

DANCING GIRL.

Japanese children have much amusement provided for them, and the most popular of all the theatres, for old or young, were those where some fairy tale or story was recited, to a running illustration of magic-lantern views. It is seldom one sees children without a toy of some sort, and in every town there is a "children's street," generally one of the avenues to a great temple, where little theatres abound, little archery grounds, Aunt Sallies, small zoological gardens, performing monkeys, and what not, with endless toy shops where porcelain toys, dolls, kites, flags, battledore and shuttlecocks, balls, and tops, may be bought by fond parents for their jolly, laughing, happy children.

One of the favourite amusements of the Japanese are the

performances of the singing and dancing girls. The ladies of our party had heard so much of these performances that Mr. Ito undertook to arrange a private display for their benefit at one of the principal tea-houses in Kioto. These girls are quite a class by themselves. They begin their profession at twelve years of age, and are apprenticed to their employer, who is bound to teach them not only their art, but to give them a very high general education. Half their pay goes to their parents, and the rest accumulates for their own benefit until they marry. They are jealously looked after and taken care of. Their performances consist of an acted story, some of them in pantomime acting the part, while others sing the tale. In our sense of the word they do not dance at all, they simply place themselves in tableaux illustrative of the sung story.

We were shown, on arrival at the tea-house, into a large upper room, where chairs had been placed for us, all the rest of the space being covered with the usual matting, and lighted with tall candlesticks and candles. Presently the performers came in. There were eight in all. Two were dressed in pretty silk robes of brown and dove-colour combined, and took their seats against the wall, each with a samisen, or Japanese guitar, which they played with a broad strip of ivory. The other six were dressed in long robes of bright red and dark blue, and were the actors of the tableaux. They all sat on their heels in a row in front of us, and appeared to be young girls of fourteen or fifteen. They were very modest and well-behaved, but at once began a merry conversation with us through Ito, displaying all the amusing curiosity of the Japanese. They were greatly interested in the ladies' dresses and jewellery, asked all sorts of questions about England, and evidently despised a maiden lady of our party of some fifty summers, because she had lived to such an age without a husband. We asked a few questions in our turn, and found that they had all entered the profession to help their parents, speaking of them with much love and affection. I asked the names of each, and had them translated by Ito. The literal translation of the two singing girls' names was "Singing Pine Tree," and "Noble Soft Lady." The tableaux girls were "Singing Leaf," "Thousand Years Old Pretty," "First Happy," "Small Sour Plum Blossom," "Pleasure," "Deer," "Chrysanthemum." I won't attempt the Japanese equivalents.

Conversation over, one of them brought in tea, and the usual sugar-plums accompanying it. In return I handed round a box of compressed chlorate of potash tablets, which I always carry in my pocket, which the young ladies munched up and swallowed with many faces, quite under the impression that they were very choice English sweatmeats. They are as palatable as Japanese sugar-plums, anyhow.

The performance then commenced. Mr. Ito was in raptures with it, and assured us it was the highest art Japan possessed. The music was horrible and ear-splitting. The song was extremely lengthy, and droned in a monotonous minor. We had two—one was thirty-five minutes long, the other forty. The first was descriptive of the pairing of birds in spring and the love passages of the lion and peony. It was illustrated by a series of tableaux, in which bright fans and coloured handkerchiefs were brought into much requisition. The second was a dreary ditty in which a young daimio or prince is telling his nurse of all the cruel treatment he has received from his lady-love, and of the acts of heroism he has performed with a view to its abatement. We were glad when the time arrived to make the young ladies a present of pocket-money, and wish them good-night. I heartily wish that the decency and decorum of Japanese amusements could be imported into our theatres and music-halls. From the costly performance I have just described down to the poor theatres where the admission is less than a halfpenny, an English girls' boarding school might witness everything.

The only places where ribaldry and indecency is to be seen in Japanese performances is at the Treaty Ports, for the sole benefit of Europeans, and chiefly for Englishmen.

The Japanese have nothing approaching to our Sunday, either for religious worship or a day of rest. They have, however, about twenty public holidays in the year, and judging from the way in which all classes throng the theatres and tea gardens during the daytime, they are not slack in taking as much rest in one way and another as will make up for our fifty-two Sundays and four bank holidays. They resort to the temples in great crowds on religious holidays, but as a rule they leave religion till they are old, like other nations of the world.

CHAPTER XIV.

JAPANESE ARTS AND MANUFACTURES.

AMONG the sights which most attracted me at Kioto, were the palace of the Mikado and the ancient castle of the Shoguns. These are both difficult of access, as permission must be obtained from the minister of the Royal Household. This was secured for our party by the kindness of Mr. Trench, the British Charge d'Affaires, and we lost no time in availing ourselves of the privilege.

We first visited the palace, which is a modern building, re-constructed after a great fire about thirty years ago. It is built entirely of cedar, and is a huge wandering one-story building, without any pretensions to architectural beauty. Its great attraction, like that of all other Japanese buildings, is found in its internal decorations, for which this palace enjoys great repute, the best artists in the country having been employed upon it. We felt somewhat of a shock, therefore, when on arrival we were shown into a reception room covered with a detestably bad tapestry carpet of the loudest pattern, surrounded with cheap European chairs covered with "Solferino," the worst of aniline dyes; I fear but a foreshadowing of what will happen to all the rest of the palace as "Western civilization" continues to prevail at the Mikado's court, especially if its influence be German, as at present.

In this room we were speedily joined by two Court officials, who had been instructed to show us round. Each room led out of the other by a series of sliding walls. The first suite consisted of three handsome reception rooms, covered with fine matting, bound with red, the Mikado's colour, forbidden to subjects. These rooms, like all the rest, were entirely devoid of furniture, which is never used in Japan, everyone sitting on the floor, tables and other necessary articles being only brought into the room when required for use. From these rooms we were shown into a charming suite of family apartments, consisting of seven or eight small chambers, surrounding one large parlour, in the centre of which was a raised dais, covered with a beautiful white silk canopy, within which the Mikado was secluded from the rest of his family, until the reforms of twenty years ago. Passing on through a courtyard, we enter the large hall in which the Mikado holds his court reception. This room is about 100 feet long by 80 feet wide, with a dais and canopy in the centre. The walls are decorated with a series of portraits of distinguished literati of China, Korea, and Japan. The large ante-room, in which the nobles assemble, is divided into three sections, each a step higher, on which the three distinct grades of nobility are separated. Behind these rooms is the Mikado's study, with recesses and cupboards in the wall, of decorated lacquer work, for books and writing materials. All these rooms are ornamented with paintings in distemper on a dead gold paper, the most beautiful decorative art I have ever seen. The scenes are nearly all drawn from Nature, and are mostly arrangements of animal and forest life. The Japanese have an intense affection for birds, insects, and flowers. The Buddhist religion encourages this sentiment, for it forbids the destruction of the smallest created thing. No Japanese child would try to catch a butterfly, tie a string to a mouse's tail, pull the wings off a fly, or perform any of the barbarities on dumb animals that our English children so often delight in. This harmony between human beings and the lower creatures enters largely into Japanese art, and they specially delight in decorations in which animals are represented in the full enjoyment of life. Thus, one of the walls in these beautiful rooms represents storks on reedy sandhills, with seashore and waves; another a mass of blossoming briers with song birds fluttering about them; a third a pleasant river, overhung with wisteria in blossom, with swallows skimming over the surface; a fourth represents mountain deer drinking at a rush-grown lake, over which curlews are disporting themselves; a fifth, of singular beauty, one of the few which escaped the fire, had one panel decorated with a vine in full fruit, in which squirrels were chasing one another about, while the three other panels of the same room displayed a woodland scene of marvellously painted foliage, under which the various animals of the forest were moving about in perfect grouping, the whole forming a picture of which Landseer himself might have been proud.

We had spent three hours in admiration of this charming series of decoration, and had arrived at the end of what Mr. Ito, our interpreter, informed us was all that was ever shown. The two officials, after a little consultation, then informed Ito that it was so seldom that any of their foreign visitors cared for the beautiful work on the walls as we had, that they would relax the rule in our favour, and show us the Mikado's private apartments as well. These were the most exquisite of all. They consisted of nineteen or twenty small rooms, even more perfectly decorated than the public reception rooms. The Mikado's bedroom contained a wardrobe in sixteen panels, representing flowers, birds, fruits, insects, and fishes, that constituted, to my mind, as perfect a specimen of decorative art as the world could produce.

The next day we visited the Shogun's Castle. This building is about 250 years old, and is entered by a magnificent gateway 20 feet wide and 50 feet high, richly decorated on every inch of available surface with gilt bronze and carved wood panels of birds and flowers. The "Castle" is a large, one-storey house, similar in character to the Mikado's palace, and decorated in the same fashion. The interest, however, is greater, as the decorations of the castle are of the same date as the building, and painted by the great artists of the finest period of Japanese art, while those of the palace are modern reproductions of similar work destroyed by the fire. The various rooms of the castle are divided, for ventilation I think, by wide friezes of pierced woodwork of finely-carved subjects of birds and flowers, which, in combination with the distemper panels below, had a very striking and beautiful effect. It is very curious, in studying these two palaces, to notice how much that is best and loveliest in modern European decorative art has borrowed its inspiration from the great artists of Japan. It would be wise for the authorities at South Kensington to try to obtain a series of the finest of these decorative panels, copied by competent Japanese artists. I can conceive of nothing that would be of greater service to those clever students who are doing so much to raise the standard of decorative art in England. They would show how perfectly the Japanese, in their marvellous work, discard all unnecessary detail, and seize simple and symmetrical forms only.

As we came away from the castle, my daughter and I could not resist the temptation of entering one of the charming tea gardens to which Japanese families resort when they give festivities. The garden was at the back of a tea-house, and consisted of about twenty raised wooden platforms, some 10 or 12 feet square, each of which was completely surrounded and rendered private by flowering bushes of chrysanthemums in pots. On entering, the garden looked like a fine flower show. These compartments were filled with merry parties at dinner, and as we passed in front of each entrance the host would politely invite us to enter and partake of his hospitality. Mr. Ito informed us that it would be considered polite if we accepted one of these invitations after we had walked round the gardens, and we did so, joining for a short time a family party of seven or eight, who were celebrating a birthday of one of the children. We declined the food, but took tea and sweets, chatting with them through our interpreter. They were very anxious to know if my daughter was married, and at first rather despised her, in that she was not. But on my explaining jocularly that she was waiting for the young Mikado (a lad of eight), they accepted the statement with perfect gravity, and saluted her with profound respect. Ito afterwards told us that they would consider it ill-bred to show doubts of any statement, however preposterous, made to them by a stranger and a guest. No intoxicating liquor was being consumed on the premises; all were drinking tea with their little banquets. The only sign of strong beverage visible was in a picture of Mr. Gladstone, with Hawarden Castle in the background, laying aside his axe while he imbibed a pot of stout with keen enjoyment depicted on his countenance. This was the highly-coloured advertisement of the beverage, and was evidently a treasured specimen of the finest English art, dear to the soul of the tea-house proprietor, who called our attention to it with justifiable pride.

During our stay in Kioto, I visited several manufactories of some of the staple industries of the country, with which we are familiar in England, such as pottery and porcelain, cloisonnée enamels, lacquered wares, bronze and metal work, and textile fabrics.

Perhaps the finest of all the arts of Japan is that of lacquering upon wood. This ware is in universal use in Japan, and is largely exported as well. Boxes, trays, bowls, dishes, cabinets, cups, vases, bottles, and, indeed, almost everything which we make of glass, in Japan is made of lacquered wood. The manufacture is not carried on at large factories, but in the homes of the workpeople, in rooms scrupulously clean and free from dust. The cup, bowl, or other article is cut out of a piece of perfectly dry wood, and finished in a curious lathe, whose spindle revolves first one way and then another, with the same action as a bow drill. When a perfectly smooth surface has been secured, coat after coat of lacquer is laid on, and the whole ground down to a fine hard surface by means of charcoal, and polished with the ash of deers' horns. The finest specimens are decorated with gold; thick lacquer is laid on by a fine hair pencil in floral and other designs, powdered gold being shaken over the sticky surface, and burnished when dry. The designs are often in high relief, and sometimes are quite elaborate pictures. I have a little medicine box in gold lacquer, about three inches by two inches, on which the artist has drawn about one hundred wild horses in every possible attitude, the whole forming a most delicate and beautiful work of art. Often the lacquer is inlaid with pearl and ivory carved in relief, and, indeed, there is no end to the variety of treatment possible in this interesting manufacture.

The lacquer tree is one of the commonest in Japan, and the clear varnish is taken from it when the tree is from five to eight years old. The bark is sliced from the trunk and the stem nicked here and there with a knife. The exuding juice is scraped off, and when no more will come the tree is cut down, chopped into small pieces, and soaked in water for some days, after which a quantity of the varnish is skimmed off the surface.

The Japanese export large quantities of pottery to all the countries in Europe, producing artistic porcelain at a price and of a quality that defies competition. There are upwards of a hundred potteries in Japan, employing many thousands of the population, but I could get no statistics. The pottery produced in Japan during the seventeenth and eighteenth centuries is the most beautiful in the world, and has been copied in every great centre of porcelain manufacture in Europe. The well-known "Crown Derby" is directly copied from the products of Imari, in Japan, while the ware known as "Satsuma" has furnished the motive for the best work of the Royal Worcester potteries. We visited a great many of the shops where various kinds of pottery was produced. Those working on a large scale had little to show that was really fine, and it seemed to me that the enormous demand for their wares which has set in lately, and which gives no sign of abatement, is slowly deteriorating the high quality of both decoration and workmanship. But in some of the smaller factories, where the work was carried on by a single family, aided by one or two specially-trained assistants, we saw specimens that were as fine as anything Japan has produced at her best period. There is, unhappily, everywhere a tendency to overload with decoration, and to depart from that charming simplicity which characterised the old art of Japan, and this is visible not only in pottery, but in their enamel, bronze-work, and textile fabrics. I bought from a curio dealer at Nikko an old kettle of forged iron, round which twined a single spray of blossom inlaid in gold and silver, with two or three figures seated under it. It is an exquisite piece of work, its special charm lying in its simplicity of treatment. I was told at Kioto that a silversmith was reproducing this old inlaid work, **and I went to his shop to see what it was** like. He was producing excellent **results,** but his kettles were so overloaded **with decoration as to lose all** suggestion of being intended **to boil water in.** An old **Satsuma cup** is decorated with a single chrysanthemum only, **or perhaps a golden** pheasant in flight, or a tender spray of plum or **cherry blossom just** straying round it. A modern Satsuma **cup will have a flower** garden spread over its entire surface, and the vendor will **urge** you to buy it because **it has fifteen** different **specimens of** butterflies and insects perched **on the** blooms.

If the Japanese maintain the **old** traditions of their decorative **art, their trade in** pottery, bronzes, enamels, embroideries, **silk fabrics, lacquer, and** art work generally, already of great pro**portions, will increase** indefinitely. In America alone, where **there are no art manufacturers** worth naming, they ought to find **a market that** will employ every pair **of** hands they can train. But if they push their mania for Western influences too far I think they will find that Western ideas are best **carried** out by Western brains, and that it is Japanese **art in its integrity, and** not Japanese imitations **of** English **and** French **art, that** will succeed in bringing prosperity **to their workshops.**

On the 14th of November we left Kioto, with many regrets, and took the **train** to Kobe, embarking **the same** evening on board the P. **and** O. steamer "Thibet" **for** Nagasaki and Hong Kong. **Next** morning **found** us in the famous Inland Sea of **Japan, a long** strait between **the two principal** islands, from 10 **to 30 miles wide, stretching 240 miles east to** west, and expanding **into six great** lagoons, dotted over with rocky and well-wooded islands. **There is** about 700 miles **of** seaboard **to** the Inland Sea, densely populated, every inch of available soil on the islands and the mountain flanks being under fine cultivation. I counted on the **chart** 407 islands between Kobe **and**

A STREET SCENE, KIOTO.

Simonoseki; on each side ranges of lofty mountains rise 6,000 or 8,000 feet above the sea, and the combinations of mountain, island, and village, with stretches of blue water dotted with junks and fishing boats, formed one long succession of charming pictures from dawn to sunset. We passed the narrow straits of Simonoseki, about half-a-mile wide, at dusk, and were soon out in the open sea, heading for Nagasaki, which we reached about nine o'clock next morning. The Inland Sea, though full of swift currents and whirlpools, is perfectly safe navigation, and as it is well lighted throughout, it is navigable night and day.

THE INLAND SEA OF JAPAN.
From a sketch by the Author.

Entering Nagasaki harbour, the terrible island of Pappenburg is pointed out to us, the scene of the martyrdom of the last of the Japanese Christians, in the seventeenth century. Early in that century there were over two millions of Christians in Japan the disciples of Jesuit missionaries. The Ruler of Japan, dreading the increase of the new religion, and alarmed at the number of Franciscans, Jesuit priests, and Spanish mendicant friars who were pouring into the country, determined to suppress Christianity altogether, and decreed the expulsion from his dominions of all the foreign priests. The Christians, headed by their priests, rose in rebellion, and were defeated. No quarter was given, and the new religion was stamped out with fire, sword, and torture, prisoners being offered the choice of recantation or crucifixion. But few of these Romanist converts abandoned their faith, and hundreds of thousands were horribly slaughtered. The history of Christendom furnishes no greater instance of sacrifice and heroic constancy. The Christians made a final

PAPPENBURG ISLAND, NAGASAKI.
From a sketch by the Author.

stand against the Shogun in an old castle near Nagasaki, which they fortified strongly. Two months' siege reduced it, and the garrison, amounting to many thousands, were hurled from a steep rock on the island of Pappenburg, now a favourite pic-nic resort for the people of Nagasaki. The great Shogun thus obliterated the last trace of a hundred years of Papal Christianity. It remains to be seen whether the determined efforts which are being concentrated on Japan by English and

American evangelical Christianity will succeed with a people who once accepted in such numbers, and with such devotion, the ritual of Rome. I think it will. Japan has moved on since then.

Nagasaki is one of the famous harbours of the world. It is about six miles long and a mile wide, land-locked by high hills, with good anchorage and deep water throughout. It is an important coaling station, some thousands of tons of good coal being raised every week from an island about ten miles off. We remained there about seven or eight hours, and then proceeded to Hong Kong, where we arrived on Sunday morning at 10 o'clock.

CHAPTER XV.

HONG KONG.

FORTY years ago Hong Kong was only a barren island in the midst of an archipelago at the entrance of the Canton river, inhabited by a male population, who combined the innocent pursuits of fishing and stone-quarrying with the more exciting pastime of piracy, an amusement of long standing, the name of "Ladrones" (thieves) being given to the islands by the Portuguese of Macao, two hundred years ago. From all I hear the name is still well deserved, for Hong Kong is the Alsatia of Canton, and whenever a citizen of that blackguard city goes a step too far he bolts for Hong Kong. Piracy, too, still exists. Every Chinese sea-going junk carries a couple of cannon and a stand of small arms, ostensibly for protection from pirates, but in reality to enable them to do a little piracy on their own account when opportunity offers, in the shape of a weaker junk than their own, when they destroy all evidence of their crime by slaughtering all on board.

The island of Hong Kong presents a very picturesque appearance from the sea. It is a single rugged mountain ridge, broken into several striking peaks from 1,500 to 1,800 feet high, with wooded ravines running down between them to the sea shore. It is about 11 miles long and from two to four miles wide, enclosing an area of 29 square miles. The main entrance to the magnificent land-locked harbour is by the Lymoon Pass, only half a mile wide.

HONG KONG.

The harbour is one of the finest roadsteads in the world. It is surrounded by mountains from 1,000 to 3,000 feet high, with a depth of water varying from 20 to 60 feet, covering an area of over 10 square miles, every inch of which affords good safe anchorage. There are three good entrances from the sea, well lighted at night.

It is impossible to imagine a more beautiful spectacle than

THE KOWLOONG HILLS, HONG KONG HARBOUR.
From a sketch by the Author.

that presented from the deck of our steamer as we dropped anchor in Hong Kong Harbour. Steamers and sailing ships of every nationality were riding in the roadstead, the surface of the water swarming with junks and boats of every description, lending life and animation to the scene. On one side the island of Hong Kong, with its lofty peaks steeped in the morning sunshine, the white villas and gardens of the Europeans on the slopes above the town glistening like pearls and emeralds; the brown native town, the blue sea flecked with a thousand little sails, and "the British fleet a-riding at anchor" in the foreground. On the other side the busy wharves and graving docks of Kowloong, the frowning forts of Stonecutter Island, and the lofty mountains of China beyond. It is not always thus. In summer terrific hurricanes, called typhoons, brew in the misnamed Pacific Ocean beyond the Philippine Islands, and visit Hong Kong in the full strength of their devastating circle. One of the finest of the noble buildings on the Kowloong side of the harbour is the Observatory, on the roof of which is a pole and red ball, the dreaded typhoon's warning. When the glass begins to fall anxious watch is kept on the red ball, and when it is run up to the top of the pole a sight worth seeing begins. The 2,000 junks, sampans, hakans and other boats bolt hot foot from the quays of Hong Kong, every sail set and every oar out, and pack themselves out of harm's way under the sheltering wing of Stonecutter Island. Every steamer gets up steam promptly, and all who can get in huddle into a sheltered corner with Her Majesty's fleet. The population get indoors with all speed, securely closing every window, shutter, and door, and all wait the arrival of the dreaded enemy. The barometer falls an inch an hour, till it gets round almost to "set fair" the wrong way, and then a blast like a shot from a hundred-ton gun falls upon the town and bay. Junks and boats which have not gone to Stonecutter's are blown ashore and piled in matchwood on the beach, verandahs fly down the streets like kites, even the great granite blocks of the sea wall are torn from their position, and ocean steamers have to drive their engines at full speed to keep their anchorage. The loss of life and property is sometimes very great in spite of all precautions. Steamers have been driven together and broken like pipkins, and large ships have been stranded far above high-water mark. Two days after a great typhoon in 1874 ninety-six corpses were picked up on the smallest island in the harbour.

The P. and O. launch took us ashore about eleven o'clock on Sunday morning, the other passengers waiting for the hotel launch. On reaching the jetty fifty Chinese 'long-shore coolies leaped on board, seized our portmanteaus, and began tugging and fighting over them like vultures over a carcase. Our luggage and they, in "one wild burial blent," tumbled on shore, and we gave it up as lost. To our great relief, however, a small man who had come ashore with us, a P. and O. luggage clerk, rushed into the mêlée, belaboured the coolies with fist and boot, and in about three minutes an orderly procession of twenty, four to each portmanteau and two to each Gladstone bag, started for the hotel, the energetic P. and O. at the head, my daughter and I bringing up the rear. The procession briefly halted at the hotel office for the number of our rooms, then solemnly ascended to the third floor, and the luggage was deposited in our two respective chambers. I asked P. and O. how much I was to pay, and he instructed me to give a halfpenny each! I gave them a penny, P. and O. rebuking me gravely for "spoiling the market," and they appeared abundantly content. Presently, however, P. and O.'s back being turned, they all came clamouring for more on the plea of "too much piecy top side," by which they meant to signify three pairs of stairs, but P. and O. suddenly returning, swept them out of the hotel with many thumps and kicks.

Stick and fist seem to be the only treatment meted out to the coolie population of Hong Kong. It may be quite true, as some Europeans urge, that no other argument prevails, but I am not surprised that "China boy" in return steals whatever he can, and sticks a sly knife into a European skin every now and then.

Immediately after lunch we started out to see what we could of the only real Chinese town we shall visit in our travels, as we cannot spare time to visit any portion of the Chinese Empire. Hong Kong is virtually two towns. In one the European merchants and their clerks, with the military and naval forces, live; in the other the Chinese.

There are 8,000 population in the one, 160,000 in the other, and the smaller population covers the most ground. Two leading thoroughfares, Queen's road, and the Praya or Quay, run through both quarters. The Queen's road contains the shops, clubs, banks, and hotels, the Praya the merchants' offices and warehouses, with wharves and jetties innumerable. It is in contemplation to extend the Praya sixty feet further out into the harbour, as the traffic of the port is becoming congested for want of space.

China town consists of three or four good wide thoroughfares, parallel with the Praya, out of which wander narrow filthy lanes, swarming with people of all ages and both sexes, and suggesting a very maggoty, mouldy cheese more than anything else. The people are rough, brutal, uncivil, villainous-looking, in marked contrast to the charming and delightful population we have left behind us in Japan. The open shops and pleasant tradesmen we saw there give way to grimy, dark little dens, the windows of which are covered with glass, it being unsafe to leave goods exposed to view in Hong Kong, thieves being not only abundant but universal, while escape in the crowded streets is certain and easy.

The wide distance which is usually maintained between precept and practice is amusingly illustrated by the scrolls one sees hanging up in every shop, on which are printed exhortations from Confucius in praise of honest traders, and commending civility to strangers.

The Hong Kong shops are famous emporiums for Chinese curiosities, and here one may purchase silk and satin embroideries, filagree work, pipes, gold bangles, and earrings, sandal wood boxes and fans, carved ivory, carved walking-sticks, carved horns, tortoise-shell work, and dead birds of wonderful plumage; the workmen who are manipulating these various articles sitting in the window to be stared at by the passers by.

CHINESE TOWN, HONG KONG.

The signboards are often in Chinese and English, the latter being generally of the kind known as "pidgin." Many of the shops hang out wooden emblems, a practice common enough in our own country.

As one wanders further and further from the English town, Hong Kong gets frowsier and more ruffianly every yard, till Tai-ping-shan is reached (the Hill of Great Peace, as it is facetiously called), where a seething mass of blackguardism exists. Here are the sailors' and soldiers' grog shops and their inevitable associations and surroundings, resorted to by seamen of all nationalities, and women of the most degraded character. Low music halls, liquor bars, old clothes shops, pawnbrokers, filthy cook shops, and filthier opium dens abound everywhere, with dirt, squalor, and population to match. I have never seen a city so lovely as Hong Kong, when viewed from a respectful distance, nor one in which beauty of situation and magnificence of buildings was laid so completely cheek by jowl with ugliness and horror of every kind.

In the better part of China town the streets are very quaint and picturesque, running up the side of the hill in a series of long steps, with shops on each side. The whole population is on foot, everyone being either carried in a sedan chair or walking. There are a few jin-rickishas plying for hire on the level ground, but there are only two carriages in Hong Kong, the governor's and Mrs. Jardine's, the wife of the leading merchant of the place. The streets are full of perambulating tradesmen; water-carriers, with buckets at each end of a bamboo pole; fruit sellers with baskets of pears, grapes, oranges, brilliant persimmons, and shaddocks; while others vend pieces of sugar-cane, pea-nuts, and sweetmeats. Coolies go round the houses carrying huge cages of live chickens, ducks, turkeys, quails, and other birds. At street corners are open-air restaurants with fearful viands displayed for sale, and at which Chinamen stand devouring the dainties with great gusto, a dish of grey greasy cabbage with fids of fat pork being the favourite. In some shady corner is a letter-writer, who varies his occupation with a little fortune-telling and quackery. The only open shops are the barbers', who are kept busy all day long shaving their customers' heads and faces, and trimming and anointing their long pigtails. The Chinese are so particular about their shaving that they have the inside of their ears and nostrils shaved with delicate dainty little razors. All these, with many similar incidents, make a Chinese street a perfect kaleidoscope of movement and colour.

After spending two or three hours in China town we called on Sir William des Vœux, the Governor of Hong Kong, to whom we had introductions. Government House is about 150 feet above the town, surrounded by private grounds, and a public garden beautifully situated and charmingly laid out, in which palms, cactuses, poinsettas, bougainvilleas, aloes, hibiscus, ferns, orchids, passion-flowers, and a score of other plants which only flower with us in hothouses, were blooming in the November sunshine. The Governor asked me to dine with him that evening, to meet some of the leading officials of the colony, from whom I got a large amount of interesting information, some of which I will record presently.

The following day the Governor proposed we should spend with him on board his steam launch, visiting the various points of interest in the harbour and round the island ; and on the day after Colonel Storer placed the Royal Engineers' launch at our disposal, Major Camperdown, R.E., kindly accompanying us, to show us the fortifications and explain the defences of the port. We thus were enabled to see more in the three days we were in Hong Kong than, unaided, we could have seen in a week.

HONG KONG.

At Kowloong, when finished, there will be the largest dry-dock in the world, capable of holding the new ironclad, the "Trafalgar," or the longest merchant steamer afloat. It will be completed next March. When busy, the Hong Kong and Whampoa Dock Co., who are building this dry-dock, employ in their engine sheds and shipbuilding yard over 4,000 hands, all of whom, except the foremen, are Chinese.

The harbour and its inlets swarm with fish of many kinds, and the Hong Kong fish market is one of the best in the East.

I thought I knew most of the methods pursued in different parts of the world to catch fish, but I find a new one at Hong Kong. All round the island and on the mainland opposite are small clusters of huts where the fishermen live. In front of this a stage runs out into the sea, on which is a rough wooden windlass, attached to a huge drop net. This net is lowered to the bottom, and all the boats put out from the shore, form into a circle, and slowly close in upon the net; the fishermen, by means of long poles with which they beat the water, by striking gongs, and uttering fearsome yells, frighten the fish over the drop net, which is then wound up from the platform full of the spoil of the sea. It sounds very primitive, but they catch fish, and that's the great thing after all.

Hong Kong is a Crown colony, with a Governor and Council. Its revenue is about £230,000, and its expenditure about £200,000, with an extraordinary expenditure last year, mainly on fortifications and other public works, of £135,000. Its revenue is derived as follows :—From Crown lands and quarries, £30,000 ; markets and piers, £12,000 ; licences—spirit £7,000, opium £32,000, miscellaneous £4,000 ; stamps, £30,000 ; municipal rates, £52,000 ; postage, £22,000 ; fines and fees of courts, light dues, junk licences, and other miscellaneous items, £40,000.

The expenditure is roughly—Military, £22,000; police, £32,000; post office, £21,000; judicial, £13,000; prisons, £9,000; fire brigade, £2,500; harbour, £8,000; gardens and plantations, £3,000; Surveyor-General's department, £9,000; various police offices, £15,000; education, £7,500; roads and bridges, £6,000; works and buildings, £12,000; the Governor's pay, £6,000.

There is a magnificent water supply brought to the town from the hills by a fine aqueduct, which is a marked feature in the landscape. £35,000 of the extraordinary expenditure of last year was in connection with this; about £16,000 was also spent in sanitary improvements.

The Council, which constitutes the Government, consists of the Governor, the Colonial Secretary, the Commander-in-chief, the Registrar-General, Treasurer, and Surveyor-General, and the Registrar of the Supreme Court. These eight form the Executive Council. The Legislative Council, which makes the laws for the colony, consists of the eight above named, the Chief Justice, and five unofficial members, all of whom are justices of the peace, and one of whom is a Chinese.

The pension list of the colony reaches £4,500 annually, about half of which goes to the police.

The following nations are represented by resident consuls:—Austria, Belgium, Brazil, Chili, Denmark, France, Germany, Hawaii, Italy, Japan, Netherlands, Peru, Portugal, Russia, Siam, Spain, Sweden, and United States. This gives a good idea of the various nationalities which throng the wharves of Hong Kong.

The places of worship are the cathedral, with about 400 worshippers; a seamen's mission, 70; a union nonconformist church, 300; a small German chapel, 100; four Roman Catholic churches, with 2,800 worshippers, mostly Portuguese. All these are European churches.

The London Missionary Society (Congregationalist) has four services in chapels or rooms in China town, with an aggregate congregation of about 500. The Church Missionary Society has got a little room which holds about 50, seldom full, and German missionaries have three congregations, numbering altogether about 200. The Roman Catholics have five Chinese chapels, with a total attendance of 500.

It does not speak great volumes for Hong Kong Christianity that forty years of English government and influence shows but 1,200 Christian worshippers in a population of 160,000 Chinese subjects. Missionaries do best the further they get away from "Christian" colonists.

The educational statistics of Hong Kong do not make one too proud of the department. There must be at least 16,000 children of school age in Hong Kong, yet there are not 6,000 in school attendance. There are any number of schools. Sixteen are Government schools, one of which costs £3,000 to administer, and is a school for the better class of Europeans, with an M.A. at the head of it. Fifteen are Government-aided schools, the masters of which are granted £10 a year, and 50 are missionary schools, which receive small grants in aid, and which educate 4,000 out of the 6,000.

The currency of Hong Kong is the Mexican silver dollar, and about four millions of paper money issued by three banks. There is also a Colonial silver currency of 20, 10, and 5 cent pieces.

The shipping returns for Hong Kong ought to silence those who are so fond of quavering about the decadence of British trade and commerce. Hong Kong is the greatest trade emporium in the East, the heart from which pulsates the commerce of a third of the human race, China, Japan, and nearly all Oceana. It will be interesting to analyse, from the shipping returns of Hong Kong, what is the share of all this trade which falls to England as compared with her many competitors for the trade of the East.

27,222 vessels of all nations, with a gross tonnage of 6,324,000 tons, and crews amounting to 470,000 men, entered and left the port of Hong Kong last year. Of these vessels 23,100, with a tonnage of 1,753,000, were Chinese coasting vessels, bringing their country's produce to this great distributing centre; thus leaving for all other countries 4,100 ocean-going vessels, with a total capacity of 4,570,000, or an average of about 1,100 tons each. Of these three-fourths of the whole, both in number and tonnage, were English, leaving just one-fourth for all the other nations of Europe and the world.

I will give, in order of precedence, the exact returns for each nation.

	Vessels.	Tonnage.
British.	2,982	3,372,000
German	676	488,000
French	123	176,000
United States	111	149,000
Danish	55	23,000
Dutch.	38	50,000
Spanish	33	19,000
Austrian	23	45,000
Norwegian	22	22,000
Siamese	16	7,500
Italian.	13	19,000
Russian	8	12,600
Japanese	7	5,000
Belgian	1	850
Hawaiian	1	350

This most satisfactory return is not due to the fact that Hong Kong is a British port, for pretty nearly the same results would be shown by an analysis of the foreign carrying trade of New York, Odessa, Genoa, Alexandria, Antwerp, Havre, or Hamburg.

The number of fishing boats frequenting the harbour and bays of Hong Kong is estimated at 3,000; the families all live on board their boats, and, it is said, reach a total of 30,000 souls.

The average rate of wages for labour in Hong Kong is very low. Domestic servants (all male), 4s. 6d. a week without food; 1s. 3d. per week with food. Chinese workmen at trades, 3s. 6d. with food. Day labourers, 8d. per day; blacksmiths, 2s.; carpenters, 1s. 4d.; masons and bricklayers, 1s. 3d.

The Chinese are terrible thieves. Nearly 17,000 persons were brought before the police magistrates last year for various offences, larceny and unlawful possession being the majority; about 400 for drunkenness, piracy, and kidnapping. Burglary, highway robbery, and assaults make up most of the balance. The daily average number of prisoners in prison is about 700. It must, however, be borne in mind that many of these criminals ought to be in Canton prison instead of Hong Kong if they got their deserts.

CHAPTER XVI.

SINGAPORE.

ON the afternoon of November 22nd we were dropping slowly down Hong Kong Roads on board the Pacific and Oriental steamer "Ancona." We had about a score of cabin passengers and some 200 Chinese coolies, who were being taken out to Singapore by a labour company. These coolies engage for a term of years. The company pay them so much a month, and contract to bring them back at the end of their term of service. About a mile from Hong Kong I heard a sudden splash. Running to the side and looking over I saw a Chinese coolie calmly striking out for a small boat a quarter of a mile off, which pulled to meet him, and into which he climbed. A small steam launch, which had been following the "Ancona," swooped down upon the boat, and we could see the coolie through our field glasses dragged into the launch, and thrust into its hold. It was explained to us that these rascally coolies get a month's pay, about 30s. in advance, and that if any of them can slip overboard undetected they make for shore, and engage in the next gang, pocketing the month's pay. In consequence the steamer conveying them is followed out to sea by the agents of the Labour Company, who pick up their man as he jumps overboard, and then send him to prison as a warning to his fellows. During the passage of the "Ancona" from her anchorage to the open sea no less than six jumped overboard, of whom only two were retrieved by the launch, four escaping in boats, every fisherman apparently being in the swindle.

We had a pleasant and uneventful passage to Singapore, which we reached in less than five days, arriving on Sunday morning about noon. We moored alongside the coal wharves of the Pacific and Oriental Company, which are about three miles from the town. The heat was very great. Singapore being almost on the equator, the same temperature prevails almost all the year round, and although the sun had been clouded over all the morning the thermometer stood over 90° in the shade. After lunch we started off in a carriage to see what we could. The carriages are covered with a thick roof, and the sides and ends are open all round, with windows of open woodwork, which can be drawn up as a shield from the burning sun. It has long been one of my dreams to see the tropics, and I looked eagerly out of the carriage for plants and trees familiar to me as a horticulturist and cherished in hot-houses at home, which I longed to see growing in their native heat. The first hedge we came to contained a shrub and two creepers in bloom, which were familiar greenhouse friends, and every garden we passed was a mass of bananas, palms, pineapples, cactuses, and flowering plants. I have never seen such greenery. Talk about Ireland as the Emerald Isle! Singapore is an emerald all the year round, for here it rains eighty inches in the year, with a vertical sun blazing on everything between the showers.

We drove through the town to the botanical gardens, a park of some 300 acres, beautifully situated on the sunny slope of an evergreen hill, the most delightful garden imaginable, nearer to Eden than I could have believed anything on earth to be. Here were great forest trees a mass of crimson bloom, delicate-leaved acacias forty or fifty feet high, with vermilion blossoms at the end of every twig, shathodeas covered with their great orange flowers, bushes of yellow allamanda, brilliant crotons, with ixoras, begonias, hoyas, eucharis lilies, stephanotis, callistemons and every variety of orchids, blooming in the open air. In the ponds were the wonderful Victoria Regia lily and the scarlet lotus. In spite of the burning sun we wandered through the garden for nearly two hours, at the end of which we were thankful to adjourn to a friend's house in the neighbourhood for a cup of refreshing tea. Thence we repaired to the cathedral for evening service. We found it a very fine church, with a choral and processional ritual. It was strange to see three rows of huge punkahs or fans running down the whole length of the cathedral, waving back and forward all through the service over the heads of the congregation. I was glad to escape from the pompous cathedral service to a hearty little meeting of soldiers and blue jackets at the Sailors' Rest, a coffee house and recreation room established for their benefit by an excellent lady who lives in Singapore, Miss Cook, to whom I was introduced after the service, which was conducted by Col. Cardew, who commands the regiment of infantry stationed at Singapore.

On Monday morning we again drove into the town, as the steamer was not to sail before four o'clock. Singapore appears to consist of three towns. The business or English town, Malay town, and China town. They are all connected by a wide esplanade facing the harbour, between two and three miles long. There are many fine buildings. The Post-office, the City Hall, the Police Barracks, the imposing Public Library, the Cathedral, and the Government Buildings are all handsome stone edifices of considerable pretensions. The town is full of open spaces, beautifully laid out, especially the Chinese park, a charming little garden of four acres in the middle of the most densely populated district. There is another pretty garden of ten acres, in the middle of the esplanade, facing the cathedral, covered with a green sward like velvet, and surrounded by magnificent trees. The esplanade itself for more than a mile is shaded by a double avenue.

The great business centre is Commercial Square, surrounded by banks, shops, and warehouses. Seven leading streets radiate from this centre, presenting the usual gay and lively scenes peculiar to an Eastern commercial city, in which the 140,000 inhabitants of Singapore swarm, clad in the brilliant and picturesque dresses of their twenty-five nationalities, relieved by the rich brown skins of those who wore no dresses at all. I suppose there is no place in the world where such a conglomeration of peoples is gathered together as appear in the busy streets of Singapore. The Blue Book of the Colony distributes the population among the following nationalities:— Achinese, Africans, Anamese, Arabs, Armenians, Bengalis, Boyanese, Bugis, Burmese, Chinese, Dyaks, Eurasians, Europeans, Japanese, Javanese, Jawi, Pekan, Jews, Malays, Manilamen, Parsees, Persians, Siamese, Singhalese, and Tamils. About half the population are Chinese, next come Malays, and third in strength Tamils from Southern India.

One is much impressed by the scarcity of women in the streets. Chinese women, however, do not leave their country readily, and although there are 72,000 Chinese males in Singapore, there are only 14,000 Chinese women; there is also but one Tamil woman to four Tamil men. The Malays, being the natives of the place, have their population pretty equally divided between the sexes.

The smart dresses of the Malays form the most striking feature in the scene. It consists of a single piece of silk, woven in as many and various colours as Joseph's coat, twisted round the waist, and hanging down petticoat fashion to below the knees; a piece of white muslin or cotton cloth thrown picturesquely about the shoulders, with a noble turban of crimson silk.

This finery is for the streets only, for a glimpse into house or shop reveals these same dandies squatting about on floor or counter with nothing on but a loin-cloth, the children contenting themselves with a tin fig-leaf about the size of a penny tied round their waists with a string.

The chair of Hong Kong and the jin-rickisha of Japan find no place in Singapore, though there are a few of the latter. The conveyances here are the Indian "gharry," drawn by active wiry little ponies about eleven hands high, which bowl you along at the rate of eight or nine miles an hour with wonderful endurance. Their drivers are all Malays dressed in full native costume.

I always like to visit the markets in every strange town. Singapore, like every other Eastern town, is well off in this respect, and the supply of food of all sorts is as usual in the hands of the industrious Chinese, who catch the fish, grow the vegetables and fruit, raise the ducks and poultry, and import the beef and mutton. The food dearest to the Chinaman's soul is duck and pig. All round Singapore are small farms in which pigs are reared for the market, and ducks are hatched by artificial incubation. One of these hatching establishments rears from 25,000 to 30,000 ducks every month. The hatching house is just a small hut, roofed with tiles, with arrangements for so modifying and retaining the sun's heat within the building that it is maintained at one even temperature day and night. Ducks alive, ducks dead, and ducks roasted and baked, are the leading feature of the Singapore markets. After ducks come fish, which are caught in great quantities in the bays and straits of the archipelago of islands, of which Singapore is the centre, and which are brought to market fresh, or rather alive, twice a day, at daybreak and at two in the afternoon. Cuttle-fish are in great demand; crabs shaped like long-tailed fans, whose tails are full of green eggs about the size of a pea, are also a great delicacy. Prawns, six inches long, are prized for curry, and the variety of fish of all sizes ranged from a 12-foot shark to the tiniest transparent whitebait.

The shark appeared the staple food of the poor in fish diet; but the bonita, a fish that looked like a two-foot herring, small sword fishes, gar-fish, a creature that seemed all fins and head, another with a head so big that its eyes look out from the middle of its sides, and a fish about the size and character of the chad of the English channel, were all plentiful and cheap. One whole side of the market is given up to dried and salt fish, which made one thirsty even to look at. Another avenue is devoted to "chow chow," or cooked food of all sorts, where groups of Chinese and Malays were squatted about enjoying fearsome-looking dainties of various kinds and flavours. The meat supply comes from Siam and India, and the fowls mainly from Cochin China and the Malay Peninsula. In the market we brought some fruit for lunch. The far-famed mangosteen was in season, and is a delicate pulpy fruit about the size of a large strawberry, with a fine subtle sub-acid flavour, embedded in a husk about $\frac{3}{8}$ inch thick. Nothing could form a prettier study of colour for a school of art student than the freshly-broken mangosteen, with its kernel of shining pulp, milk white streaked with a little yellow, embedded in the bright chestnut brown of its husk. Large pineapples at $\frac{1}{2}d.$ each, great clusters of golden bananas and mangoes, green-skinned oranges, persimmons from China, lychees, custard apples, cocoa-nuts, and other tropical fruits were displayed in tempting profusion, but a punnet of Kent strawberries or a pound of

Mayduke cherries are, in my opinion, worth the whole fruit market of Singapore.

From the market we drove some three miles into the country to see the garden of a wealthy Chinese millionaire merchant, who has made a hobby of it for years. I don't know how much money the wonderful tropical houses at Chatsworth have cost the Duke of Devonshire, nor how many thousands a year it takes to maintain them, but Mr. Whampoa knocks them into a cocked hat with a dozen coolies at wages of less than 1$s.$ per day. He wants no costly conservatories designed by a Chinese Sir Joseph Paxton. His two lakes covered with Victoria Regia leaves as big as open umbrellas, with their gorgeous flowers as big as a wide-awake hat, thrive better under the blazing canopy of the equator than they can ever hope to do at Chatsworth or at Kew under glass and over coals. All the shelter he wants for his vast collection of orchids is a little open matting stretched across a bamboo frame, or the natural foliage of some tree on whose trunk the orchid clings. Even Mr. Chamberlain must take a back seat behind Whampoa as an orchid grower. Here and there in the garden are summer-houses on tiny islands, reached by miniature bridges, exactly like the pictures on willow plate china. Trees and shrubs are cut into the shapes of dogs, birds, horses, cows, mandarins, and what-not, the effect being heightened by the introduction of fierce glass eyes, artificial hands, heads, and feet, which give a very ludicrous grotesqueness to the garden generally.

Singapore harbour is wide, deep, and well sheltered. The great demand of every steamer which enters it is coal; lying, as it does, just half-way between Colombo and China, it is one of the most important coaling stations in the world. It is well fortified with three excellent, newly-constructed forts, which look formidable enough, but which are dumb dogs for want of guns, long promised by the Home Government, but not yet forthcoming—the Ordnance Department of the British Government being the worst-managed and most exasperating branch of the public service.

There are four fine graving docks in the port, the largest of which is 475 feet long, 60 feet wide, with a depth of water 21 feet. There are about one and a half miles of wharves, alongside of which ocean steamers can lie, with a stock of 300,000 tons of coal, a tempting bonfire to an enemy's cruiser in times of war.

The Straits Settlements consist of the Islands of Singapore and Penang, and the town of Malacca on the mainland; subsidiary to the Government of the Straits Settlements are the dominions of the Sultans of Johore and Perah, whose territories lie along the Straits coasts of the Malay Peninsula, and who are virtually under the care of a Resident; and some smaller native states, who look to the Straits Government for counsel and help.

The annual revenue is about £600,000, of which two-thirds is derived from opium and spirit licences (some £380,000). The revenue from land is £65,000; from pawnbrokers' licences, £25,000; stamps, £50,000; port and harbour dues £12,000; postage, £18,000; profit on coinage, £10,000; miscellaneous receipts making up the balance. The increase of 1886 over 1885 was nearly £40,000, denoting very satisfactory material progress.

The expenditure consists of the following items: for salaries in all the civil departments, £26,000; for administration of justice, £80,000; for police and gaols, £20,000; for medical service, education, £20,000; ports and harbours, £12,000; postal services, £10,000; works and buildings, £160,000; roads, bridges, and canals, £22,000; military expenditure, £40,000;

pensions, £15,000; which, with a series of miscellaneous items, makes up a total expenditure of £580,000, leaving a good surplus, and a decrease on the previous year of about £15,000.

The exclusive privilege of retailing opium and spirits is farmed out for a term of three years, and the Chinese are the principal competitors for both. A licence to keep an opium shop costs 40s. Spirit licences vary from £16 to £8 for hotels and saloons; small spirit shops, 40s.; toddy and bhang shops, 40s. The income from opium and spirit licences is greatly on the increase, showing that in Singapore, as everywhere else where English influence sways the habits of natives, intemperance is increasing instead of diminishing. The revenue from these farmed licences has grown in twelve months, 1885-1886, from £340,000 to £380,000. No check of any kind seems to be placed on the issue of any number of these licences, which appear to be issued at the discretion entirely of the man who, for a lump sum, farms the right to grant them. I drove a circle of 15 or 16 miles round Penang Island, and every little village and hamlet had its spirit or toddy shop. Surely a Government whose revenue shows a steady increase and regular surplus, might devote some of its energies to reducing the appalling number of opium and spirit shops. I was not surprised to hear that missionary efforts in the Straits Settlements met with but scanty success.

The local revenues of the municipality of Singapore are £80,000, and the expenditure about the same. This is raised by assessment on houses, taxes on carriages, rent of markets, water rates, &c. The administration is all that can be desired. The water supply is excellent, the roads level and well made, the streets clean and well swept, the town well lighted, and the same may be said of Penang, whose local revenues are £40,000.

The public debt of the colony is the modest sum of £40,000.

There is a volunteer corps in Singapore, which claims to be the first ever started in the East Indies, and indeed it is older than any of our existing corps at home, except the 1st Lancashire, having been established in 1854. It consists of one officer, and fifty-one non-commissioned officers and men. It drills between thirty and forty times in the year, and costs £160.

The composition of the Executive and Legislative Councils is much the same as that of Hong Kong, described in the last chapter. There is one Chinese on the Legislative Council.

The Governor draws a salary of £4,000 a year, with free quarters at Government House, and various allowances and perquisites; the Colonial Secretary is paid £1,600, with free quarters; the Treasurer £1,000, the Surveyor-General gets £1,200 a year besides his pay as Colonel of Royal Engineers, the Commissioner of Lands £1,000, the Harbour Master £700, the Postmaster-General £700, the Chief Justice £2,000, the Puisne Judge £1,400, the Registrar £700, the Attorney-General £1,300, the Police Magistrates from £600 to £800, the Bishop £100! the Colonial Chaplain £600, the Inspector of Schools £700, the principal Medical Officer £800, the Inspector-General of Police £800, European policemen £80 and free quarters with rations, the Superintendent of Prisons £800, with free quarters; and the superintendent of the Botanic Gardens £400, with free quarters and £70 travelling expenses. I don't think the salaries paid to these leading officials can be considered excessive, taking into account the responsible work they have to do and the blazing climate in which they have to do it. At Penang and Malacca the Resident Councillor gets £1,000 a year and free quarters, and the Resident at Perah, who is to all intents and purposes the actual governor of the country, receives £3,000 a year.

The total population of the three towns of Singapore, Penang and Malacca is 424,000, of which 174,000 are Chinese, 174,000 Malays, and 3,400, including military, are Europeans.

The heathen of the Straits Settlements are not much troubled by missionary zeal. How is it, I wonder, that we so persistently neglect the conversion of the heathen at our own doors in our various Crown colonies? Can it be that the specimens of Christianity who form our governing and merchant classes are of such quality that missionaries find it impossible to get the heathen to believe in the religion whose products they are? The fact that a "Christian" Government draws the bulk of its revenue from the encouraged vice and degradation of the population, may go far to account for the obstinate preference of a Mohammedan native for a religion which enjoins total abstinence, and forbids the social habits which produce Eurasians? The merchants say the missionaries are idle and worthless, the missionaries retort in kind, and for myself, I fear that in Singapore, at any rate, there is truth on both sides. There is a magnificent cathedral at Singapore, with a Right Reverend Bishop, a Venerable Archdeacon, and an Assistant Colonial Chaplain. There is a surpliced choir to boot. The S.P.G. has also a missionary, who gets £300 or £400 a year. The only natives visible at the cathedral services are the fifteen or twenty Malays who, standing outside the building, pull the punkah strings to cool the fashionable worshippers inside. The only attempt to reach the heathen by the Church of England is a small school chapel, at which there is an attendance of fifty or sixty at most.

The Presbyterians have a fine handsome chapel for themselves. I surveyed it from the outside, and it had a fashionable congregation of 150 or 200. Fifty or sixty carriages were waiting outside, with as many native servants as there were good Presbyterians inside. The minister gets £500 a year and a free house. The English Presbyterian Mission have one clerical and one lay missionary. They have four small rooms in Singapore in which they hold services, and in none of which do they muster a congregation of fifty souls. I do not venture to judge these gentlemen. I am quite sure from all I heard that they were excellent and pious men, but the results of their labours are miserable and unsatisfactory, and I cannot but think that their methods and plans of working must be wrong.

In Penang the Nonconformists have no missionary whatever, but the Church of England (S.P.G.) maintain an excellent native missionary to the Tamils, who seems to be meeting with some measure of success. He has an average congregation in Penang of eighty-five out of a total Tamil population of 25,000.

In Province Wellesley there is an undenominational Protestant mission, with an English minister and four native assistants. They have services in five places, and possess three small chapels, none of which will hold a hundred persons. They have sixty or seventy Chinese worshippers among the lot. The Church of England people keep a clergyman for themselves at a salary of £350, and have three "Catechists," who work among the Tamils.

At Malacca, the Colonial Chaplain ministers to English residents at a salary of £550, and they pay Mr. Chong Sin Tai, to convert the Chinese, a salary of £30! Nonconformists do not put in an appearance at Malacca.

So much for Protestant zeal for the conversion of our heathen fellow-subjects in the Straits Settlements. But what are the Roman Catholics doing? may be asked. They have twenty-five chapels in the colony. They have forty-one priests, missionary priests and Catechists, with aggregate congregations of 6,500. I think it would be well if the secretaries of our various missionary societies spent **twelve** months in the East trying to find out how it **is that** Jesuits succeed so well when they fail so completely.

What I fail to understand is the comparative zeal and success of Roman Catholicism and the comparative failure of Protestantism in the conversion of the **Eastern** heathen to the Christian faith. The fact is there, **and is stubborn. I draw** the figures just quoted from returns furnished **to the Government of** Singapore by the various denominations themselves, and published in the Blue Book for 1886.

The imports from all countries into the Straits Settlements are £12,800,000, **and the** exports **to all countries** a shade over £10,000,000, **the bulk of this enormous trade** being the collection at this great "**corner** shop" of the **world of the produce** of the surrounding islands of the Malay Archipelago, and its distribution to England, **Europe, and America.**

The Straits Settlements **are free** ports, open on equal terms **to** the commerce of the world. The total imports and exports from **and** to the British Empire reach **a total of** £8,400,000. The total imports from and exports to every other nation in Europe and their colonies, including French India, French Cochin China, Java, Sumatra, **Celebes, and all the other** Dutch islands, Portuguese India, **and** the Philippine Islands reaches **£6,500,000.** This is a remarkable instance of the supremacy of **British commerce,** drawn from **a free port in** the very centre of **all the most** important colonies of our European competitors, containing populations **of over** fifty millions, on an area of 470,000 square miles; **in the** midst of which we are squatted on two small islands and **a tiny** province.

This is brought out more forcibly **by a** comparison **of** shipping statistics, which demonstrate how completely Englishmen and English trade dominate in every part of the earth, and how British traders manage to get the best of it, even in colonies settled by other European nations.

The following shows the number of ships and tonnage entered and cleared from the port of Singapore alone during 1886 with their flags :—

	Ships.	Tonnage.
United Kingdom	535	776,000
France	89	159,000
Germany	87	110,000
Austria	41	79,000
Belgium	None	—
Holland	5	8,000
Italy	9	13,000
Russia	26	43,000
Spain	7	11,000
Colonies.		
British Possessions	1,162	1,491,000
French „	167	197,000
Dutch „	1,033	707,000
Spanish „	91	108,000

These figures show conclusively how impossible it is for Colonies not British to get their imports and get away their exports except with the help of British bottoms and through British emporiums. All this we owe to John Bright, Richard Cobden, and Free Trade.

We left Singapore, after a stay of nearly two days, for Penang, where we remained six hours, from 7 A.M. to 1.30 P.M. We went ashore with Sir Hugh Low, the British Resident at Perah, who, with Lady Low, were our fellow-passengers. He and I had foregathered on the voyage, in sympathy as orchid growers. He is a very distinguished colonial official, but I confess his name was more familiar to me as the discoverer of some of the most beautiful orchids in Borneo, which bear his name. We drove together to the Botanical Gardens, about five miles out of Penang, and spent two pleasant hours with Mr.

Curtis, the superintendent, who showed us many rare and beautiful plants which he had brought into the gardens from Malayan jungles.

We then breakfasted with Mr. Brown, the leading merchant of Penang, who had been our fellow-passenger also from Singapore, at his beautiful country house, and the wonderful curries he gave us will linger in our memories.

SINGAPORE—A MANGO BREAKFAST IN JULY.

CHAPTER XVII.

KANDY.

ON Sunday morning, December 4th, the Island of Ceylon was eagerly watched for from the deck of the "Ancona" by all its passengers. Perhaps it would be more correct to say it was eagerly smelt for, as both captain and first officer at breakfast assured their somewhat sceptical passengers that

> "The spicy breezes
> Which blow from Ceylon's isle,"

was no poetical fiction, but a pleasant reality when the wind was blowing off the land, which it was kindly and very softly doing that morning. Certainly about eleven o'clock I perceived a distinct odour of aromatic wood, not unlike the smell of a larch plantation in spring, which I was informed came from the numerous cinnamon gardens along the coast.

We had had a delightful five days' run from Penang. The sea was calm enough all the way for a Rob Roy canoe, while the gentle zephyr of wind, dead ahead, increased by the speed of the ship, kept the deck and cabins cool and breezy; an important addition to our comfort, as the thermometer seldom stood below 85°, even at night.

At noon Point de Galle, which was the old coaling station before Sir John Coode's famous breakwater was made at Colombo, hove in sight, the "Ancona" steaming near enough to shore for signals to be telegraphed on to Colombo, and to enable us to see vast cocoanut plantations on shore, with Adam's Peak, the sacred mountain of Ceylon, rising high in the dim distance. The Peninsular and Oriental mail steamer from Calcutta, and also the one from Australia met the "Ancona" twenty or thirty miles from Colombo, and the three fine vessels kept each other company to port, where mails were to be

ADAM'S PEAK, CEYLON.
From a sketch by the Author.

exchanged, a not unusual instance of the admirable punctuality of the great Peninsular and Oriental Company.

It was nine o'clock, and quite dark, when we dropped anchor in Colombo harbour, too late to go ashore, so we decided to sleep on board and disembark in the early morning. Six o'clock found us on deck to take a first look at the harbour. It is enclosed by a magnificent breakwater nearly a mile long, of which I shall have something to say later on; right opposite to the ship is the busy wharf and Custom House, with the useless old fort; northwards the crowded and picturesque native town; and southward the bright suburb of Kolpetty, the whole standing "dressed in living green" of cocoa palm, plantain, bread-fruit, and mango trees.

The ship was surrounded with native boats, clamouring for jobs to take passengers ashore, and I saw for the first time in its native waters the "Catamaran," which had excited my interest two or three years ago at the Fisheries Exhibition in London. This singular boat consists of a tree-trunk, about 20 to 25 feet long, hollowed out like a canoe. The two sides have a sort of bulwark 3 feet high, made of upright boards lashed on, the width between being 18 or 20 inches. If this were all, the "Catamaran" would be the crankiest boat ever made; but some feet away from the canoe and parallel to it is a stout log of bamboo or other light wood, the same length as the boat, both being fastened together by two curved bars of bamboo. This outrigger lies on the surface of the water, and by its weight on one side and its resistance to the water on the other renders the "Catamaran" one of the best sea boats in the world, and they are often met with far out of sight of land and in very rough weather. We were, however, glad to find that Captain Webber had kindly placed his gig at our disposal, in which, with our luggage, we went ashore, to find that a polite Custom House officer not only declined to search our trunks, but volunteered to take care of them for us till two o'clock, when we had decided to go on to Kandy, the ancient capital, leaving Colombo till the end of our visit.

We spent the morning in driving about Colombo, but as we shall be there three or four days before going to Madras and Calcutta, I will leave any remarks on the capital of Ceylon to the next chapter. At two o'clock we drove to the station and took our seats in the train for Kandy, with a 75-mile journey before us. The Ceylon railways are a Government monopoly, and there are 185 miles open for traffic. The carriages are horribly uncomfortable, the first-class being no better than the third-class on an English trunk line. I had to pay heavy excess on our luggage. The journey lasted five hours, an average speed of 15 miles an hour. For some miles out of Colombo the train runs through a flat country chiefly under rice cultivation, or in grass for cattle. The whole area is one vast swamp, every crop being profusely irrigated, the cattle, all black buffaloes, feeding knee deep in water. Wherever there is a knoll, or a bit of rising ground, a beautiful tropical picture forms itself; a clump of quaint cottages and barns, surrounded by palms, jack-fruit trees, bananas, and vegetable gardens, the dark red tiles of the buildings, the bright yellow and crimson dresses of the peasants, and the brown skins of the naked children relieving the intense and somewhat monotonous tropical green. Presently the Kelani-Ganga River, the greatest stream of water in the island, is crossed by a very fine iron bridge, and on the other side a branch line turns off to the quarries from which were got the stones for building the breakwater at Colombo. Fifty miles from Colombo the railway begins the great climb of 6,000 feet to Nuwera Eliya. It creeps up the flank of a magnificent mountain, Allagalla, whose high peak, crowning a sheer precipice, dominates the whole valley. From the summit of Allagalla, the old Kandyan kings used to hurl those whom they suspected of treason. On the opposite side of the great green valley of Dekanda are the Camel Mountain, so called from its resemblance to that animal, and the Bible Mountain, with a chain of connecting peaks 4,000 to 5,000 feet above the sea. In the valley are seen terraced fields of pale green rice, the flower-like branches

KANDY. 265

of the Kekuna trees, magnificent forest trees covered with purple and pink blossoms, palms of all kinds, with here and there noble specimens of the great talipot palm, and patches of luxuriant

THE DEKANDA VALLEY.

tropical jungle, bright with a score of different brilliant flowers or creepers which throw themselves from one tree-top to the other, as they tower above the tangled undergrowth. Beautiful waterfalls are seen up the glens, as the train climbs slowly by, while others rush under us as we cross them on bridges, to leap into mid-air, and lose themselves in clouds of mist and spray,

ON THE KANDY RAILWAY—SENSATION ROCK.

in which the sun dances in all the colours of the rainbow. Every now and then we get a glimpse beneath us of the fine road constructed long since by the English Government, to enable them to take and keep possession of the ancient capital, which had been wrested from the Portuguese and Dutch by the valiant old Kandyan kings; this road is now superseded by the railway. A few miles from Kandy the train, after passing through several tunnels, runs over what is called "Sensation Rock," skirting the edge of the cliff so closely that the sight drops a thousand feet before it rests on anything on which a blade of grass or a tropical creeper can lay hold. Just beyond this exciting scene we cross the dividing ridge of two water-sheds, and in a very short time reach the lovely valley of Kandy, run into the station, and by seven o'clock find ourselves comfortably settled at the Queen's Hotel.

Ceylon is an island of villages, and Kandy, though the ancient capital, is not much more than a group of two or three villages, containing in all a population of 22,000. It has little of general interest, the only buildings of any importance being the gaol, the barracks, three or four churches and chapels, the Government office, and the world-renowned Temple of the Sacred Tooth of Buddha; this latter being an insignificant little shrine of no great antiquity or architectural beauty, its only interest lying in its peculiarly sacred character, rendering it the heart from which all Buddhist sentiment ebbs and flows.

The temple is a small building with a good-sized courtyard surrounding it, the outer walls of which are decorated with hideous ill-executed frescoes of the various punishments inflicted in the Buddhist Hell, differing very little in character from those one so often sees depicted in Roman Catholic churches in Italy. The deepest and hottest hell, with the most gruesome fiends to poke the fire, is reserved for those who rob a Buddhist priest, or plunder a Buddhist temple. The great relic, which is two inches long and one inch thick (what a tooth to ache!) is preserved in a gold and jewelled shrine, covered by a large silver bell, in the centre of an octagonal tower with pointed roof. It is only exposed to view once a year, but I was privately informed that five rupees would open the door for me. I preferred my five rupees.

In the porch of the temple were groups of horrible beggars, who display their various wounds and defects of nature with much liberality. The most popular appeared to be a monster with a huge tooth growing through his under lip. I suppose his popularity was due to the fact that this horror was nearer to the genuine article in the shrine than could be found outside the mouth of a hippopotamus.

The kings and priests of Burmah, Siam, and Cambodia send regular yearly tribute to the Temple of the Sacred Tooth, and more or less reverence is paid to it in India, China, and Japan.

The real charm of Kandy lies in its beautiful situation. The town itself is lost to view in green tropical foliage. It is built on the banks of a large artificial tank or lake, about three miles in circumference, surrounded by beautiful hills five or six hundred feet above its surface, on which are dotted here and there the pretty bungalows of missionaries and other well-to-do inhabitants. We spent a morning wandering about the lovely lanes of these hills, in any of which you may gather from the hedgerows bunches of "hot-house" flowers, which would fetch a guinea at Covent Garden market. From their heights magnificent views of the high mountain ranges of Ceylon are obtained, all richly timbered to the summits.

I found growing wild on these charming hills sunflowers, roses, dracœnas, poinsettas, mimosas, lantanas, balsams, iconias, petreas, passion-flowers, and a dozen other varieties of beautiful blooms familiar to me in English hot-houses, but whose names I cannot now call to mind.

In the afternoon we drove out to the Government Botanical Gardens at Peradenia, whose distinguished director, Dr. Triman, I had become acquainted with in the train, and who showed us much kindness and hospitality. The entrance to the garden is through a fine avenue of tall india-rubber trees, towering into the air a hundred feet, spreading out into enormous leafy crowns fifty or sixty feet in diameter, their huge roots, longer than the tree is high, creeping over the surface of the ground like great

THE INDIA-RUBBER TREE.

snakes, sometimes growing straight up in the air till they attach themselves to the lower branches, thus forming stout props to support the weight of heavy foliage, and enable it to resist storm and tempest.

There is no need in this garden for the familiar notice, "Keep off the grass." If you venture on the lawns, especially in damp weather such as we are having, nasty little leeches the thickness of a hair wriggle through your trousers and stockings, and suck your blood till they swell out to the thickness of a lead-pencil. Instances are known in which men have gone to sleep on the grass in Ceylon, and have been found dead, sucked to death by hundreds of these horrible creatures. It is also necessary to beware of "snakes in the grass." The day before our visit one of the gardeners was bitten by a snake, and was lying dangerously ill in the hands of a native doctor, who possesses secret remedies handed down to him from his forefathers by word of mouth only. While we were enjoying a cup of tea at Dr. Triman's bungalow, another gardener brought a fine lively cobra which he had just caught, tied by a string to a stick, striking its fangs vigorously into every object that was thrust towards its head. On the whole, therefore, we kept to the paths and beaten tracks as much as possible to avoid these gentry, as well as centipedes and black scorpions, which are equally plentiful. Immediately inside the garden gate is a wondrously beautiful group of all the palms indigenous to the island. Here is the cocoa-nut, with its cylindrical trunk two feet thick, soaring up into the air 150 feet, crowned with a huge tuft of feathery leaves eighteen or twenty feet long, with great bunches of fruit clustering in their shade. The Palmyra palm, which, according to a famous Tamil poem, can be put to 801 different uses. Its leaves are circular, with seventy or eighty ribs, opening like a great fan. These leaves are used by the natives to thatch their cottages, to make matting for floor and ceiling, bags and baskets, hats and caps, fans, umbrellas, and paper. The fruits, as well as the young seedlings, are cooked and eaten as a nutritious vegetable, and from the flower-spikes, alas! the native obtains palm wine or toddy, which can be distilled into stronger arrack. The Sago palm and its relative, the Kitul palm, yield not only the nutritious pith which makes the familiar pudding of our childhood, but also produce excellent sugar and splendid fibre for rope-making and other purposes. The Areca-nut palm produces the well-known Betel nut, which, rolled up in leaves of the Betel pepper, with a little lime and tobacco, makes the favourite "chaw" of the natives of Ceylon and India, a harmless, though nasty practice, for which they will sacrifice meat, drink, washing and lodging. More beautiful than these is the queen of all palms, the Talipot, which for thirty years from its birth pushes up its straight white shining trunk, with its crown of dark green leaves, till it reaches a height of a hundred feet or more. Then it blooms—and such a bloom! a tall pyramidal spike of white blossoms forty feet above its crown of huge green fans, perhaps the noblest flower the world produces. Each bloom forms a nut, and the tree, having scattered its seeds to become palms in their turn, dies of the supreme effort. We were fortunate enough to see a magnificent Talipot in full bloom, and to obtain a good photograph of its marvellous beauty. The travellers' palm is one that contains quantities of perfectly pure water in the thick ends of its leaves. The Cabbage palm has a capital edible imitation of that homely vegetable as its fruit, and the Oil palm, with a dozen other varieties, were all to be found in flourishing growth in the remarkable clump of palms I am trying to describe so feebly.

The next point of interest was a plantation of nutmeg and clove trees, further on were Jack-fruit trees, with their huge fruit growing from the trunk and weighing fifty or sixty pounds each; bread-fruit, pomeloes, the candle tree, the magnificent *Anthurium Regale*, with its vari-coloured leaves, three feet long by two feet wide, were all passed and examined with interest and curiosity. We then were taken into a dense piece of jungle, in which giant creepers, with stems six or eight inches thick, climbed to the tops of the highest trees with profuse blossoms of all sizes and colours, while the ground was covered with all kinds of tropical ferns, including the lovely *Adiantum Farleyense*, the gold and silver ferns, great tree ferns, *Adiantum Peruvianum*, and a hundred other varieties of ferns, lycopodiums, and ground plants.

THE GIANT BAMBOO—PERADENIA GARDENS.

But the great sight is the giant bamboo, which grows in mighty clumps by the bank of the fine river that flows round the gardens. These form enormous green thickets more than

100 feet high, and the same in thickness, consisting of 80 or 100 tall cylindrical stems, each from one to two feet thick. They grow so closely crowded together that a cat would find it difficult to find her way through. They shoot 70 or 80 feet into the air without a break, and then spread out into immense branches of slender little leaves, that give the appearance of gigantic green ostrich feathers. As every one knows, the bamboo is one of the most useful plants that grow in the tropics, and I might fill my book with a description of all the uses to which it may be put.

The garden swarms with pretty striped squirrels and with bright-plumaged tropical birds, while hanging from the branches of the trees are swarms of great flying foxes, which live upon the different kinds of fruit, and very often get drunk on the sweet palm sap, being found lying helplessly incapable in the vessels which the natives leave out all night to catch the juice. But there is no end to the botanical wonders of this unrivalled and fascinating garden of Peradenia.

The next day we left Kandy in company with Dr. Triman to visit the great health resort of the English residents in Ceylon Nuwera Eliya, 6,200 feet above the sea level. In the advertisements of one of the hotels here the attraction is held out that it is "so cold as to make it possible to burn open English fires all the year round." The great desire of a European who has been baked for eight or ten months in the oven of Colombo is to feel cold, to wear a great coat and comforter, to sleep without mosquito nets, and with half a dozen blankets over him. So he goes to the most detestable place on the whole island, where the rain-clouds of a radius of 1,000 miles love to dwell; where the climate is cold and damp; where the thermometer is at freezing point at six in the morning and eighty in the shade at noon; where the rainfall is 150 inches and the sun shines only

T

sixty days in the year. Here the Anglo-Cingalese love to play at "being in England." They build themselves feeble imitations of English cottages; despising the fine flora of the country, they fill their gardens with pallid pinks, roses, and other English flowers, which look as miserable as a Hindoo beggar in a November London fog. They grow wilted specimens of English vegetables, and on rare occasions really clever gardeners have been known to ripen a strawberry; then a solemn dinner party is given to intimate and valued friends, and that strawberry is reverently divided and eaten in solemn silence. It is the dream of their lives to grow a cherry, and the man who succeeds will have a monument. They have cherry trees, but they all turn into weeping willows, and blossom feebly all the year round. These cottage gardens gave me a nightmare, and I dreamt that Nuwera Eliya was a bit of England, dying of a bad cold in the head. The only English plant that has acclimatised itself with any vigour is gorse, which was all about the hedges in odorous profusion.

Dr. Triman took us to see his hill garden at Hakgala, six miles from Nuwera Eliya, where his clever deputy, Mr. Nock, grows with some little success various English plants and flowers, and with distinguished success a wonderful variety of semi-tropical flora; he also experiments on possibilities for the advantage of Ceylon planters. Here we saw the magnificent New Zealand tree ferns, the huge shield fern, splendid rhododendron trees as big as oaks, with trunks 2 feet thick, beautiful ground orchids, lobelias, large gentians, balsams, an endless variety of ferns and lycopods, and a brace of magnificent jungle cocks, which flew out of a tree as we passed by, resplendent in their gold and crimson plumage.

Nuwera Eliya is a great plateau, on which is a fine lake about two miles long, which has recently been stocked with English trout. One was caught with the artificial fly the other day, and the intelligence was immediately cabled to the English press. They are said to be thriving, but Dr. Triman fears that as soon as the natives find out they are there they will manage to clear the lake out somehow or other. Fish have a poor chance in this Buddhist country. A Cingalese won't take life, so he never tastes butcher's meat; he has, however, no scruple to help a fish on to dry land and let him die if he can't get back to his native element, and by this amiable quibble he is able to add fish to his mess of rice without any breach of conscience. Your Buddhist is a true Pharisee. The highest peak in the island, Peduru Galla, rises just behind our hotel, and is a favourite excursion, but as we were not fortunate enough to get one of the rare sunny days, we did not ascend it. Peduru, and all the peaks round Nuwera Eliya, are forest-clad to the summit, and are the chosen home of the wild elephant, which still exists in considerable numbers in Ceylon. There were five or six of these huge beasts in the jungle, within half a mile of Hakgala gardens, and every now and then they had a tramp through them, to the sore dismay of poor Mr. Nock. There are also leopards, cheetahs, tiger-cats, jackals, elk, wild boar, monkeys, and a fine crested eagle, all plentiful in the ancient and sombre forests which clothe these lofty mountains.

Instead of returning to Kandy by the railway we determined to drive from Nuwera Eliya through a fine mountain pass to Gampola, a distance of forty miles, taking the train thence back to Kandy. It was very curious, in our descent of nearly five thousand feet, to watch the gradual change from temperate vegetation to all the luxuriance of the tropics. Half-way down we stopped at the Government Rest House at Ramboda to bait our wretched pair of ponies, and get some refreshment for ourselves.

These Government rest houses are placed at intervals of

T 2

fifteen miles along all the roads in Ceylon. They contain a good guest room and five or six bedrooms, rudely furnished, but tolerably clean and comfortable. The charges are moderate. For the use of the house, 9d.; for a bed, 1s.; for sheets and blankets, 1s.; a lamp, 4d.; breakfast of tea or coffee, toast, eggs, and meat, 2s. 3d.; dinner of three courses, 2s. 6d. There is also accommodation for poor people at reduced rates, and for horses and cattle.

Ramboda is situated in a wide amphitheatre of mountains, and has a dozen fine waterfalls within a few hundred yards of each other, the amphitheatre indeed being one great spring of water. From Ramboda to Gampola we passed through a succession of coffee, tea, cocoa, and chinchona plantations, of which I shall have something to say in my next chapter, when I shall refer to the natural resources of this rich and fertile colony, and we finally arrived at the station in a deluge of tropical rain.

We spent a quiet Sunday at Kandy, visiting some of the missionary stations and native churches. Next day we came down to Colombo to spend two or three days previous to sailing for Calcutta and Madras.

CHAPTER XVIII.

COLOMBO.

WE spent four days pleasantly and profitably at Colombo, the capital of Ceylon. While at Kandy I had written to Mr. A. M. Ferguson, the proprietor of the *Ceylon Observer*, who had long been known to me by repute as the man of all others best acquainted with the social condition of the Cingalese people, asking him if he would give me the opportunity of making his acquaintance. I got a reply from his nephew and partner, Mr. John Ferguson, saying that his uncle was up country, but that he himself would call on me on my arrival, and be glad to help me all he could to some knowledge of the country and its people. He kept his promise, and treated us with a princely hospitality. His time, his carriage, his library, his bungalow, and himself he placed unreservedly at my disposal, and the more I drew upon him the better he was pleased. A. M. and J. Ferguson are sound authorities on all Cingalese questions; the one has been forty-seven years, and the other twenty-five years editor and proprietor of the leading newspaper on the island, and both have written many books and pamphlets on the resources of Ceylon, marked by great shrewdness and research. Mr. John Ferguson at once constituted himself our "guide, philosopher, and friend," and by his help we saw and learnt more in four days than we could have acquired in four weeks without him. I was also favoured with long interviews with Sir Arthur Gordon, the Governor of the Colony; Mr. O'Brien, the Colonial Secretary; Mr. Campbell, the Inspector-General of Police and Prisons; Mr. Pigott, the senior Baptist, and Mr. Scott, the senior Wesleyan missionary, both of whom have had twenty years' experience of Ceylon; Mr. Grinlington, the leading merchant of Colombo, and many others; and in this and my next chapter I desire to tell my readers some little of what I have gleaned from these authorities with regard to this valuable possession of the British Crown.

Colombo owes its existence as a seaport to the genius of Sir John Coode, the great engineer. Before the existence of the breakwater, Galle was the chief port of Ceylon, the coaling station of the Peninsular and Oriental Co. and other lines of steamers trading with Calcutta and the East. Poor Galle is now quite extinguished by its powerful rival, whose harbour, easily accessible by day or night, provides safe and easy anchorage for the entire passing trade of the East, as well as for the bulk of the export and import trade of Ceylon. The harbour is over 500 acres in extent, more than half of which has a depth of from 26 to 40 feet at low water spring tides. In this deep water twenty-four sets of double screw moorings, suited for vessels of the largest class, drawing 25 feet and over, have been laid down, furnishing accommodation far in excess of the present requirements of the trade, which, however, will in good time require it all and more.

The first block of the magnificent breakwater was laid by the Prince of Wales on December 8th, 1875, and the lamps of the lighthouse shone out over the Indian Ocean on the night of January 27th, 1885. The breakwater thus took nearly ten years to complete. The shore portion, or "root work," extends over $4\frac{1}{2}$ acres, reclaimed from the sea, having a solid wall of concrete blocks to the sea front, and a fine wharf about 1,000 feet long on the harbour side with a depth at low water of 14 feet, accommodating a considerable number of good-sized vessels engaged in the coasting trade. From this wharf the breakwater starts, in 16 feet of water at low tide, extending northwards for over 3,000 feet, then curving inwards for another 1,000 feet or more, which, with the shore portion, makes a total length of 4,877 feet, or close upon a mile in length. The breakwater ends in about 40 feet of water at lowest tides with a circular head 62 feet in diameter, on which there is a fine lighthouse visible for 10 miles. This circular head is formed of concrete in mass, in a wrought-iron caisson under low-water, and of concrete blocks above the level. The breakwater itself is composed of a mound of granite rubble stone, raised by convict labour from quarries about 12 miles distant. The rubble mound, after being allowed twelve months to consolidate, was levelled off by means of divers to depths varying from 13 feet below water at the land end to 24 feet below water at the breakwater head. Upon the mound, thus levelled, huge concrete blocks from 16 to 32 tons in weight are founded, extending up to eight feet above low water, the whole being finished off with a capping of concrete in mass, four feet thick, throughout the whole length of the breakwater.

During the south-west monsoon the sea breaks over the whole length in columns of spray 50 feet high, a marvellous sight which I was not privileged to see, the north-east monsoon blowing while we were at Colombo. But I remember having seen a fine photograph of it in Sir John Coode's office at Westminster, which was more like Niagara Falls turned upside down than anything else.

The total cost of this wonderful feat of engineering skill was a little over £700,000, but its value to the colony is far beyond price. Before its construction vessels were often delayed days, and even weeks during the south-west monsoon, owing to the impossibility of loading and unloading shore boats in the tremendous swell which rolled across the open roadstead, while even during the lulls of the monsoon the damage to cargo and the loss overboard, as well as the extra cost of operation, was very great indeed. The value of the breakwater to the port of Colombo is best shown by the fact that since 1882, when the breakwater first began to afford material protection to shipping, the tonnage of the port has increased from 1,700,000 to very nearly 3,000,000 tons.

It is proposed some day to meet the breakwater with a northern arm from the opposite shore, which would make the harbour smooth water in every wind that blows. The mercantile interests press this further development of the harbour upon the Government with some vigour, but the present Government prefer, and as I think rightly, to push on other public works, viz., railway extension, irrigation tanks, and the further fortification of Colombo. But if the trade of the port continues to increase in anything like the proportion of the last few years, some extension of the harbour and the building of a good dry-dock will become imperative.

The breakwater makes a very fine promenade when the wind is off shore, but is very little resorted to by the inhabitants. We walked to the end and back one fine evening, but it was deserted except by three or four natives lazily fishing, and by small processions of crabs making short cuts over the breakwater from the open sea to the more succulent feeding grounds of the harbour.

The Grand Oriental Hotel at Colombo is one of the sights of the East. It is a caravanserai with 100 bedrooms, and when two or three Peninsular and Oriental steamers are in port these rooms are all filled, and couches are laid out in the verandahs and passages for the surplus. Its dining-room will seat 300 people, and its huge verandah, facing the sea, is crowded with pedlars and vendors of the precious stones for which Ceylon is famous, a trade largely supplemented by Birmingham enterprise. These brigands are mostly Moormen, descendants of a colony of Arabians who have waxed mighty in the retail trade of Ceylon. They address their customer with bland confidence, introducing themselves in various guises. One informed me that he was "Streeter's confidential buyer"; another introduced himself as

SIR JOHN COODE'S BREAKWATER, COLOMBO.

"the personal friend of Lord Rothschild"; and a third as the "favourite jewel broker of the Prince of Wales." They vary their list of distinguished patrons for Americans, substituting Tiffany, General Grant, and Vanderbilt, while they dazzle Australians by enormous prices. I was told over and over again, "If you was Australian my price would be a thousand rupees, but for Englishman I take 200," finally coming down to 20. No one escapes in the long run. Scornful sceptics begin by treating every stone as "Brummagem glass," and threatening the pedlars with a stick, but they always end by being taken into a dark corner to see a sapphire gleam in the light of a wax match, and come on board with a dozen bits of coloured glass wrapped up in cotton wool, for which they have given £2 or £3 each. If glass, these so-called precious stones are only worth a few pence; if genuine, they are worth £50 each. You may, however, go to respectable shops, known to bankers and merchants, and buy very pretty things made of third-class sapphires and cat's-eyes cheaply enough, after two or three days' patient chaffering; there is one jeweller who has a small stock of really good things, but every fine stone that is found finds a ready market at its full value in Calcutta, London, or Paris, and the splendid stones purchased by transient passengers are either flawed or otherwise inferior in colour or quality, or are other stones than represented. The finding and cutting of gems is an important trade in Ceylon. At Kandy the cutters are seen in their little shops working a cast-iron cylinder with a bow, like a drill, on which they grind the uncut sapphire or ruby, which are the gems most frequently discovered. The zircon, a smoky-coloured diamond, the amethyst, the chrysoberyl, or cat's eye, a gem which has lately come into fashion, and for which great prices are demanded, garnets, spinel rubies, tourmalines, and the pretty moonstone which was so popular a purchase at the Colonial Exhibition in London a year or two back, are all found in various parts of Ceylon, mostly about Ratnapura (the city of gems).

Ceylon is also celebrated for fine pearls, gathered from oyster or mussel banks on the north-west coast.

The pettah, or native market-place, is, as is always the case in the East, a scene of busy life, full of varieties of costume, race, and colour. The traders in Ceylon are Moormen and Cingalese;

the labourers are mostly Tamils from Southern India. The Moormen wear cotton trousers and jacket, with a curious beehive-shaped hat of plaited grass, dyed in various colours. The Cingalese wear a sheet of brightly-coloured calico twisted round the hips, and reaching to the feet like a petticoat, with a white jacket. They delight in long hair, which they twist up into a chignon, combing it back all round the forehead. Their only "hat" is a round tortoise-shell comb, which every Cingalese wears as a sacred duty. The Tamils wear as little as possible, and the children of all sorts nothing at all except a bit of string round the waist or neck, from which is suspended a charm to ward off the attacks of their favourite devil. The Cingalese women and men dress very much alike, and it is often difficult to tell which is which until you realise that the men wear a comb, and the women hair-pins. Besides the pettah, or central market, there are others clustered round the suburbs, to which the villagers on their own side of the town resort. One of these is on each side of a curious bridge of boats, about 500 feet long, two miles out of the town on the Kandy road, composed of twenty-one boats anchored at each end, from which two are slipped every day for two hours to let the traffic through. The Cingalese are a rice-eating people; rice and some curried vegetable, such as cocoa-nut, jack-fruit, or plantain, with a little dried fish, forming their diet all the year round. Fish, fruit, and vegetables, therefore, are the chief stocks of all the markets. The vehicular traffic of the country, except a few carriages in Colombo and Kandy, is drawn by bullocks. These animals are often very beautiful, being all of the Zebu breed of India, which are generally to be seen attached to Wombwell's Menageries under the name of "Brahmin Bull." There is a pretty little variety, about the size of a small pony, that are used in gigs and other carriages, and travel 30 miles a day at a trot of about 5 miles an hour. The bit is a piece of rope passed through a hole in the nostrils. The Buddhist religion, though forbidding the killing of any animal, does not seem to forbid their torture, and these poor brutes are most cruelly treated by their drivers. The Government has been obliged to enact severe penalties for this offence.

The streets of Colombo are broad and well made, with a gravel of rich, dark red colour, which contrasts pleasantly with the profuse foliage of the endless gardens and trees which line the footpath, the poorest hut having a bit of garden about it. The town is placed on a neck of land between a magnificent sheet of fresh water and the sea, so that every street has its vista ending in bright and sparkling water, giving a special charm to the town that I have never seen anywhere else. There are no fine buildings in Colombo. The Governor's residence, called Queen's House, the Government Buildings, the Cathedral, Clock Tower, and other public institutions call for no comment on the score of architectural merit. The Museum is the finest building in the town, well situated in the midst of the Cinnamon Gardens, now a public park.

The Barracks are a series of buildings capable of accommodating 5,000 soldiers. We are able, however, to "hold down" our Cingalese subjects with a single regiment. I was glad to find that in this hot tropical station over 200 soldiers out of 1,000 found no difficulty in being staunch total abstainers.

The total population of Ceylon is 2,800,000, of whom 1,850,000 are native Cingalese, 700,000 are Tamils from Southern India, 200,000 Moormen and Malays, and 22,000 Europeans and Eurasians. The religious census shows that 1,700,000 of the population are Buddhist, 600,000 Hindu, 200,000 Mohammedan, and 270,000 Christians.

The Roman Catholics are in overwhelming majority among

Christian denominations (220,000 of the whole), being as successful in Ceylon as everywhere else throughout the East.

The Buddhist priests are very ignorant, and exercise little or no moral restraint over their people, who are more attached to their ancient superstition of devil worship than they appear to be to Buddhism, which they only respect so far as the outside of

DEVIL-DANCER AND TOM-TOM.

the cup and platter is concerned. The devil-dancer and his curate, the tom-tom beater, have a good time in Ceylon, and there are 2,735 of these scoundrels distributed throughout the island. They are simply professional exorcists, and as everything untoward—bad weather, sickness, and what not—is the direct result of devils, they are in continual request. It speaks ill for Buddhism that 2,000 years of influence over the Cingalese has not destroyed this base and grovelling superstition, which has rooted itself so deeply that even native Christians will resort to it secretly in great emergencies.

During the brief fortnight I have been in Ceylon I have endeavoured as far as possible to find out what is being done by Christian missionaries to conquer this headquarters of Buddhism. The Roman Catholic Church has been at work longer than the Protestants, having entered the mission field with the Portuguese conquerors 350 years ago, who brought with them the usual army of ecclesiastics. Their methods of conversion were bound to succeed more or less. The Inquisition played its part, "conversion" was the only gate to employment open to the natives, and the priests didn't object to these converts "bowing in the house" of Buddha, if they were reasonably often at mass. But whatever the methods pursued by the Roman Catholic missionary, they get and keep disciples.

The Dutch cleared out the Portuguese in 1656, and, although they had no inquisition, they refused employment to any native who refused to make profession of the Protestant religion. In 1796 the English cleared out the Dutch, and in 1815 were in possession of the whole island. There was not much missionary spirit in English churches during the dawn of this century, but as early as 1812 the Baptist Missionary Society commenced operations in Ceylon, followed in 1818 by the Church Missionary Society, and a little later by the Wesleyans, who are now the most active of all in the island.

Seventy years of Protestant missionary enterprise has produced 22,000 Episcopalians, 20,000 Wesleyans, 13,000 Presbyterians (a large proportion of whom, however, are descendants of the Dutch), and 5,000 Baptists, in all 60,000 Protestants, old and young, of all sorts, as contrasted with 220,000 Romanists.

Does this reflect credit on English Christianity? The result is hardly pentecostal! I can find no fault with the men who are at work; I had ample opportunity of judging of their quality, and I did not find any missionary who was not full of zeal and devotion, shrewd, practical, and sensible. But these results appear to me so poor and inadequate to the expenditure of men and money that it is impossible to feel satisfied with them. For instance, the Baptist Church in Kandy was commenced in 1841, and has less than fifty members, or about one member for every year it has been in existence, and is not self-supporting. Yet this church has a native pastor of great merit, and has from its origin been under the residential superintendence of the best men the Baptist denomination could furnish. I have had the pleasure of becoming acquainted with three men who, in succession, have been in charge at Kandy: Rev. Mr. Carter, who is not only a capable and experienced missionary, but the most distinguished Cingalese scholar living; Rev. H. R. Pigott, a man of much energy and power, and the present resident, Rev. H. A. Lapham, who was for some years colleague of Hugh Stowell Brown, in Liverpool. Better and fitter men could not be found. For fifty years such men have been at work for the Baptist Missionary Society, and I have no reason to suppose that the men sent out by the Church of England and the Wesleyans are one whit inferior. Yet, in my humble judgment, they have failed to do more than scratch the surface of Buddhism.

The Salvation Army has now entered the field, and I went to some of their meetings. They are pursuing entirely different methods to those hitherto employed. Their missionaries dress like Buddhist priests in a piece of yellow cotton cloth, bareheaded and barefooted, and their female captains in Cingalese women's dress. They throw themselves upon the hospitality of the natives, and live upon rice, which they beg from door to door. They claim to have made 700 converts this year, but the other missionaries say they are sheep-stealers, and that the 700 consists of the flotsam and jetsam of other native churches. However that may be, no one who knows anything about them can question their genuine earnestness and enthusiasm, and although I doubt if methods which have been so wonderfully successful with the English blackguard will succeed with the mystic Buddhist of Ceylon, I think the Salvation Army will make and keep its converts like the rest. Their temperance zeal may perhaps do something to diminish the growing appetite of the Cingalese for "Christian" liquors, and their untiring energy will infuse fresh zeal into other missionaries. There is some evidence of this latter result in the fact that the Colombo district of Baptist missions has baptized 163 converts this year, as compared with only 33 during 1886.

Although I cannot concede the praise of unqualified success to the efforts of Protestant missionaries to convert the heathen of Ceylon to living Christianity, there is no need to qualify the recognition of the services they have rendered to education and morals throughout the island. There are 3,460 schools in Ceylon, giving instruction to 112,652 children. These schools and scholars are assorted in the following list, taken only from those schools receiving grants in aid from Government:—

	No. of Schools.	No. of Scholars.
Church of England	243	13,917
Roman Catholic	208	16,466
Wesleyan	223	14,988
Baptist	46	2,356
American missionaries	136	8,088
	856	55,815
To which must be added children being educated in other mission schools, unaided	132	3,733
Total to credit of missionaries and Christian churches	988	59,548

It is therefore clear from these figures that more than half the education in Ceylon is due to the efforts of the various denominations of Christian missionaries. It is, however, a powerful testimony to the tenacity of Buddhism that while the children of Cingalese parents are sent in such numbers to missionary schools, so few of them become Christians in after life. The Wesleyan schools of the Galle district have 3,253 children in attendance, of whom 320 only are Wesleyans, while 2,752 are Buddhists.

There are only fourteen Buddhist schools on the whole island, receiving grants with 902 scholars. It is an extraordinary fact that the religion of Ceylon can safely afford to allow half its children to be educated by the missionaries of a rival religion, and yet maintain its hold upon them when they reach maturity.

I went with Mr. Lapham, the Baptist missionary at Kandy, to visit some of his village schools. One of them had about 120 boys on the books, with seventy-six present, a head master, and two assistants. The elder lads could speak English fairly well, and the average appeared good, as far as I could judge by some test questions. The school hours were from nine to three, with religious instruction quite optional. The boys were mostly the sons of small farmers, and some of them came five or six miles to school. They rise to an eighth standard, to pass which boys must explain a passage from some Cingalese classic, pass an examination in all the rules of arithmetic up to interest and discount, in the geography of the world, the history of Ceylon, and advanced English reading and writing. I also visited Mrs. Pigott's training school for female teachers at Colombo. She has thirty or forty young Cingalese women boarding with her, who are trained by her two daughters, who hold certificates from the College of Preceptresses in London. These girls have all professed conviction to Christianity, and their future lies in the village and other elementary schools of the Baptist mission, and in many cases as wives of native Christian pastors and schoolmasters. Mrs. Pigott has been unusually successful in this excellent work, and I hope the Baptist Missionary Society will enable her to extend it far beyond its present limits.

I heard much that was good of the work being done at Jaffna, in the north of the island, by the American missionaries, who are said to have been more successful with the Tamils than any other mission agency. I tried to go and see what they were doing, but as it would have involved three days and nights in a bull-cart, I did not venture. Since my return home I have had as my guests two ladies connected with this work at Jaffna, the Misses Leitch, who are endeavouring to raise money for a college for training young Tamils of both sexes.

It is well worth while for our missionary societies to give more and more attention to Ceylon. It is the home and heart of Buddhism, and if Ceylon were converted to Christianity it would have a marvellous effect on Buddhism all over the East. A few good medical missionaries would do much to strengthen the hands of those already at work. Native medicine is a very feeble institution in Ceylon, and the devil-dancer is the most popular practitioner.

While in Colombo I paid a visit to the exiled Arabi Pasha. I was warmly welcomed by him in an excellent bungalow, in which he appears to lead a happy and contented life. He would converse upon any subject but Egypt, on which he maintained a discreet reserve. He takes a leading position in Mahommedan society, and both he and the other exiled Pashas are settling down, some of them taking up land and becoming planters. He still pretends to sigh for his native country, but I shrewdly suspect that if he were offered the chance of returning, without his comfortable pension of £500, he would beg to be excused. A man who heads an unsuccessful revolution has no place in his country for ever afterwards.

CHAPTER XIX.

THE RESOURCES OF CEYLON.

WE have been in possession of the Island of Ceylon since 1815, when we finally subjugated the savage ruffian who was then the King of Kandy. My friend Mr. John Ferguson kindly furnished me with some particulars which he had carefully compiled, showing the condition of the island at that time, and which compared with the statistics of the Blue Book for 1886, give striking evidence of the material prosperity which sixty years of British rule brings to such a country as Ceylon, and such a people as the Cingalese and Tamils, which form its population.

I give a few of these facts in comparison one with the other.

	In 1815.	In 1886.
Population	750,000	3,000,000
Number of houses	20,000	500,000
Military force required	6,000 troops	1,000
Revenue	£226,000	£1,300,000
Imports and exports	£546,000	£8,400,000
Roads	Sand and gravel tracks only.	2,250 miles of good roads.
Railways	None	183 miles
Tonnage of shipping	75,000 tons	4,000,000 tons
Expenditure on education	£3,000	£70,000
Health expenditure	£1,000	£60,000
Post Offices	4	130
Area under cultivation	400,000 acres	3,100,000 acres
Live stock	250,000 head	1,500,000 head
Carts and carriages	50	20,000

But besides, there are in the island 1,100 miles of telegraph, a Government savings bank with 10,000 depositors, 120 excellent hospitals and dispensaries, with a first-rate medical College for natives. If Ceylon had remained under the rule of the Kandyan kings none of this progress would have been visible. Ceylon is a purely agricultural country, as its lists of exports clearly show. The following is a short list of the exports of some of the principal crops of Ceylon for 1886:

	£
Cardamoms	22,000
Areca nuts	100,000
Quinine	300,000
Cinnamon and cinnamon oil	115,000
Cocoa nuts and fibre	70,000
Cacao	40,000
Coffee	600,000
Cotton	20,000
Cocoa-nut oil	24,000
Tea	370,000
Tobacco	80,000

Fifteen years ago the great staple crop of Ceylon was coffee, which, in the years 1868, 1869, and 1870, reached an average export of £4,000,000. This industry is, unhappily, being slowly destroyed by a minute fungus which has attacked the leaf, working deadly mischief all over Ceylon, and especially in the young plantations which, at a capital outlay of nearly £3,000,000, were brought under coffee cultivation in the years 1870–74. The slow but sure destruction of this valuable industry is shown by the list of exports from 1877 to 1886, which are as follows, in cwts.:—

Year.	Cwt.	Year.	Cwt.
1877	620,000	1882	260,000
1878	825,000	1883	323,000
1879	670,000	1884	315,000
1880	454,000	1885	224,000
1881	564,000	1886	180,000

THE RESOURCES OF CEYLON.

Many of the coffee planters of Ceylon have been hopelessly ruined, and if it had not been possible for the valuable cleared lands to be brought under other profitable crops, it would have gone hard with the colony. The planters of Ceylon are shrewd industrious men, with a large Scottish element among them, and they seem to be finding their salvation in TEA and QUININE.

In 1872 there were not 500 acres of chinchona (quinine tree) in all Ceylon, with an export of bark not reaching 12,000 lbs.; while to-day there are at least 30,000 acres under cultivation, with an export of 14,000,000 lbs. of bark.

In 1876 the exports of tea were 23 lbs.! This year they will exceed 14,000,000 lbs., and Ceylon bids fair to rival the most important districts in Northern India in its tea-growing capacity. The teas are of a high character, fine flavour, and perfectly pure, and I see no reason why India and Ceylon should not in course of time supplant China teas to a very large extent. I visited several of the finest tea plantations in Ceylon, and in many cases found the young tea plants growing up in a forest of stumps, all that was left of what was once a valuable coffee estate, destroyed by the fell fungus. Tea will prove of greater value to the colony than coffee growing, as it employs rather more than twice the number of hands per acre. I should think that there are few better opportunities open to a young Englishman with a little capital than to come out to Ceylon, serve a two or three years' apprenticeship to tea growing, and then start an estate for himself.

Other coffee planters are turning their attention to the cacao tree, on which the bean grows which gives us our cocoa and chocolate. The export of this product has grown from 10 cwt. in 1878 to 14,000 cwt. in 1886, and is likely, in a very few years, to reach ten times this amount. Cardamoms have risen in the same space of time from 14,000 lbs. to 240,000 lbs. It will be readily seen from these figures that although the destruction of the coffee tree has been disastrous to a large number of planters, the colony is recovering itself with great buoyancy, and is probably more solidly prosperous to-day than at any previous period of its history.

The only industry in Ceylon which is not agrarian, is plumbago mining. This is entirely in the hands of the Cingalese, who work mines up to 300 feet in depth in a very primitive fashion, obtaining some £350,000 worth of the finest plumbago in the world.

It appears to me, in the short visit I have been able to pay to this interesting tropical colony, that its main dependence in the future must be on tea, and the best authorities tell me that the export will in a very few years reach thirty or forty million pounds, worth some two millions sterling. I am also told by coffee planters that the ravages of the disease is abating, and that the colony will be able to produce in future an average export of coffee of about one million sterling, or one-fourth of what was produced at the highest period of its prosperity. It is quite evident, however, from the figures I have given, that the deficit of three millions on coffee is fast being overtaken, and that the general prospects of Ceylon agriculture are bright enough.

There is no doubt that the change of culture in Ceylon from coffee to tea will be of great benefit to the masses of the population, from the largely increased employment which it will afford. Almost all the plantation labour is carried on by Tamils, from Southern India, the Cingalese refusing to do coolie work, devoting themselves entirely to trading, small farming, carting produce (a large industry), and to handicrafts. To these Tamils Ceylon is a heaven upon earth. In their own country their average earnings per family of five reaches about £6 in the year, or less than 1*d.* per head per day, a condition of things that appears almost incredible to English minds, and in which recurrent famines, terrible in their results, are certain. The Tamils employed on a Ceylon tea estate have the wealth of Crœsus compared with their relatives at home. They have good huts, cheap food, small gardens, medical attendance, and can earn from 6*d.* to 9*d.* per day. I doubt if, considering the climate and cost of living, there are any labouring classes in the world better off than the Tamil families settled on the plantations of Ceylon.

The revenues of the colony average about £1,000,000, of which £650,000 comes from taxation, and £350,000 from land sales, railways, and other miscellaneous receipts. The expenditure is slightly in excess of revenue for 1886, being £1,040,000. The public debt is 2¼ millions, and has been incurred for Colombo harbour, railway extension, water works, &c.

The trade of Ceylon, as everywhere else in the East, is overwhelmingly in the hands of the English. Of 6,341 vessels entered and cleared last year at Ceylon ports, 413 only were foreign, 4,928 were British.

Of £6,500,000 of commerce in the year 1886, foreign countries got £780,000, while £5,720,000 fell to the British. And yet the Conservative caucus in England passed last year, amid loud acclamations, a resolution condemning the Free Trade policy which makes and keeps us supreme in every neutral market in the world, and enables us to open our own ports and those of India and our Crown Colonies to the commerce of other rival nations with impunity, and without a single protective duty.

Ceylon gets on without a poor law. A very few old persons get a charitable allowance from the Government, varying from 2*s.* to 25*s.* each per month, but it amounts to very little on the whole. Employment is plentiful, the people are thrifty, the cost of living is extremely small, and the young and strong are glad to care for the aged and weak.

The Local Government of Ceylon consists of the following Boards:—

1st. *The Executive and Legislative Councils*, which are of the same composition and exercise the same functions as I have already described with regard to Hong Kong or Singapore. None of the members are elective, but there is always a Cingalese and a Tamil member on the Legislative Council.

2nd. *Municipal Councils*, of which the majority are elected by occupiers rented at £7 a year, the rest being nominated by the Governor. In Colombo there are five official and nine elective members. The other two boroughs in the island are Kandy and Galle.

3rd. *Local Boards* in populous districts, composed in the same manner as the Municipalities. There are ten of these Local Boards in Ceylon. The qualification is an occupancy of not less than £3 10s.

4th. *The Village Council*.—This is a Council elected by a constituency composed of every male inhabitant of the village, or groups of villages, who is twenty-one years of age. There are forty-eight of these Village Councils. Anything approaching party politics is quite unknown in Ceylon. There is a tendency to jobbery, which, however, is kept in check by the official members. On the whole the system of local government appears admirably suited for the budding intelligence and education of the people, and will no doubt be extended as the social conditions improve and justify.

I have already spoken of wages paid on tea, coffee, chinchona, and other plantations, as ranging from 6*d.* to 9*d.* per day. The general rate of wages for labour in Colombo and other towns, for such work as stablemen, messengers, porters, gardeners, &c., is about the same, 12 to 15 rupees a month, the rupee being worth 1s. 5d. Men in more responsible positions, such as warehousemen, foremen of gangs of coolies, &c., are paid 35s. to 40s. per month. Skilled workmen, bookbinders, machinists, compositors, cabinet

A CINGALESE WORKMAN.

makers, and carpenters get 45s. to 50s. per month. Good clerks and bookkeepers, £40 to £50 a year. These wages will appear very meagre to an English workman, but I expect the Cingalese is better off with these wages than the English workman with his. The Cingalese wants no fire, no meat, no woollen clothes, no beer; his house costs a tenth of the English workman's; he dresses in a shilling's worth of cotton cloth, and only wears a pennyworth of it when he is working. He is content with two meals a day of rice, at 5*s.* per bushel, and vegetables flavoured with curry, and has half a farthing's worth of dried fish on Sunday. He has never felt cold in his life, and the climate he lives in enables him to thrive as well on his simple vegetarian diet as an Englishman at home can on beef and mutton. Everywhere they give the constant impression of being a joyous, contented, sober, well-nourished people.

The Government of Ceylon, like that of every Crown colony, is virtually a despotism tempered by the Colonial office, and "question time" in the House of Commons. The Governor selects such men, in addition to his leading permanent officials, as he believes can best advise him, and the decisions of this Council become the will of the Government. The influence of a really able, energetic, independent Governor, thoroughly just and impartial, is practically paramount, and every successive Governor strives to leave behind him as the record of his term of office some public work of utility—an education scheme, a college, a hospital. A bronze statue of Sir Edward Barnes stands opposite the Queen's house in Colombo, but his real monuments are the great macadamized road to Kandy, the bridge of boats on the Kelani river at Colombo, and the superb satin-wood bridge at Peradenia. The railway to Kandy keeps green the memory of Sir Henry Ward; Sir Hercules Robinson has left his record in every province of the island, especially in irrigation works, and Sir William Gregory's massive stone monument is a mile long—the famous Colombo breakwater. The present Governor is set upon restoring to their ancient usefulness the great tanks at Kalaweava, which, when completed, will be seven miles square, 20 feet deep, and will send water down a canal 54 miles long, irrigating a vast area through the dry season; an area now almost unpeopled, but which 2,000 years ago, watered by these ancient tanks, had a population of at least a quarter of a million, whose ancient cities and temples, smothered in jungle, are still among the wonders of the East.

Plenty will be left for successive Governors to accomplish. A great development of the railway system is imperative, and its profitableness assured by past experience; the Lords of the Admiralty join the Colombo Chamber of Commerce in the urgent demand for a good graving dock at Colombo, the only dry dock in India being at Bombay; vernacular education is but in its infancy; the codification of the civil laws is unaccomplished; an agricultural college would aid greatly in the development of Crown and other lands; and nothing would add to the importance and wealth of Ceylon more than the abolition of its Custom House, and the establishment of Colombo and Galle as free ports.

This is a political programme well within the reach of the Government of Ceylon. Many of the public works named would be self-supporting from the first, and the rest might be carried out by loans. The public debt of the colony is not much more than a single year's revenue, and in recent years the splendid network of roads, the series of restored irrigation works and many public buildings, costing in all over six millions sterling, have all been paid for from the general revenue.

Among the social difficulties perplexing successive Governors is the question of the sale of alcoholic liquors, the consumption of which is undoubtedly on the increase, and to meet which temperance societies are being formed, and total abstinence is being urged on the natives. Missionaries, both European and native, are adding temperance advocacy to their Christian work, and most of them appear with a conspicuous blue ribbon.

They find that "Christian" vices are the chief temptations to Christian converts, and one missionary whom I knew in England as a strong opponent of total abstinence has been forced by circumstances to adopt it, and is now making up by his zeal in the cause for his previous opposition. We cannot be held responsible, however, as in so many other heathen countries, for the introduction of intoxicating liquor into Ceylon. The inhabitants of Southern India manufactured them long before they ever beheld an Englishman, and have used toddy, the fermented sap of the cocoa-nut palm, for many centuries. The Portuguese and Dutch taught them to distil toddy into arrack, and we are now making them familiar with the infernal cheap spirit of Europe, which is sold in the village toddy shop to a considerable extent.

The licensing system of Ceylon is akin to that of India and Singapore. The exclusive privilege of manufacturing and selling arrack and toddy is reserved to Government, being farmed out by public auction every year in each province. These farmers in turn sub-let the privilege to the village pot-house keeper, at a handsome profit, compelling the sub-tenant to buy all his supply from them, like the monopolist brewers in England. The head farmer usually manufactures for himself. He pays to Government 100 rupees for each still of a capacity of not less than 150 gallons. Wholesale dealers, who may not sell less than 35 gallons at once, also pay 100 rupees for a licence. Retailers arrange as best they can with the head farmer, who has paid a lump sum by auction. About one-seventh of the whole revenue is derivable from the arrack and toddy farming, which makes it very difficult for the Government to restrict its consumption without seriously disturbing the finances—a step from which every well-regulated Governor shrinks with dismay.

The liquor trade is virtually uncontrolled. No excise officers exist, and the Government has to depend upon the Renters to detect and check illicit sales in their own districts. Adulteration is largely practised, and no efforts are made to prevent it.

It is very difficult to find any statistics by which it is possible to test absolutely the increase or decrease in the consumption of strong drink, but the rough test of the money the farmers are willing to pay for the monopoly gives a fair gauge. Here is an instructive little table which I have extracted from the Blue Book :—

Year.	Population.	Revenue.
1830	962,000	283,000 Rupees.
1840	1,400,000	410,000 ,,
1850	1,590,000	557,000 ,,
1860	1,876,000	735,000 ,,
1870	2,128,000	1,279,000 ,,
Average for the last 10 years	2,650,000	1,905,000 ,,

It will thus be seen that the farmers are willing to pay progressive prices for the monopoly, far in excess of the progressive increase in the population. A simple rule of three sum will show that the average for the last ten years gives nearly 900,000 rupees of revenue in excess of that of 1860, taking into account the increase in the population. The consumption of liquor by natives has therefore increased per head nearly double in twenty years, a fact that ought to cause the gravest alarm to any responsible Government. It must further be remembered that the last ten years has been one of very unusual depression, caused by the destruction of the coffee plant.

The consumption of spirits in Ceylon is estimated at twelve million bottles a year, which gives an average of four and a half bottles per head, and a total expenditure of about eight millions of rupees. When it is remembered that apart from infants and young children, a large proportion of the population are Mohammedans, who are strict teetotallers, and that many others avoid intoxicants on grounds of religion or caste, it is not to be wondered at that this large consumption of spirits produces a great deal of drunkenness, enough to cause anxiety in the mind of every thoughtful Cingalese. A few years ago an administration report of one of the remote country districts said, "the habit of indulging in spirituous drinks increases. A glass of arrack has taken the place of a cup of coffee as the early morning beverage of many; others drink raw spirits immediately before their meals, while many, including not a few head men, have the reputation of being habitual drunkards."

Native opinion is universally against the village arrack shop, and I have had abundant assurances that if the Government prohibited the distillation of arrack altogether, and only permitted spirits to be imported by the consumer, forbidding the retail sale, such restrictions would be warmly welcomed by all native society. It would without doubt be difficult to prohibit the use of toddy, which can be tapped from any hardy cocoa-nut palm. But compared with arrack, toddy is an innocent beverage, containing about four per cent. of alcohol, and is preferred by the natives perfectly fresh when it can be got, before fermentation has set in. The large amount of spirit drinking in Ceylon by the natives ought to alarm greatly the paternal Government of the island, and it should not be beyond the great ability of Sir Arthur Gordon to devise some fresh tax by which the revenue could be recouped. But loss of revenue from a diminished consumption of spirits would in itself result in a great saving of expenditure, as well as adding largely to the general prosperity of the population, and some serious effort ought to be

A VILLAGE SHOP, CEYLON.

made to check the evil, before its growing revenue increases indefinitely the difficulty of facing it. It is a scandal that a Christian Government of a heathen country should depend for its revenue on the vices and improvidence of its subjects.

The farming system, dependent as it is upon an unchecked stimulus to extended sale, is the very worst and silliest licensing method that could be devised. I was glad to find, in conversation with Sir Arthur Gordon, that he entirely condemned it, and is very anxious to exchange it for an excise duty, and a severely restricted system of wholesale and retail licences controlled by the police and magistracy. I have no doubt that by this a larger revenue could be obtained from a smaller consumption, and that severe measures against adulteration might render the liquor sold less noxious. The really sensible course, however, would be to prohibit absolutely the sale and manufacture of distilled liquors, and face the disorganization of finance boldly; it would not be long before it would right itself by the increased prosperity, sobriety, and industry which would accrue. The problem is a difficult one, but I think that any Governor who solved it would go down to posterity with a greater name than any of his illustrious predecessors.

We left Colombo with much regret in the Peninsula and Oriental steamer Rosetta for Calcutta on the 15th of December. We reached Madras on the 18th. Madras is one of the oldest settlements in India, and is the third port in importance. It is a large town, with a frontage to the ocean of some three miles. A tremendous surf breaks on the beach, and the swell even in the finest weather renders it difficult to load and unload ships. Some years ago £600,000 or £700,000 was spent on two breakwaters, but they have been destroyed by successive gales, and the sea now flows fourteen feet deep over the greater portion of it. We were landed in huge boats, built of planks sewn together with cocoa-nut fibre, with twelve or fourteen oarsmen. It was difficult and dangerous to get in and out of these boats, as one had to jump into the arms of the crew, as she lurched up to the steps of the steamer, and afterwards to the pier. The Babel of tongues caused by thirty or forty of these boats round the ship was a perfect pandemonium. We spent a few hours ashore, wandering about the streets, but being Sunday, had no opportunity of visiting any of the institutions of the town.

IN THE BAY OF BENGAL.

CHAPTER XX.

CALCUTTA TO BENARES.

We reached Calcutta at ten A.M. on the 24th of December. I had telegraphed from Madras to that beneficent providence of modern travellers, Messrs. Thomas Cook and Son, asking them to engage an intelligent native servant to travel with us through India. The steamer had hardly moored when a polite person in a blue striped turban and white calico suit introduced himself as "Aino Deen," whipped us ashore in a small boat, and sent us off to the Great Eastern Hotel, following an hour later with all our luggage. Calcutta is crammed with strangers from all parts of Bengal and Northern India, who have come up to the capital, to pay their respects to the Viceroy at the Levee and Drawing Room, to see the races, and enjoy the Christmas Holidays, which are four days, during which the banks are closed and all business suspended. I had telegraphed from Madras for rooms; we got one, divided by a screen, and we felt ourselves lucky to get that. Many of our fellow-passengers had great difficulty in getting a roof to shelter them, some being put into dormitories with a dozen beds, and others gladly taking tents pitched on the roof.

Calcutta is a handsome modern town, and likes to be called "the city of palaces," a name it does not in any way deserve. There are a good many fine buildings, handsomely grouped in the occupation of the Government—the Town Hall, the High Court, the Post Office, the Telegraph Office, the Currency

Office, the Bengal Secretariat, the Dalhousie Institute, and Government House, but as they are none of them to be compared for a moment to any good Lancashire Town Hall, I need not inflict any description of them on my readers.

Calcutta spreads itself along the banks of the Hooghly, a branch of the Ganges nearly a mile wide, for a distance of four-and-a-half miles. Its area is seven square miles. The centre of the town is occupied by the buildings just referred to, the Eden Gardens, where a band plays by electric light every evening to the fashionable people of the city, white, native, or mixed, and the Maidan, a great open space of grass, in the middle of which is the old historic fortress of Fort William, erected by Clive at a cost of two millions sterling. Round this great common the roads are lined with the fine houses of English residents and wealthy natives, beyond which are miles of native streets and lanes crowded with a teeming population of Bengalis.

The finest sight in Calcutta is the magnificent line of shipping along the quays and wharves of the Hooghly, taking in cargoes of jute, cotton, indigo, grain, hides, silk, and tea, or discharging the different manufactures which England exchanges for Indian produce, a trade reaching nearly sixty millions sterling every year. Nowhere in the world is such a display of shipping to be seen at a glance as from the great Hooghly Bridge. First comes a mile of noble steamers, few of them under 2,000 tons register, and then two miles of full-rigged iron ships, many of them carrying four masts, and with an average capacity of 3,000 to 4,000 tons of dead weight.

Calcutta has not greatly interested me. The historic spots connected with Job Charnock, Holwell, and Clive have all disappeared. The famous Black Hole has vanished *in toto*, and a spick and span post-office covers the almost forgotten site.

Calcutta is a brand new English city, with a fashionable drive, a Rotten Row, modern European shops, a fine cathedral and Methodist Chapel, with native India thrust into the background; and a very dirty and unwholesome background it is, in which cholera darkly lurks.

We have not been able to see any of its institutions, educational or otherwise, as they are all closed for the Christmas holidays, and they are not worth waiting for, as in almost every instance better and more characteristic institutions may be seen in the great inland towns we are about to visit.

We were not allowed to eat a lonely Christmas dinner at an hotel. The Hon. J. F. Norris, Q.C., one of the judges of the Supreme Court of Calcutta, who contested Portsmouth in 1880 as a Liberal, carried us off to his hospitable board, round which we met a pleasant and merry company. I had never met Mr. Norris before in my life, and only made Mrs. Norris's acquaintance on the steamer, which she joined at Madras, but this hearty and spontaneous hospitality is characteristic of Englishmen in India, and we expect to experience plenty more of it before we leave the country.

On Sunday afternoon we went with my friend Rev. G. Kerry, the senior Baptist Missionary in Calcutta, to Beadon-square, where the different missionaries speak in the open air to a regular audience of educated Bengalis, who come there to listen and discuss. There were about a hundred present, who from their dress and general appearance appeared to belong to the richer middle class. I had an interesting discussion with them on the liquor question, and found them, without exception, strongly opposed to the existence of spirit shops at all, and that they had evidently followed with interest the agitation which has set in at home with regard to the trade in liquor with subject races of England.

Young Bengal is highly educated. They are beginning to despise the venerable superstitions of Brahminism, and it is common to meet with young clerks in the public service or in merchants' offices to whom the writings of Comte, Herbert Spencer, Darwin, Huxley, and Tyndal are familiar friends, and who, though preserving the outward respect for the faith of their fathers, are really atheists, or at best theists. Young men of this stamp begin by eating prohibited food. They eat mutton, but still abstain from beef, as to eat the sacred cow would be open sacrilege that would lead to instantaneous loss of caste. They frequent the hotels, and beginning with a glass of lemonade, soon slide into wines and spirits. Drinking is quite common among high caste young Hindoos in Bengal, especially in large towns. A party of educated young natives is hardly respectable without wines, and toasts are the order of the day. There is also much clandestine drinking in the country amongst educated natives. It is easy to see that leaders among enlightened Bengalis are deeply anxious that the Government should discourage the sale of liquor to the uttermost, and are filled with dread at the certain results which must follow the present senseless out-still system.

We left Calcutta at nine o'clock P.M. on Monday night for Benares, by the mail train for Bombay. There are no sleeping carriages on the Indian railways; but a hard bench, thinly covered with padding, is provided in the first-class carriages, and it is necessary to provide one's self with mattress and pillow. There is a lavatory attached to the carriage, but no soap or towels. Indian railways are twenty years behind time with their railway accommodation. The refreshment rooms furnish plain meals, badly cooked, all along the 1,450 miles from Calcutta to Bombay, for the daily mail trains. Messrs. Cook and Son very kindly sent to the hotel for all our luggage, engaged a carriage for us, and all we had to do was to drive to the station and get into the train. It is always a pleasure to have any transaction with this enterprising firm, who attend to the smallest and most trifling wants of their clients as readily, cheerfully, and as thoroughly as they would if you wanted a ticket for a voyage round the world.

At daybreak we were 200 miles from Calcutta, in the midst of the vast and fertile plain of Bengal. During the night, stopping at wayside stations, we heard the howls of the jackals, which swarm throughout India. It was pretty cold and sharp, and we found overcoats and ulsters very welcome up to nine o'clock, when the heat of the sun made us glad to throw them off again.

The scenes from the carriage window were full of interest and variety. The mud-built villages teeming with population, the great tanks and irrigating canals, the abundant wells from which the coolies were raising water by means of the primitive shadouf, a long pole swung on a pivot with rope and bucket at one end, and a huge lump of clay at the other; every now and then vast green plains without a tree or hut, stretching away to the horizon; the enclosed gardens of some wealthy zemindar or landowner; a Hindoo temple on some rising mound, herds of zebus, buffaloes, and goats, rows of bright green parrots and jays sitting on the telegraph wires, a flock of 300 or 400 ducks dashing down from the sky with a great splash into some tank, or great white storks and brown kites circling overhead, kept our interest excited till we crossed the great Ganges at Benares, on the new iron bridge, one of the finest in the world.

At Benares station we were met by Dr. Lazarus, one of the oldest medical practitioners in India, who has lived in Benares for forty years, and to whom I had letters of introduction. He ushered us into a magnificent open carriage, drawn by two horses, with coachmen and two footmen in gorgeous livery of crimson and gold. I thought this was pretty smart for a doctor, the "profession" generally affecting sober and quiet equipages, but Dr. Lazarus presently informed me that he had told the Maharajah of Vizianagram that a friend from England was coming to see Benares, and he promptly placed this carriage at our disposal day and night as long as we remain here. The Maharajah resides chiefly at Vizianagram, which is in the Madras Presidency, but, having large estates round Benares, he keeps up three or four palaces, to one of which he comes for a few weeks every year, and the rest are lent to distinguished Hindoos who come to visit the Holy City. He takes much pleasure in showing attention to English visitors.

We have spent nearly three days in Benares. It is probably the most ancient city in India, and is supposed to date back to times when the Aryan race first colonized the country; it is certainly coeval with the earliest days of Hindooism, and has held the first place in the hearts and affections of the Hindoos through every century of their history. For thousands of years it has been the holiest of holy places, resorted to by pilgrims from every part of India. To the pious Hindoo Benares is what Mecca is to the Mohammedan, what Jerusalem was to the Crusader. The longing of his whole life is to visit this place of spotless holiness, and wash away his blackest sins in the waters of the sacred Ganges. Truly blessed is he if he may die there, and most of the fine palaces which fringe the river have been built by Rajahs, princes, and rich bankers from different parts of India, as homes for their aged relatives, who wait patiently, but with ecstatic happiness, the summons of the dread angel of death. Benares is the gate of heaven, and in its whole precincts there is not the smallest chink by which any faithful Hindoo may be squeezed into the "other place" by mistake. Benares is equally revered by the other great church of the East—the Buddhist. Twenty-five centuries ago Buddha chose this city as the centre from which to spread his reforming doctrines, for even then it was a place of such power and influence throughout the East that it was of paramount importance that a teacher of the power and pretensions of Buddha should secure the countenance and support of its pundits and teachers. Tradition says that from Benares Solomon got his apes and peacocks, both of which are to be seen as sacred animals in the Hindoo temples of the city to-day; and further, that among the wise men of the East who came to Jerusalem at the time of our Saviour's birth was a Rajah of Benares. However that may be, there is probably no sacred city in the world with so ancient and unbroken a record, or which to-day exercises its sway over so many millions of devotees; dear alike to a religion which above all others is saturated with the grossest and vilest idolatry, and to its great rival, which, despising idolatry and polytheism, teaches that each individual man, by a holy life, can himself become absorbed into the Divine.

Buddhism has long since been swept out of India, and has not even a shrine within the boundaries of Benares. But at Sarnath, four miles away, is a great tope, or solid tower, built at the time when, eight centuries after Buddha, Asoka, the ruler of Benares, tried to make this religion the creed of the whole country. To these sacred ruins distinguished Buddhists from Hionen Thsang, who came a pilgrim from China in the seventh century, on to the author of "The Light of Asia," love to resort, that they may see the spot where their beloved master sat under his Bo tree and evolved his wondrous doctrines.

This marvellous tope consists of a stone basement, 93 feet in diameter, the stones being clamped together with iron to the height of 43 feet. Above the stone-work, the building is of brick, the whole rising to a height of 128 feet above the plain.

Encircling the monument is an exquisitely beautiful band of sculptured ornament, of which enough remains to show what the whole must have been. The central part of this band, which is about 15 feet wide, consists of a geometrical pattern, with above and below a variegated pattern of foliage and flowers. This very interesting monument is the finest tope in Bengal, and well repaid us for a hot and dusty drive.

Modern Benares is a city "wholly given to idolatry," and is said to contain 1,454 temples to the honour of various gods of the Hindoo mythology. I have not visited them all, but I have seen enough to justify me in accepting the statement. It is finely situated on a bend of the river Ganges, which in the rainy season is about a mile wide, but now flows deep under the city, with great bare sandbanks on the other side. It used to be approached by a bridge of boats, which has just disappeared in favour of a very fine iron bridge, nearly a mile long, with roadways for rail, carts, and foot-passengers. The town itself is ranged for 3½ miles along cliffs of 100 feet high, crowned with magnificent palaces, temples and mosques, whose glittering and picturesque pinnacles, domes, and minarets sparkle like jewels in the bright morning sun. Down the face of this cliff, pious and wealthy Hindoos have built magnificent flights of steps leading down to the river, at the foot of which crowds of devotees and pilgrims are constantly bathing themselves in the sacred Ganges. These steps are called Ghâts, and there are more than thirty of them altogether.

We got up at daybreak, that we might see these Ghâts at sunrise, their busiest time. Our hospitable friend, Dr. Lazarus, had arranged for the Maharajah's barge to be ready, and we drove at once to the Dasasamed Ghât, passing on the way the Church Mission College, where 500 or 600 native lads are taught. We stopped a little short of the Ghât, to visit the

THE BATHING GHATS, BENARES.

curious observatory which rises loftily at the top of the steps, giving a noble appearance to the Ghât, when viewed from the river. In the passage leading up to the entrance, we passed a Temple sacred to the Rain God, who is drenched with water in dry weather to remind him he is neglecting his duty, but who is allowed to get covered with thick dirt in the rainy season. If the drought is great, they put him in a cistern and keep him wet till he is fairly roused to a sense of his responsibility. This god, whose name is Dalbhyeswar, is also the friend of the poor man, but they do not seem to have much faith in him, as he is not much noticed, unless circumstances necessitate his removal to his cistern. His wife or companion, who shares his temple, is a lady named Sitala, who is the goddess of small-pox. Next to this is the Temple of the Moon, where diseases of every kind may be healed. The good people of Benares, however, seem to have more faith in the excellent hospitals and Dr. Lazarus.

The observatory contains some curious structures for making astronomical observations and calculations, a huge mural quadrant and an equinoctial circle; the view from the roof looking over the principal Ghâts was very curious and interesting.

We then descended the great flight of steps and got on board the Maharajah's launch, painted red, with a huge prow shaped like a peacock, a necklace of pearls round its neck, and a gilded canopy over our heads. We rowed slowly down the river past all the principal Ghâts. These were thronged by thousands of earnest men and women from all parts of India, who, removing their upper garments, stepped into the river up to their waists, immersing themselves over and over again in the sin-cleansing Ganges. It was a very sharp morning, the thermometer having gone down to 45 degrees during the night. It was a pitiful sight to see tottering aged women, with scanty white locks, stepping into the cold river, and then crawling feebly up the steep steps with their wet clothes clinging to their poor shivering lean legs. When we landed we were begged to be careful how we passed them, for if our infidel shadows fell upon them the unhappy creatures lost the virtue of the wash, and had to creep back and do it all over again. Many of these aged creatures of both sexes had left home and family a thousand miles away, never to return, happy and glad to chill themselves slowly into heaven at holy Benares.

After bathing at the Ghâts the devotee betakes himself to Manikarnika, the famous well of healing, which will wash away the foulest and blackest murder, or even the still greater crime of having cheated a priest of his dues. This well was dug by the God Vishnu, who worked so hard at it that he filled it with his perspiration. When he had finished he invited a rival god, Mahadeva, to come and look at it. Mahadeva was so pleased with it that he shook with delight, and one of his earrings fell into the well, thus giving it a double sanctity.

I saw the contents of this well, and if it be Vishnu's sweat he must have been a very dirty god indeed, worse than any of his worshippers, for the stink is horrible. It is thicker than gruel from constant bathing, and the flowers which each worshipper throws into it, to decay uncleansed. A fat priest sits at the mouth of the well dispensing ladlefuls to an eager crowd, who drink it up greedily. A collection is, of course, being continually taken up. Cholera is seldom absent from Benares, and in hot weather has a high time.

From this the pilgrim (if cholera permits) goes to the Well of Knowledge, Gyan Kup, and has another drink of rotten liquid flowers; he may then wander from temple to temple and shrine to shrine, till the time comes for his return, surfeited with holiness, to his native village, or till he dies on the sacred soil of

Benares. This well is in the courtyard of the famous Golden Temple, dedicated to Shiva, the Poison God. This temple is a quadrangle covered with a roof, above which rises a very picturesque tower. At each corner is a dome, with a larger dome in the centre. These are all covered with gold plates, presented by Runjeet Singh. The courtyard is thronged with worshippers and sacred bulls and cows, and the jostling of the dirty smelling crowd is not pleasant in the heat of the day.

We passed from temple to temple, through streets like pictures from the "Arabian Nights," past shops in which skilful artists were making the chased brass dishes and bowls so familiar to us in England, or cutting out clever wooden toys, boxes, and puzzles. Here were a group of weavers, squatted on the ground waiting to be hired by the merchants of the richly-embroidered gold and silver cloth for which Benares is famous; there in some open space were groups of pilgrims, with their worldly goods in two bundles hung from each end of a bamboo, decorated with red ribbons to denote their object, footsore and weary, from a tramp of many a hundred miles along the hot and dusty roads of India, but overjoyed at reaching the holy spot at last. Brahmins, priests, bellowing street preachers of Hindoo dogmas, vicious pariah dogs, horrible beggars who showed their horrible deformities, sacred bulls and cows, street hawkers, palankeens, and flocks of poultry throng the narrow streets and lanes, making locomotion difficult, but presenting a busy swarming mass of bright colour and movement, such as I have only seen equalled in the bazaars of Cairo. The sacred bull is a distinct nuisance. These are animals performing much the same religious function as the scapegoat did for the Jews, but instead of being turned loose in the wilderness he is turned loose in the narrow streets of a busy town, whose pious inhabitants tempt his pampered appetite with dainties put out for him in an iron pot on the doorstep, and who permit him unchecked to walk into any shop he fancies, and help himself to any fruit, vegetables, or grain for which his soul may lust. Everybody makes way for my lord, and if any scoffer were to twist his tail he would have to run for his life. The municipal authorities used to kidnap them at night, and turn them loose on the other side of the Ganges, but they swam back the next night, and turned up holier than ever. Now they are darkly stolen by the police, disguised, and utilised for carting away the town refuse. But in spite of this their name and nature is Legion. I never saw a

NOTHING IS SACRED TO A SNAKE!

more self-righteous looking Pharisee than a fat old white bull in one of the temples, levying blackmail from every worshipper, who brought him each a cake, some rice flour or a dainty bit of fruit. I have been told that suburban snakes have a pleasant trick of shackling the hind legs of the sacred cows, and helping themselves to milk, a dainty of which serpents are inordinately fond.

A great feature of the Ghâts are the Fakeers or Ascetics, who resort hither from the uttermost parts of India. We saw one of these sitting in a circle of low mud wall which he had built for himself. His hair and beard were long and matted, and his face and body covered with ashes from a small fire which he had provided for the purpose. The expression of his countenance was one of rapt ecstacy. The admiring bystanders said he had been there for eight days without moving or speaking. If any pious person placed a cake or a bit of fruit on his stone he would eat it in an absent manner, washing it down with Ganges water. There are hundreds of these Ascetics constantly at Benares. We heard some very eloquent preaching from Hindoo pundits, who sat on a raised platform, and discoursed to large assemblages, chiefly veiled women. These men are all Brahmins, the highest caste of Hindoos, and there are some 20,000 or 25,000 of these in Benares, none of whom do a stroke of work, all fattening on the alms devout Hindoos are always ready to bestow. They superintend the worship in the temples and control all the holy places of the city, but their work consists chiefly in holding out their hands for money, and it is little wonder that where the highest caste are the loudest beggars all the rest follow suit, making India the worst place in the world for this pest.

Among the many curious sights of Benares is the temple of the goddess Durga, about three miles out of the town. The temple is a fine building, set off by a large tank in front and trees all round, but with no special architectural interest. In front of the shrine is an altar, bedabbled with blood, on which many goats are sacrificed. Durga is the terrific form of Shiva's wife, and delights in destruction and bloodshed of all kinds. Whenever a Hindoo wants a meat dinner he brings a kid to Durga, and sacrifices it. The priests levy toll on the carcase, and then he may take it away and eat meat offered to idols to his heart's content. In the trees around this temple, peering over walls and round pinnacles, are hosts of monkeys, about the size of dogs. These animals are all living deities, gods, and

Y

goddesses, and it would be a horrible crime indeed to injure one of them. They are so mischievous, that it is impossible for any one to live within half a mile of the temple, as all their household belongings would be destroyed by these creatures, which are numbered by thousands. They became such an intolerable nuisance some years ago that the magistrate of Benares removed all he could catch to a distant jungle. We bought a few handfuls of rice, and whenever we threw it on the ground scores of these monkeys appeared in a few seconds.

The finest building in Benares is the lofty mosque of Aurungzebe. Its foundations are laid deep below the river's bed, and rise from its level in great stone breastworks, on the summit of which are the four walls and domes of the mosque. Soaring high into the air, like the tall stems of some beautiful flower, are two delicately graceful minarets, 150 feet from the floor of the mosque, $8\frac{1}{4}$ feet in diameter at the base, tapering to $7\frac{1}{4}$ feet at the summit, overtopping every temple and palace in the city. The river is 150 feet below the base of the minarets, so that the whole structure rises some 300 feet sheer. Mohammed, the worshipper of one god and the greatest breaker of idols the world has seen, thus looks down with lofty and desolate scorn on the hundreds of temples which not even the savage persecution of the great Aurungzebe, or eighty years of Christian missions, has been able to reduce by one. We climbed laboriously to the summit of one of these pinnacles, and got a glorious view of the city, and the great sweeping river bearing away the sins of its devotees to the great ocean, and wondered sadly when the most religious people on earth would turn from their hideous superstitions to the truth of Christianity. There are two or three earnest missionaries pecking at this mass of horrible idolatry, which but for the restraint of British rule would burst out again into all its ancient cruelties of Juggernaut and Suttee; but they are making about as much impression on it as a woodpecker trying to cut down an oak, and I doubt if there is a single convert to Christianity in Benares who is not in some way or other dependent upon the missionaries. This dense ancient mass of priest-ridden heathendom has resisted alike the attacks of Buddhism, Mohammedanism, and Christian missionaries.

Benares used to be a great dépôt for all the agricultural produce of a vast area of India, whence it was sent down the Ganges to Calcutta for distribution over the whole world. Fleets of boats and steamers were used for this purpose, but the railway has almost extinguished them; another instance of many others I have noticed in my journey round the world, of the destruction of the traffic on great water-ways by railways, tending to confirm the distrust I have always felt of the success financially of such schemes as the Manchester Ship Canal, and this new proposal to take ships up to Leeds *viâ* Goole. Only an absolutely free water-way like an open sea appears able to compete successfully with railways, and not always then, as the trade between the Bristol Channel and the Mersey proves.

Benares is full of sad pathos, its streets, its temples, and the Ghâts all affording evidence of the powerful roots which the Hindu religion has struck deep down into the affections and devotions of this ancient people. For beauty of situation and picturesqueness of detail it has few rivals. I would fain have prolonged our stay for weeks, but our time is short, and the shadow of St. Stephen's looms dark in front of our pathway round the world. So with a reluctant good-bye to Benares, hoping it may be only *au revoir*, we take train to Agra to see a new phase of past Indian life in the wondrous monuments which tell of the vanished greatness of the Mogul Empire.

The natural course of our trip should have taken us somewhat out of our way to Lucknow and Cawnpore, but the main interest of these places consist in the scenes and memorials of the mutiny, a dark and terrible episode in our history of which I am content to have read about, and we pass on, without reviving its horrid memories

CHAPTER XXI.

THE CITY OF THE GREAT MOGULS.

A LONG and weary night's journey on the 29th of December brought us in the early morning to Agra, the city which Akbar, the great Mogul Emperor, chose as his metroplis in the middle of the 16th century. Akbar was seventeenth in descent from Timour, or Tamerlane, the great Tartar conqueror of India, whose descendants have sat on the throne of Delhi till Hodson slew the two sons of the last king during the mutiny. The Mogul Empire reached its zenith during Akbar's reign, and nearly all the wonderful buildings and palaces, which attract visitors from all over the world to Agra and Delhi, are the monuments of his splendour and extravagance, or of his immediate successors, Jahangir, Shah Jehan, and Aurungzebe.

Agra is situated on a great bend of the river Jumna, which is crossed by a clumsy bridge of boats, and also by a fine railway bridge. The fort is placed in the angle of the peninsula formed by this great bend, on the very edge of the bank, commanding the river. The old walls of Agra enclose an area of 11 square miles, about half of which is covered with dwelling houses, containing a population of 150,000. The town is better built than most Indian cities, and has a larger proportion of well-to-do citizens.

In viewing the city from across the river, the great central object is the huge crenelated fortress of sandstone, with its vast red walls and flanking defences surmounted by the white marble domes of its royal palaces. This enormous fortress, impregnable at the period in which it was built, is a mile and a half in circuit, and its frowning walls are 70 feet in height. During the mutiny in 1857 it sheltered the whole of the European population, over 5,000 in number, within the walls of its barracks and palaces. The fort is placed in a position to command the whole town, as well as every possible approach by the river.

The only entrance to the fort is by the Delhi gate, a magnificent building of red sandstone, reached by a drawbridge across the wide moat. Passing through this gateway, guarded by tall Sikh soldiers, a winding road brings us to a long flight of steps leading up to the famous Moti Musjid, or pearl mosque, the private chapel of the Court of the Mogul Emperors, occupying much the same relative position to the great Palace of Agra as St. George's Chapel does to Windsor Castle. When the door of the gateway was thrown open I was literally blinded with the dazzling beauty of the mosque, standing in the full blaze of noonday sun. Against a cloudless sky of the purest azure stood a corridor of three rows of beautifully-proportioned Saracenic arches, crowned with a row of lovely cupolas, surmounted in their turn by three lofty domes. These three aisles stood open to a great courtyard, surrounded by cloisters, with a large fountain in the centre. Courtyard, cloisters, corridors, cupolas, and domes were all alike of the most beautiful white marble, decorated with fine carving in low relief. The mosque itself, *i.e.*, the three arched corridors, is 142 feet long by 56 feet deep, the courtyard being 100 feet wide from the mosque to the gateway. At each end of the mosque are marble screens of floriated tracery, and the columns, arches, and ground vaults, exquisitely decorated, intersect one another with infinite grace and beauty when viewed from the outer corners. This mosque

THE JASMINE TOWER, AGRA FORT.

was built by Shah Jehan in 1654, and the only ornament which is not strictly architectural is an inscription in black marble, inlaid in the frieze of the mosque itself. This inscription tells us that "the mosque may be likened to a precious pearl, for no other in the world is lined throughout with marble." The gateway is well worthy of careful study. In the centre of the court is a large square tank of white marble for ablutions. A cloister runs all round the courtyard, containing 58 slender twelve-sided pillars, on square bases. During the occupation of the fort by the British refugees at the time of the mutiny this pearl mosque was used as the hospital.

A few minutes' walk further brings us to the great Divan, or public audience hall, 192 feet by 64 feet, the roof being supported by a succession of colonnades of red sandstone, covered with plaster, and painted white and gold. In the centre of this hall is a curious alcove of marble, inlaid with mosaics of precious stones, in which the Emperor sat, watching the administration of justice in the court immediately beneath him. The Prince of Wales, the future Emperor of a vaster India than that of the Mogul, held a durbar, or public reception of native princes, in this great Divan during his visit to India in 1876.

Passing through a small door at the side of the alcove, a flight of steps conducts us into what is probably the most beautiful and unique monument of Saracenic domestic art. We wander on through a succession of great courtyards, surrounded by arcades, on the top of which are a series of white marble palaces and pavilions, elaborately decorated with carving and inlaid work of precious stones. One of these vast courtyards is 500 feet long by 370 feet wide, with a broad walk 20 or 30 feet wide all round the top of the cloisters, from which lead innumerable chambers.

The Harem surrounds a beautiful Eastern garden, bright with

fountain and blossom; three sides of this garden are occupied by the ladies' apartments; the fourth, overhanging the outer wall of the fortress 100 feet above the river, is composed of three white marble pavilions of exquisite grace, whose walls, pillars, and roofs are adorned with inlaid flowers of agate, cornelian, lapis-lazuli, onyx, porphyry, jasper, bloodstone, and other precious stones, and are topped with golden domes. On a lower level, down six or eight marble steps, is the Jasmine tower, the boudoir of the chief Sultana, a wonderfully perfect specimen of carved and inlaid marble, which has been finely restored at the expense of Lord Northbrook, when he was Governor-General of India, and a projecting belvedere, in which the Emperor sat to view elephant fights and other savage sports on the plains below. Another curious apartment is the Shish Mahal, or palace of glass, being the Hammam or Turkish bath, used by the ladies of the Harem, a series of chambers adorned with thousands of small pieces of talc or mica, disposed in intricate designs, giving the appearance of innumerable little mirrors.

I cannot attempt to do justice to this gorgeous home of the great Mogul Emperors, probably the most magnificent palace the world has ever seen. We spent many hours of our stay in Agra, wandering through its beautiful courts and chambers, finding fresh cause for admiration every moment.

From every window and terrace of the palace the view closed in with the shining dome and minarets of the sublimely beautiful tomb which Shah Jehan erected over the body of his beloved wife Mahal, who died in giving birth to her eighth child. The famous Taj Mahal is probably the most renowned building in the world. Like that other great tomb, the pyramid of Cheops, at Cairo, one's enjoyment of its wondrous loveliness is marred by the recollection that it was built by forced labour, and was reared on the lives of hundreds of its makers. Twenty thousand

THE TAJ MAHAL, FROM THE SUMMIT OF THE GREAT GATEWAY.

workmen were employed for seventeen years in building and decorating the Taj. They were half starved, and their families wholly starved, producing great distress and mortality among them. The total cost is estimated at over forty million rupees, or about four millions sterling.

The road to the Taj Mahal from Agra passes the ruins of many ancient palaces, leading up to a superb gateway of sandstone, inlaid with floral ornaments, and passages from the Koran, in white marble. We had chosen noon for our first visit to the

VIEW FROM THE TERRACE OF THE FORT, AGRA—THE TAJ MAHAL IN THE DISTANCE.

Taj, for I love the blaze of the midday sun beyond all other times of the day if there is anything to be seen worth seeing. Passing through the gateway, we stood upon a flight of steps looking down an avenue of sombre cypresses, the floor of which was of white marble, covered with water about a foot deep, reaching away for three or four hundred yards ; the vista closed in with a vast dome of white marble, posed on a building whose perfect symmetry and absolute finish of every detail, flashed like some priceless jewel in the glorious blue setting of the Indian noonday sky. The beauty of it literally struck us dumb. Words were worthless. I had come disposed to carp a little at what had been so continually praised, but I found the building as a whole, its details and its surroundings, its exterior and interior, absolutely faultless. My daughter said, "It was never made, it has grown like some beautiful flower."

The enclosure in which the Taj is placed is a great garden in which orange and lemon trees, pomeloes, pomegranates, palms and flowering shrubs and trees, with marble fish ponds and fountains, speak of the East in every whisper of their leaves and plash of their waters. This garden is a third of a mile long, and nearly as wide. The marble paved avenue of cypresses runs through its entire length, closed at one end with the dazzling marble Taj, at the other contrasted by the rich red sandstone gateway. The tomb itself is 186 feet square, and 220 feet high to the top of the dome; it is raised upon a plinth of white marble 313 feet square, and 18 feet high above the level of the garden. At each corner of this plinth stand four tapering minarets 137 feet high, also of white marble. At each side of the Taj, about 400 feet back across a great court flagged with marble, are splendid mosques of red sandstone, richly decorated with mosaics of white marble, and topped with three white marble domes, only inferior in beauty to that of the Taj itself. During one of our visits one of these courtyards was occupied by a little pic-nic party of thirty or forty Hindoos in every variety of bright holiday attire, the colours of which formed an admirable foil to the white brilliance of this wonderful building.

We were fortunate enough to see the Taj by the light of the full moon on two consecutive evenings. It is even more beautiful in the silver dress of moonlight than in the golden robes of the noonday sun. By day or night alike it has made an impression on my memory that nothing can ever obliterate.

THE CITY OF THE GREAT MOGULS.

Inside the Taj, the Emperor Shah Jehan and his beloved Mahal lie buried side by side in marble tombs, inlaid with rich gems. The great Mogul Empire, over which they ruled, has passed away, and on this gorgeous remnant of its splendour we saw "Tommy Atkins" sitting in the seat of the scornful, carving the broad arrow of a greater Empire on its topmost stone.

There were originally two great silver doors at the entrance, but these were taken away and melted by the Jats. The architect was a Frenchman named Austin de Bordeaux.

The interior of the Taj is lighted through double screens of white marble trellis-work of the most exquisite design, one on the outer, the other on the inner face of the walls. In England a building thus lighted would be gloomy and almost dark, but in the blazing sun of India, in a building composed entirely of pure white marble, it only tempers a glare that would otherwise be intolerable, while giving light enough to see the lace-like details of the open trellis-work.

The great sandstone gateway to the garden in which the Taj stands, is a worthy entrance to this splendid monument. It is 140 feet high and 110 feet wide, built of warm red sandstone inlaid with ornaments and inscriptions from the Koran in white marble, and surmounted by twenty-six marble cupolas.

After gazing at this gateway of sombre hues, it is a marvellous contrast to pass through, and behold the soft and pearl-like whiteness of the Taj, dazzling in the noonday light, framed in green cypress and orange trees, against the deep blue background of the Indian sky.

About five miles from Agra, at Sikandra, an ancient place supposed to take its name from Alexandra of Macedonia, is the last resting-place of Akbar, the greatest of the Mogul Emperors. A fine gateway of red sandstone admitted us into what had once been a great garden, as well cared for as that of the Taj, but which is now a wilderness of infinite beauty. In the centre of this rises a singular building of five stories or arched causeways, of hewn stone richly carved, the bottom story of which is 300 feet square, and the top story, 74 feet high from the base, is a cloistered quadrangle of white marble, 70 feet square. The outer walls of this cloister are formed of marble screens pierced with a great variety of intricate patterns and designs, through

THE TOMB OF AKBAR, SIKANDRA.

which the blue of the sky and the dark green of the tangled garden glitter like some fine mosaic.

In the heart of this great pile of arched terraces lies the tomb of Akbar in a gloomy domed chamber, into which the light of day faintly struggles through narrow apertures in the walls. This huge mausoleum took twenty years to build, and is said to have employed 3,000 workmen the whole time.

The gateway at Sikandra is magnificent. It is a massive structure of red sandstone with a scroll of white marble twelve

A CORNER OF AKBAR'S PALACE, FATTEHPUR SIKRI.

inches broad, adorning it, engraved with a chapter from the Koran. It is 72 feet high, and the roof is crowned with a white marble minaret about 60 feet high at each corner. The view from the top is wide and extensive, comprising the river Jumna winding through the fertile plain like a great blue ribbon, the domes and minarets of the mosques and palaces of Agra, the Taj Mahal glistening in its great loop, with Fattehpur Sikri far away to the south.

Twenty-four miles distant from Agra is the curious and wonderful deserted city of Akbar, Fattehpur Sikri, which was to the palace at Agra what Windsor Castle is to Buckingham Palace. The ancient walls of this city are seven miles round, in the centre of which the magnificent series of buildings rise on a hill about 150 feet above the plain. The walls remain, but the city has long since vanished, fertile fields and gardens having taken its place. Some idea of its extent may be guessed from the vestiges of the great market or bazaar, a mile in length, the flint pavement of which may still be distinguished near the gate on the north side. The royal buildings cover the whole summit of the hill, completely dominating the city and plain. They are half mosque and sepulchre and half palace, for the Moguls loved to rest in their graves with even greater magnificence than that in which they spent their lives. The main entrance is by the great gateway of the mosque, the highest gateway in the world, it is said, which, standing on a flight of steps about 100 feet wide, rises 130 feet from the roadway, visible for 20 miles across the plain. At the side of this towering gateway is a large tank about thirty feet deep, into which men and boys leaped from a height of seventy feet as soon as we appeared, running up the steps breathless and wet to beg for annas in reward. These singular tanks or wells are to be seen in most of the Mogul palaces, and were used as cool retreats from the great

heat of summer. Passing through the gateway, we entered
the fine cloistered quadrangle of the mosque, 433 feet long and
366 feet wide, in which were placed two magnificent tombs, one
of carved red sandstone, and the other of pierced marble, looking
at a distance like fine lace. This latter is the tomb of a Fakeer,
a holy hermit who had great influence over Akbar, and who
must have been a shrewd and clever statesman, if the legends
which are told of him are true. Half the village claims lineal
descent from this Fakeer, including a smart young Hindoo who
acted as our guide. Over the grave is a curious canopy like
a four-post bed, incrusted all over with fine mother-of-pearl
inlaid work. Leaving the mosque, we wander on for hours from
palace to palace, through courtyards and old gardens, past
dainty white marble summer-houses and sculptured sandstone
stables, all in that fine preservation which only is possible in
such a perfect climate as India. I will try to describe one of
these royal houses, the apartment of Birbul, one of the Emperor's
favourite Hindoo ministers. It contains eight rooms, each fifteen
feet square, on two stories. Not an inch of wood is to be found
in the whole structure, which is entirely of red sandstone, built
in the most massive manner. The minuteness of the decoration,
which covers every inch of space inside and out, is more like the
work of some Chinese ivory carver than of a stonemason. The
ceiling of the rooms on the ground floor is made of long slabs of
sandstone fifteen feet long by one foot wide, resting on bold
cornices, as richly decorated as the rest. The rooms in the
upper story are crowned by massive domes, got by putting a
capstone on the top of sixteen sloping slabs, each of which
stands upon an abutment, the whole supported on eight sides,
rising from the walls of the room. One is puzzled whether to
speak of it as "the most diminutive of palaces or the most
gigantic of jewel cases," but the prevailing impression in my

BIRBUL'S HOUSE, FATTEHPUR SIKRI.

mind was that it ought to be removed to South Kensington and put under a glass case. There is a cast of two pillars from this wonderful little palace to be seen at that museum, which give a good idea of its infinite beauty of decoration.

It is at Fattehpur Sikri that the great Akbar must be judged as a builder. During the whole of his reign of fifty years it was his favourite residence. It has been fitly spoken of as "a

THE MAUSOLEUM OF PRINCE ETMAD DOWLAT.

romance in stone, and a reflex of the mind of the great man who built it."

A pleasant morning's drive is to be had by crossing the Jumna by the old bridge of boats, a gay and busy scene, thronged with bull-carts from the country, the gravelly banks of the river on each side being crowded with washermen and water-carriers. About a mile up the river stands the tomb of

Prince Etmad Dowlat, one of the most beautiful mausoleums in India, a masterpiece of pierced and carved marble, and pietra dura. Like all other mausoleums, it stands in a lovely garden overhanging the river. From the terrace of the garden a fine view is obtained, and we found some amusement in a number of enormous tortoises or turtles, swimming about in the river. Some of these were 4 or 5 feet long, with great horny-beaked mouths; we were told that they have been known to attack men swimming across the river, and pull them under water, drowning them.

I suppose the various palaces and magnificent tombs erected by the Mogul Emperors during a period of less than a century must have cost ten or twelve millions sterling, although chiefly erected by forced and unpaid labour. The jewelled peacock throne of Shah Jehan was worth seven millions sterling. This pomp and show was paid for out of a revenue wrung out of the very life-blood of the people, equal in amount to the whole revenues of British India. The beneficent change from the rule of these wasteful tyrants to that of the present Empress of India is shown by the fact that for a less sum of money than that spent upon three palaces, two tombs and a throne, the British Government has made 4,500 miles of irrigating canals, watering some three millions of acres, giving employment and food to 15 or 20 millions of population.

I visited several of the missionaries in Agra. The Church Mission consists of several excellent schools and a good church. The Baptists have three missionaries, six Zenana lady missionaries, fifteen native pastors and schoolmasters, and ten native women whose work it is to visit the Zenanas and read to the wives and children of Hindoos. They have six day schools, with 315 boys and seventeen teachers, in which they give very good elementary education. Dr. Valentine, a Presbyterian, has an excellent training college for native medical missionaries, with ten clever young Hindoo Christians as students. Dr. Wilson, an American Methodist, and his talented wife, who is paid by the Baptist Zenana Mission, conduct three dispensaries in different parts of Agra, as medical missionaries. I visited all three, and was astonished at the amount of work they got through in the day. They treat between them over 11,000 patients in the year, and their reputation is so great that villagers come long distances for advice. I saw a man who had walked twelve miles from the country, returning the same day, and he did this every three days to get medicine and advice. Dr. and Mrs. Wilson are specially commended in the report of the medical officer for the North-West Province as having the best and most successful dispensary in his district. Folk at home sometimes are apt to think that a missionary in India has a mighty easy time of it. It may be that there are some who have, and I have seen such, but not here. The day we left Agra, Mr. Daniel Jones, the senior Baptist Missionary, left for a two months' tour through the villages. He is accompanied by a native, and his home will be a small gipsy van, drawn by bullocks. He will not sleep in a bed the whole time, and often will live for days together on the poor bread of the villagers. He will preach six or seven times every day in the open air. I have found that missionaries, as a rule, know far more about the real social condition and habits of the people than the run of the civil or military services, most of whom hold themselves very much aloof from the native population. Missionaries, on the other hand, mix freely with all classes, their wives and the ladies who visit the Zenanas having a wider knowledge about the home life of the Hindoo and Mahommedan population than any other Europeans. All through India, so far, I have received more real help from missionaries in my efforts to learn something of the Indian people than from any other Englishman with whom I have come in contact. With some honourable exceptions the Anglo-Indian, civil and military, speaks of the native with distrust and contempt, and it is a significant comment on their attitude towards the humbler folk that in most of the hotels I have stayed at notices are put up in the rooms begging guests "not to illtreat the servants."

I have tried as well as I can to see something of the village and country life of India, and the journey from Agra to Futtehpur Sikri, a drive of about 50 miles altogether, took me through many villages. My companion was a Baptist missionary, Mr. Potter, a man of rare intelligence, who is very familiar with the district, and who had friends and acquaintances in every village we passed through. The scenes along the road were full of interest and variety. The animal life in India is abundant, and, as no Hindoo injures or kills any wild animal, they are wonderfully tame. The minars, a very common bird about the size of a blackbird, hardly takes the trouble to hop out of the way of the horses' feet. Vultures and crows, the scavengers of the villages, roost about on stumps and rocks, and let you come within a few feet of them, when they move lazily away for a short distance. At every pond, handsome storks, cranes, and wild ducks are to be seen, peacocks strut about the fields, pheasants run across the road, pigeons, ring-doves, hoopoes, woodpeckers, and bright green parrots fly from tree to tree, and pretty grey squirrels, full of cheerful impudence, are all over the place, on roofs of huts, walls, playing in the dusty road or chasing one another up the trunks of trees. The village well is always hard at work, with a couple of sleek oxen drawing huge leather buckets up to the surface with rope and pulley. Beggars are everywhere. In one place they were so numerous and so miserable that I gave the head man of the village the largess of one rupee, which he went off at once to change into pies (small copper coins about half a farthing in value), with the whole lot howling at his heels.

These poor creatures are all deformed or leprous, the result in most cases of chronic hunger. In one village some girls pursued us clamouring for coppers, on the strength of their being hungry. They were well-fed and well-clothed rogues, and got nothing. One of them, however, had a pretty puppy, which the ladies of our party noticed. Immediately the girl exclaimed, with a grin, "This puppy very hungry, Ma'am Sahib!"

The village communities in India may be divided into two classes, cultivators of the soil and those who render different services to the cultivators, for which they are paid in kind. These latter are, firstly, the head man of the village, elected by popular suffrage, who manages all the affairs of the community, assisted by a village council of five or seven in number. The village accountant comes next, then the priest; the barber, a very important functionary, who shaves, shampoos, cuts nails, and acts as village doctor; the potter, who makes all the pots and platters for the village, with great skill; the blacksmith, the carpenter, the dhoby or washerman, who belongs to a special caste of his own, and no family, however poor, "washes at home;" the water-carrier; the tailor, the shoemaker, who belongs to the lowest of all castes, the watchman (this functionary always followed me about the village, never losing sight of me till I was well off the premises!), and lastly the impure caste who do all the dirty work of the village. Large villages add to to these a schoolmaster, an astrologer, an apothecary, and an exorcist of evil spirits. As far as I could make out, these trades are all paid in the produce of the soil, and share the prosperity or adversity of agriculture equally with the cultivators of the land. Cultivation is very primitive. The land is fertile, and seems to need no manure. At any rate it gets none, as all the cow dung is made up into cakes with chopped straw, dried in the sun, and used for fuel. It is strange to see the sunny wall of a house covered all over with these cakes.

The shopkeeper is also an important person in large villages, though he is not in community with the rest. He is also a money-lender, and the child-like Hindoo cultivator also gets into his clutches, and becomes his mere slave. The villagers generally appear better fed and nourished than the town labourer, but the poverty of the whole country is very great, and probably four-fifths of the population of India live and die without ever once having had as much as they could eat at a meal.

In towns the average earnings of a labouring man is one rupee a week, and his wife may pick up one way or another 4 annas. A rupee is worth 1s. 6d. of our money, and 4 annas about $4\tfrac{1}{2}d$. He and his children live entirely upon bread or a kind of lentil called dhol, with a little vegetables, pepper and salt stewed together to relish the bread. If he has four children, six mouths to feed, he can only afford one meal a day, and that a scanty one. His wants are few indeed—hut, fuel, washing, clothes, and food. I have carefully inquired into the cost of these necessities for a week for such a family. Rent is 1 anna, washing $\tfrac{1}{2}$ anna, fuel 2 annas, vegetables, pepper, salt, and oil, $2\tfrac{1}{2}$ annas, $\tfrac{1}{2}$ lb. of corn or dhol per head per diem, 16 annas ; total 1 rupee 6 annas, or 2 annas more than the whole earnings of the man and his wife, leaving nothing for clothes, which must cost about 7 rupees a year for a family of six, and which must be squeezed out of the $\tfrac{1}{2}$ lb. of flour. The Zenana missionaries told me that there are widows in Agra and Delhi who are living on 1s. 6d. per month ! It is little to be wondered at that when pestilence or famine comes these poor creatures die off like flies. Before British rule, famine and cholera would often clear off millions in a single year.

The average Hindoo does about one-fifth of the work of an average Englishman, and has not physical strength for more. In the cotton mills at Agra and Cawnpore, it takes exactly three times the number of grown men to turn out as much work as a Manchester mill employing women and children as well as men. There are some terrible social problems to be solved in India, and unless by irrigation and other public works fresh tracts of land are brought under cultivation, and the price of food reduced, recurrent famines will be inevitable. In England the average income per head per annum of population is £33; in France, £23; in Turkey, the poorest country in Europe, £4; but in India it falls as low as £1 15s., with a steadily increasing population to share it.

CHAPTER XXII.

DELHI.

DELHI is one of the ancient cities of the world, and has exercised a controlling influence on the politics of India from a period which loses itself in the distance of ages. Fifteen hundred years before Christ it had a distinct history, whose traditions are as marked as those of Nineveh and the Exodus, and portions of the great ruined fortress of Indrapat, four miles from modern Delhi, are pointed out as dating back to the time of Joshua. Seven ancient and ruined cities, with colossal fortresses, marble palaces, stupendous wells, and magnificent temples, stretch for 12 or 15 miles on the great plain which lies between the Ridge and the River Jumna, any of which would be one of the wonders of Europe if situated on that continent, and attract as many travellers as Heidelberg, Venice, or the Alhambra.

Some of these ruined cities were the mere freak of despots who wished to found capitals bearing their own name and commemorative of their personal glory. They appear to have built new cities side by side with the older ones, and forced the whole population from one to the other. The Cyclopean group of buildings, known as Toghlakabad, consisting of a citadel, a vast enclosing fortress with 13 gates, and a huge hexagon of outer walls, is called after a successful military adventurer, one Toghlak Ghazi Khan, whose life was one of those wonderful topsy-turvies that are only possible in Oriental Empires. He started life as a Turki slave, and was raised by his master (the Emperor) to the Governorship of the Punjab; he showed his gratitude by murdering his benefactor, and usurping his throne. His dynasty lasted nearly a century, and was a succession of savage ruffians whose kingdom was in continual revolt, and whose subjects must have been the most miserable wretches on earth. Places are still shown where one of them used to hunt men with dogs, and slaughter them like wild beasts. When Timour, the Tartar conqueror, swept down with his hordes, the dynasty of Toghlak, sapped by Mohammedan mutinies and Hindoo revolts, fell an easy prey. Timour had a five days' slaughter, after the fashion of the times, during which the streets were impassable for dead bodies, leaving Toghlakabad the abode of vultures and jackals, whose descendants swarm there to this day.

History has repeated itself often enough in Delhi, and we passed from one ruined city to another, with wondering eyes for the magnificence of the monarchs and aching hearts for the misery of the subjects, ending with the great fortress of New Delhi, from which the last of the Mogul Emperors was driven in 1857 by the victorious English troops under General Nicholson, dying a State prisoner in Rangoon five years after.

The present ruler of Delhi lives in a modest bungalow near the Cashmere Gate. He did not attain his position by slaughter and conquest, but by the milder and more peaceful way of the Indian Civil Service examinations.

I will not weary my readers with any detailed descriptions of this vast area of ruined cities. My own mind is rather chaotic as to the identity of the splendid mausoleums, delicate inlaid tombs, carved marble palaces, bathing houses one dazzling sparkle of pearl and mica, and lovely gardens full of ruined summer-houses, which float before my memory as I write, illustrating the rise, prime, and decadence of Mussulman art in India. I will content myself with a brief account of some of those buildings which command the immediate interest of all who visit Delhi. The chief of these is that superb monument which still remains as perfect as ever, of the reign of Kutab-ud-din, the first resident Moslem sovereign of India, erected in the early part of the thirteenth century. The Kutab-Minar, the loftiest tower in the world, rises out of the ruins of the older fortress of Lallkot, a Hindoo stronghold of the eleventh century, whose massive walls encircle the mosque of which the Kutab is the splendid minaret. This magnificent tower is 238 feet high, twice the height of the Duke of York's column, tapering from nearly fifty feet at the base to a diameter of nine feet at the top. It is divided into five stories. The lower story is 95 feet high, and consists of twenty-four faces in the form of convex flutings, alternately semi-circular and rectangular. In the second story, which is 51 feet, these projections are all semi-circular;

THE KUTAB-MINAR.

in the third story, 41 feet, they are all angular; the fourth is a plain cylinder, and the highest is partly fluted and partly plain. Each story is divided by an ornate gallery running round the tower. The whole is encrusted with chapters from the Koran cut in low relief. A circular staircase of 375 steps took us to the top, where we remained for a long time picking out of the plain spread at our feet the well-defined walls limiting the great fortresses and citadels which have one by one disappeared with the successive dynasties which created them, leaving only their mighty ruined cities as the memorials of their vanished empires. The Kutab-Minar is supposed to be the most perfect as well as the loftiest tower in the world. Its carvings are as fresh as if they were of yesterday's date, and it soars into the air to its utmost height without break or flaw. I know of nothing that can be compared with it for beauty except that wonderful masterpiece of Italy's greatest architect, Giotto's campanile at Florence, erected about the same period.

The Kutab-Minar is about eleven miles from New Delhi, and the two roads by which we went and returned were one long succession of ancient monuments of the greatest architectural interest. The most notable of these is the magnificent tomb of the Emperor Houmayoun, situated in a large desolate garden of about twelve acres, whose wild and tangled shrubberies are full of a weird beauty of their own. We enter this garden through a double gateway of red sandstone, and pass along a broad walk to the great mausoleum, which is 287 feet square and 70 feet high. The front is a curious hollow, half-moon-shaped archway, with alcoves. Within are three beautiful white marble tombs. The building is of red sandstone artistically inlaid with white marble.

It was in this tomb that the two sons of Bahadur Shah hid themselves after the storming of Delhi, in the mutiny, being captured there and shot by Major Hodson.

Near the Kutab-Minar is the Mosque of Kutab-ul-Islam, now in ruins, unrivalled for its great line of arches, 385 feet long, covered with flowered tracery of much beauty and grace. Within this mosque is the famous iron pillar, a solid shaft of wrought iron, 16 inches in diameter, 24 feet in length, and weighing 17 tons. This column has an inscription cut upon it, which commemorates the victory of Rajah Dhava over the Vahlikas. This pillar is probably 1700 years old. It is a striking fact that the Hindoos, so long since as this, were capable of forging a bar

INDRAPAT.

of iron larger and heavier than any that have been forged even in Europe up to a very late date.

On the way back from these interesting monuments, we paid a visit to the ancient city of Indrapat, repaired by Houmayoun and partly rebuilt by Shir Shah in the sixteenth century. The crumbling walls of the old fortress are very picturesque. All the gates but one are now closed up, and of that I give an illustration above.

There is a noble old mosque here, deserted and grass-grown, with a tiny little Baptist Chapel just opposite the main entrance, in which a school is held, and services are conducted by the missionaries at Delhi. Near the mosque is an octagonal building 70 feet high, used by Houmayoun as a library.

Two miles nearer to Delhi is the great fortress of Firozabad, now utterly ruined, but which must have been a formidable place in old time, dominating the river Jumna, which flows at its base. Within its walls, on the top of a hill, is one of the columns on which are inscribed the edicts of Asoka. It is a monolith of pink sandstone, 40 feet high, 2200 years old, and the

THE JUMMA MUSJID, DELHI.

characters inscribed upon it are of the oldest form yet discovered in India.

The glory of New Delhi is the famous Jumma Musjid, the great Mosque of Shah Jehan, the builder of the Taj and the Pearl Mosque at Agra, described in the last chapter. This building is raised on a flattened rock just opposite the great sandstone fort. It has three splendid gateways, reached by magnificent flights of steps, opening on the great cloistered courtyard, 600 feet by 200, at the end of which is the superb mosque, roofed in by three marble cupolas, crowned with gilt spires, and flanked with two lovely minarets 130 feet high. The flights of steps by which the mosque is reached, add greatly to the grandeur of this noble building. The lowest step is 150 feet long, and this length gradually diminishes up to the top of the flight, which consists of forty steps, each eight inches high. Within the mosque are some curious manuscripts and relics, which a rupee will produce. There is an old Koran written in Kufic, dating from the seventh century, the slipper of Mohammed, a hair of the Prophet's beard, and some other kindred rubbish.

We went there at noon on Friday, which is the Sabbath of the Mohammedans, when some thousands of men, in every variety of costume, were assembled in the spacious courtyard and mosque, to pray to the one great God, and hear the Koran read aloud.

The great citadel, or fort of Delhi, is a gorgeous building of red sandstone, of which the Lahore Gate, which did such damage to the English storming column in the mutiny, is the main entrance. Inside the fort are a succession of palaces, of which the Diwan i Khan, or private Hall of Audience, is the most remarkable. It is 90 feet by 70, of white marble, beautifully inlaid with pietra dura and gold. Some of the most beautiful pierced marble work in India is to be found in the palaces within the fort at Delhi.

Opposite to the Diwan i Khan is the Moti Musjid, or pearl mosque, an exquisite little gem. It has a handsome bronze door, and the façade has three arches. The building is of pure white marble, and is about 40 feet square. It was built by Aurungzebe in 1635 A.D. and cost over £100,000.

Delhi is the great trading centre of the North-West Provinces, and the main street of the town is the celebrated Chandni Chowk, down the centre of which runs an aqueduct shaded by a fine avenue of trees. It is lined on both sides with the shops and handsome dwelling houses of its merchants, whose touts pester you to come and see their wares, pressing into your hands cards and circulars written in absurd Baboo English, advertising their stocks, consisting chiefly of Cashmere shawls, chudders, gold and silver embroidery, wonderful loom work, jewellery, metal work, pietra dura, enamels, carpets, pottery, weapons, armour, and all

THE PEARL MOSQUE, DELHI FORT.

the other artistic melangerie for which India is famous. These pests ran after us in crowds, vociferating the names of their distinguished customers. Lord Randolph Churchill must have spent a large fortune when in Delhi two years ago, as at least 100 different merchants claim to have sold him large parcels of goods. After him the Duke of Cleveland appeared the best customer, and then Lord and Lady Brassey.

We spent some days in exploring the wonders of Moslem architecture at and round Delhi, and in visiting schools and other institutions; but the narrow limit of this volume forbids enlargement. We left for Jeypore with regret, feeling that a month could be well spent in a city which, whether for architectural beauty, historical associations, or present social interest, may rank with Rome, Cairo, Athens, or Constantinople.

CHAPTER XXIII.

JEYPORE TO BOMBAY.

WE had looked forward with much interest to Jeypore, from the fact of its being the chief city of that group of independent native states known as Rajputana. It is also considered the finest native city in India. It is a modern place, with the widest streets I have ever seen. The main thoroughfares are 111 feet wide, the side streets 55 feet, and the back lanes 28 feet, all running at right angles to each other. The palace of the Maharajah, occupying a vast area in the middle of the city, is a fine lofty edifice of eight stories, in the usual florid style so popular with modern Hindoo grandees, calling for no remark except that it appeared more tawdry than perhaps it really is to eyes fresh from the pure and chaste beauty of Moslem architecture at Agra and Delhi. The stables of the palace are one of the sights of India, containing 300 horses and 50 elephants, ten times as many as can be used; but this is the custom of owners of palaces, from Buckingham downwards. We were most interested in a dozen huge man-eating tigers, confined in cages, and fed at the Maharajah's expense. The amiable creatures to which we are accustomed at Regent's Park and in Wombwell's menagerie are quiet tabby cats compared with these horrible monsters, who shook the bars of their cages with impotent rage and fierce glare, growling with every tooth exposed at any person who approached them. They were certainly the most "fearful wild fowl" I ever saw.

The present Maharajah has no ideas or aspirations beyond his Zenana and his stables, but his predecessor, the late Maharajah, was one of the finest and most public-spirited men India has ever possessed. With an income from his small State of two millions sterling, he has made his little capital one of the most modern and civilized cities in the world. The town is lighted with gas throughout, while the greater cities of Delhi and Agra have but a few dull oil lamps. He has laid out a magnificent park of 70 acres, the finest garden in India. Within its area is a building much handsomer in every way than his own palace, devoted to a museum of Indian and European art, and also a splendid hospital, called after Lord Mayo, who was his warm personal friend, with 100 beds and a distinguished English physician at its head. The water supply is pure and abundant, while the sanitation of the city and the great cleanliness of the streets is secured by a Municipal Committee. The centre of his Highness's educational system is the Maharajah's College, affiliated with the Calcutta University, with an attendance of nearly 1000 students, taught entirely by native professors. There are 33 schools for elementary education, and this enlightened prince established female schools, a great innovation in Hindoo society, in which are 700 or 800 pupils. There is a fine High School for the sons of Rajput nobles, and one of the best buildings in the city is the School of Art for technical education, in which I saw numbers of young men and boys receiving instruction in drawing, carpentry, iron-working, electro-plating, engraving, metallurgy, silver and gold-working, enamelling, watchmaking, wood-carving, sculpture, embroidery, and other native arts for which India is famous. The jail is one of the best in India,

THE MARKET-PLACE, JEYPORE.

and remunerative. It is little wonder that the Rajput people revere the memory of a Maharajah who has been patriotic enough to set aside much of the extravagant splendour of his ancestors in favour of such expenditure as this, designed for the benefit of his people at large, and all completed and paid for during a single reign of 30 years.

The streets of Jeypore are crowded with a stalwart race of men, superior in every way to the poor, ill-fed, and half-clad people of Bengal and the North-West Provinces. There are signs of wealth on every hand. The scene from the fountain where the four great thoroughfares of Jeypore meet is as picturesque as anything I have ever seen in my travels. The great open space is filled with stalls of fruit, vegetables, and cereals; gay piece goods from Cashmere, Cawnpore, and Manchester, are displayed from others; thousands of pigeons walk in and out on the pavement, taking the greatest interest in the gaily dressed bargainers in front of every stall. A continual stream of traffic flows down each broad roadway, foot passengers mingling with smartly caparisoned elephants, trains of camels, white donkeys, and bullock carts. The syces or running footmen of some Rajput noble cry for passage for their master, who prances gravely in from the country on a white horse, with green and gold saddle, armed to the teeth with musket, sword, and dagger, or some groom of the Maharajah comes along with a panther or leopard led by chains. The houses are all rose-coloured, glowing in the bright sunlight against the deep cobalt of the sky. On the roofs are gay groups of women and children, clad in wondrous colours, with flocks of pigeons, parrots, and crows perched on every corner, or fluttering about the eaves. In the shops below every possible handicraft is carried on, for nothing is done by machinery in India. Here are women in bright red dresses, grinding at the mill, singing as they work. Two men, all the colours of the rainbow, come out of a dyer's shop to wave a long piece of green or blue cloth in the warm sunlight. Men squat on the side walk to be shaved, others are washing themselves at the gutter, with a bright brass basin full of clear water. Cotton picking, wheat winnowing, copper smithing, the potter's wheel, the spinning wheel, the gem grinder, the gold and silver smith, the shoemaker, and fifty other trades, all carried on with much clatter and noise, help the busy scene, which, as a whole, forms a mass of moving colour and life such as I have not seen equalled in all my travels.

Of course we paid a visit to the famous deserted city of Amber, the ancient capital of Jeypore, eight miles away. We drove out of the town past pretty gardens and handsome mansions, the residences of Rajput nobles, and presently reached a tank or lake of about 200 acres in area, in the centre of which was an old ruined palace, with no approach except by boat. Basking on the banks and small islands of this lake were a number of enormous alligators, and others were seen slowly swimming about with their ugly backs just above water. These monsters are fed regularly, and it is a great sight to see them swarming out of the water when their meal of dead horse is brought to them.

Two miles further on we reached the bottom of the hill on which Amber is situated, and here we found an enormous elephant waiting to convey us the rest of the distance. It is not possible to visit Amber without permission from the Maharajah; but it is always granted, and an elephant provided as conveyance. In every book of travel which I have seen, and they are many, the author, when he writes of Amber, invariably says, "The Maharajah of Jeypore most courteously placed at my disposal a magnificent elephant, gaily caparisoned, etc., etc., etc.," leading the reader to suppose that his Highness had specially selected the great writer for exceptional honour. But while some are born to greatness others have greatness thrust upon them, and in this case Cook's humblest tourist, equally with the distinguished author of the 'Light of Asia,' is provided with an elephant. Ours was ten feet high, its speed two miles an hour. The first step brought my stomach into my throat, the next my throat into my stomach; going downhill they both got mixed. We were grateful to the Maharajah, and tipped the Mahout, but we walked back!

Amber is a strange place. The town is quite deserted, except by a number of Fakirs or Hindoo ascetics, who have taken possession of the empty houses. It was a weird-looking place enough, and gave one the creeps to wander through street after street, seeing no human being except some half-cracked creature looking silently out of a window or over a roof. There is nothing stranger in India than the way in which some monarch, for reasons now forgotten or only guessed at, deserted his splendid palace and well-built capital, taking not only his court, but the entire population with him.

The palace at Amber calls for no special description. It is a fine pile of buildings of the later period of Mussulman art; its situation, however, is extremely picturesque, being built along the slopes of a fine hill, immediately over the lake, the summit of the hill being crowned with a powerful fortress. The surrounding hills, connected with strong walls, are each topped with smaller castles. The old deserted garden of the palace, stretching far out into the lake, is a place of rare beauty, and its rich, dark green foliage throws up the whole façade of the great range of buildings wonderfully. As we saw it, reproduced in the mirror of the still lake, it made a picture not easily to be forgotten.

Amber was built by Mân Singh in 1592, and is the finest of all the Rajput palaces.

From Jeypore we went on to Ajmere, spending a day in its queer old streets and quaint bazaars. This town is the capital of an isolated British district in the heart of Rajputana, with an area of 2,700 square miles, and a population of 320,000 souls. It is entirely surrounded by native states.

Ajmere is a great cotton market, and the transport trade of Rajputana centres here. The city is surrounded by a stone wall, with fine handsome gates. On the southern side of the city is the Dargah, an object of veneration to all religions in India. It marks the burial place of a famous saint called Khwaja, who lived in the 13th century, and whose eldest lineal descendant is the head of the shrine to-day. At the entrance gate we had to put the shoes from off our feet, having taken the precaution to bring thick woollen socks to put on instead, to protect ourselves from the deadly cold marble floors. The enclosure contains two or three mosques, the tomb of the saint, the entrance to which is spanned by a silver arch, and a deep tank or well cut in the solid rock, in which pilgrims perform their ablutions.

On the slope of a hill just outside the town is an ancient Jain temple, which was converted into a Mohammedan mosque by Altamsh in two and a half days. It is the finest specimen of early Mohammedan architecture extant, and is most elaborate in its decoration, and delicately finished in all its details.

Outside the city, in a fine park, is the Mayo College, established by the Earl of Mayo in 1870, and supported partly by endowments given by the Prince of Rajputana, and partly by an allowance from Government. Its object is to provide an education in accordance with European ideas for the sons of Rajput nobles.

AMBER.

A mile or two further out into the country is one of the finest and most picturesque tanks in India, from which the city of Ajmere derives its water supply. This tank is a lake six or

THE DARGAH, AJMERE.

seven miles in extent, surrounded by lofty hills. On its banks is situated the house and offices of the Resident, and an old palace or summer-house of white marble, surrounded by beautiful gardens, which commands a view of the whole tank and its adjacent mountains. Ajmere is full of ancient houses, with fine carved fronts, and gay busy bazaars, and with the exception of Benares, is fuller of "subjects" for the painter than any other town in India visited by us. We were sorry we had not more time to explore the city and the historical neighbourhood in which it is situated.

The next day we continued our journey to Ahmedabad, a thriving city of 120,000 population, which has played an important part in the history of India. The town is full of beautiful buildings, illustrating almost every kind of Moslem architecture, and the houses are finely carved.

Ahmedabad has always been famous for its wood-carving, and all the towns of Guzerat have many houses, the doors and windows of which are made beautiful with this work.

This city was once the greatest and most splendid in Western India, and 300 years ago had a population of about 900,000 souls; it possesses to-day not more than 120,000. It presents an imposing front to the Sabarmate River, a fine stream about 500 yards broad, being raised well above its left bank. Its fine old walls enclose an area of about two square miles. They have 14 gates, and every 50 yards there is a tower and bastion. These walls were built in the early part of the fifteenth century by Ahmed Shah, the second Mussulman King of Guzerat, who gave his name to the city.

An old native proverb says, "Ahmedabad hangs on three threads—gold, silk and cotton," and these are to-day the main staples of its trade. Silk and brocaded stuffs employ a large section of the population, and much of the gold and silver thread that is worked up into kinkobs and other fine brocades all over India, is manufactured at Ahmedabad. In every street one sees in the open shops families of weavers working up cotton cloth.

The city is full of beautiful buildings, and its architecture has a special interest, illustrating the result of the contact of

WINDOW AND BALCONY IN RANI SIPRI'S MOSQUE, AHMEDABAD.

Saracenic with Hindoo forms. Here the vigorous aggressiveness of Moslem art, which has all its own way at Agra, Delhi and Amber, has been forced to submit itself to Hindoo and Jain influences, in which the latter predominates. Even the mosques are Hindoo in their details.

Our first visit was to see the famous windows of Sidi Said's mosque in the citadel, now used as a public office. There are five of these windows, and I suppose they are the most beautiful specimens of carved and pierced marble work in the world.

SIDI SAID'S WINDOW, AHMEDABAD.

This illustration, drawn by Mr. Sheppard Dale from a photograph, will convey some idea of the graceful elaborateness of the finest of them. Of all the exquisite examples of marble tracery which I have seen at Agra and Delhi, none are so beautiful as this charming window.

The mosques of Ahmedabad are among the finest in the East, though not remarkable for size. Those of greatest interest are the Jumma, the Queen's, Ahmed Shah's, Said Alam's, and Rani Sipri's.

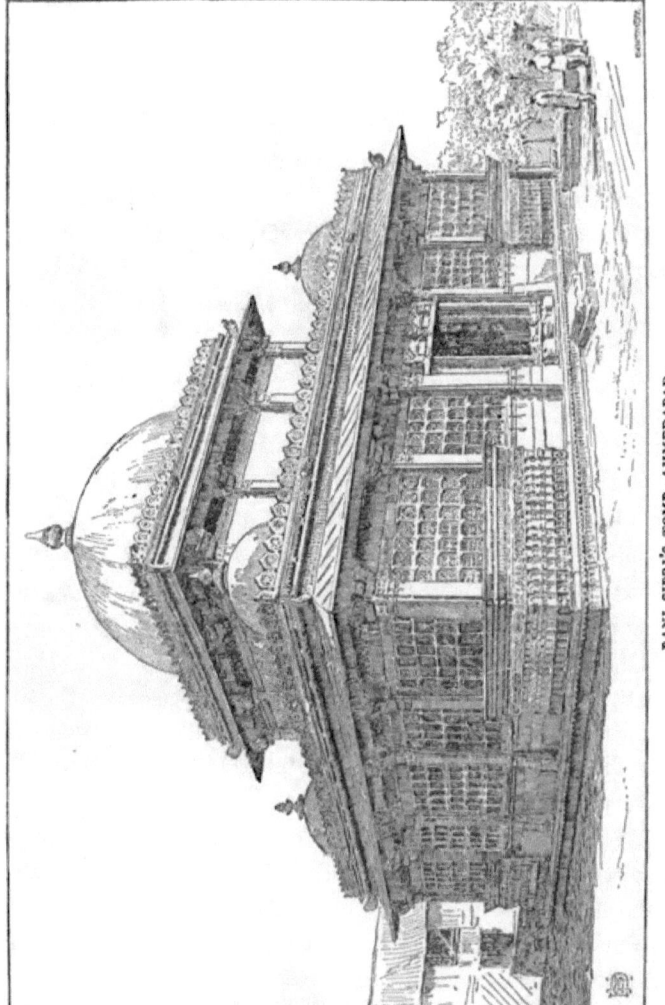

RANI SIPRI'S TOMB, AHMEDABAD.

Rani Sipri was a daughter-in-law of Ahmed Shah, and her mosque and tomb were built by herself and completed in the year 1431. They are singularly beautiful little buildings. The mosque is 54 feet long, by 19 feet wide, with six double pillars in front and single ones behind, all 10 feet high. The tomb is 36 feet square. On the opposite page is an illustration of the tomb, which will furnish a better idea of the beauty and infinite detail of its architecture than pages of description.

Another of the remarkable buildings at Ahmedabad is the fine modern Jain temple, erected about 40 years ago by Hutti Sing, a wealthy Jain merchant, at a cost of more than a million rupees. It is full of marvellous detail, though the carving is very inferior to that of the more ancient Jain temples. It is situated in a large garden behind a fine mansion in which the Hutti Sing family reside, and is entered by an archway in the house itself. The temple stands in the middle of a great courtyard 150 feet long and 106 feet wide, surrounded by a corridor of 56 arches with elaborately carved pillars.

It was impossible for us, in the one day at our disposal, to do more than glance at a few of the beautiful and interesting buildings which abound at Ahmedabad, and which would occupy a very pleasant week to see properly.

About seven miles from Ahmedabad is one of those splendid freaks of extravagance so common to Oriental potentates, which make it possible to believe any of the wildest stories of the 'Arabian Nights.' In the 15th century, Sultan Mahmoud Begada desired a country villa. He proceeded to dig out a large lake of 18 acres in extent, with 30 feet of water, surrounded it with splendid flights of steps, at the top of which rise a series of palaces. Here the Sultan buried a favourite adviser or Vizier, in a tomb that would cost £50,000 to reproduce; here he buried his queen in equal magnificence, and provided a noble mausoleum for himself when his time came; and behind them all, in a cloistered space of over an acre, he built a mosque only second in pretensions to the Moti Musjid at Agra. All this ruined grandeur of Sarkhej stands solitary and forgotten, but in wonderful preservation, the home of storks, crows, parrots, and jackals, with trees and brushwood in its stately courtyards, visited once in two or three months by some tourist who, like ourselves, is a little more adventurous than the rest.

From Ahmedabad a night's journey brought us to our last point of interest in India, the great port of Bombay, one of the most magnificent harbours in the world, with unlimited anchorage space and extensive docks and wharves. Bombay is a much handsomer town than Calcutta. Its magnificent public buildings are all grouped together along a fine esplanade, only a broad expanse of grass lying between them and the ocean. Behind them the town spreads itself, and behind the town again lies the harbour, ten miles wide, dotted with beautiful wooded islands, and backed by a noble range of mountains.

The human life of Bombay differs from that of every other Indian city by the dominating element of the Parsees, who, by their wonderful energy, enterprise and education, have become the most important and powerful influence in the Bombay Presidency. These people are the descendants of ancient Persians who fled from their native land before the Mahommedan conquerors of Persia, and who settled at Surat 1,100 or 1,200 years ago. They now number in all about 70,000, the great majority of whom reside in Bombay. They all speak English fluently, which is carefully taught in their schools. Their religion is pure theism, and the elements, fire especially, are treated as visible representations of the Deity. The founder of their religion was Zoroaster, whom tradition says was a disciple of the Hebrew prophet Daniel, and it teaches a pure and lofty morality, summed up in three precepts of two words each, viz., good thoughts, good words, good deeds, of which the Parsee constantly reminds himself by the triple coil of his white cotton girdle, which never leaves him.

One of the leading peculiarities of the Parsee religion is the method pursued for the disposal of the bodies of their dead. No one should pass through Bombay without paying a visit to the Parsee Dakhmas or Towers of Silence. These strange towers, about 90 ft. in diameter and 15 ft. high, are built in the midst of a beautiful garden on the top of Malabar Hill, looking across the wide ocean towards the setting sun, and surrounded by the villas and bungalows of the wealthy merchants of Bombay

The garden is approached by a long private road, to which all access is barred, except to Parsees, and those who, like ourselves, have received permission from the Secretary of the Parsee Society. This leads to a flight of steps, at the top of which is the house of prayer, where the sacred fire is kept burning with incense and sandal wood, and never allowed to die down. We were not permitted to enter, but from its terrace we obtain on the one side a glorious view of the whole city of Bombay, the harbour beyond, and the magnificent ranges of the Ghauts in the distance. On the other side is a lovely garden sloping down to the ocean, glorious in parterres, flowering shrubs and palms, with five low circular structures of solid granite rising solemnly out of the foliage. Ranged round the summit of these towers, crowded closely together, are rows of loathsome vultures, which, black against the sunset sky, dominate the whole scene and seem to crowd out of view all their beautiful surroundings. These birds were still and silent, but when the gate is unlocked for a funeral, they begin to stir and show signs of excitement, which increases as the procession winds slowly up the hill, followed by the mourners reciting funeral prayers. After the mourners comes a man leading a white dog, the emblem of faithfulness, and then come a crowd of priests in pure white robes, with relations and friends of the dead man, holding a handkerchief between them, in token of sympathy and fellow-feeling. On reaching the House of Prayer, the mourners enter, and chant prayers while the corpse-bearers enter the Tower of Silence with the dead body,

THE CAVE TEMPLE OF ELEPHANTA.

which they expose naked on the platform which is erected inside, but out of sight of all outsiders.

The moment they withdraw the rows of expectant vultures drop silently down into the tower, and in ten minutes have stripped every particle of flesh off the corpse, reducing it to a bare skeleton before the mourners have finished their prayers. The skeleton remains three or four weeks exposed to the tropical sun, when the bones are reverently placed in a central well within the tower, where Parsees of high and low degree are left to turn into dust without distinction.

If time had permitted, we should have liked to have visited some of the extraordinary cave temples, which are scattered over the Bengal Presidency, but we could only visit those on the island of Elephanta, about seven miles from Bombay, across the beautiful bay. These temples are quarried out of the solid rock, the columns supporting the roof being finely chiselled; against the walls are gigantic figures, the principal of which is 19 feet high. The sculpture has been much defaced by the Portuguese, when in possession of Bombay, who brought cannon into the cave, and fired them at the columns and images.

We stayed nearly a week in Bombay, which I employed chiefly in discussing, with native gentlemen of education and position, the many problems which this wonderful country presents to the politician and social reformer. The gist of these conversations I give in the following and concluding chapter of this book.

CHAPTER XXIV.

SOCIAL PROBLEMS IN INDIA.

INDIA is almost entirely a rural and agricultural country, and many of its populous towns are only vast aggregations of villages, in the midst of good agricultural land, on which the whole population are employed. In some parts of India the population is crowded densely on insufficient land, and the struggle for bare existence becomes terrible. With the least drawback, such as a few inches more or less of rain, thousands of the people die like flies, while serious climatic deficiencies bring about those awful famines of which we have so often read. In times of actual famine the Government can step in and feed the people, but no Government can deal with the certain degradation of physique and mental vigour which develops itself in a people under-fed from the cradle to the grave. In these districts the population shows a tendency to diminish instead of increase. The facilities afforded by the extension of railways drain off the more vigorous to thinly-peopled provinces, and the tea plantations of Ceylon and Assam are worked by the surplusage of Southern India and Bengal. Our new territory of Upper Burmah, though laying new and costly burdens on the Indian Exchequer, will afford fresh fields for emigration to these over-stocked districts of India, and, if we can keep out Chinese emigration, may compensate us in this way for the cost and risk of its conquest. Railways have been known to increase the population of sparsely populated but fertile districts of India, formerly remote and difficult of access, to an astonishing extent. The people, however, like the Irish at home, cling with obstinate affection to their villages and bits of poor land, in spite of misery and starvation, and this sentiment greatly increases the difficulty of solving one of the most serious of the social problems of India. There is plenty of land in the Indian peninsula for the whole of its population. We need not wish for the diminution of the population, but rather that some means may be found by which its present surplusage may be more equally distributed over the whole area, both of British India and the Feudatory provinces, which, lying interspersed among British territory, have not much more than a third of their population per acre.

The nationalities and race differences of India are as many and various as those existing over the whole continent of Europe. The Bengalee and the Sikh, the Mahratta and the Tamil, the Rajpoot and the Burmese differ as widely in every characteristic as do the Irishman and the German, the mercurial Frenchman and the phlegmatic Turk, the stolid Scandinavian and the hot-blooded Greek or Spaniard. In Europe, except in one small corner of Turkey, the religion is all the same, one form or another of Christianity. In India the Mohammedan, the Sikh, the Hindoo, the Buddhist, the Jain, the Parsee, the Brahmin, and the Christian range side by side all over the country. It is therefore clear that 250,000,000 of people, spread over an area of 1,900 miles long and wide, full of different nationalities, and conflicting religions and interests, conquered by a strange and distant people of widely different civilization and religion, governed and held down by less than 100,000 of their conquerors, forms a country which furnishes to the politician and sociologist a range of problems that have taxed in the past, and will tax in the future, all the skill and ingenuity of the finest Civil Service in the world. My own position towards them—dimly enlightened ignorance—can only present them to you as they presented themselves to me when I found myself face to face with them during the six weeks I was in the country.

Undoubtedly the most urgent social problem, ever present to English and Hindoo alike, is how to live at all, how to procure that daily bread to which every human being has a birthright. This problem is serious enough at home; but in India, as I have already explained, it overshadows the whole country like a huge cloud, the horrid memory of past and the dread of future famines being really the motive power of three-fourths of the administrative action of the Government.

Wherever I went in India the deepest impression made upon me was the terrible and widespread poverty of the people. The common idea amongst Englishmen is that India is a country of vast wealth and unlimited natural resources. As a matter of fact it is one of the poorest countries in the world. No doubt amongst the Rajahs and Princes, the great landowners, and the merchant class in Calcutta and Bombay there is great accumulation of wealth that is continually in evidence with much show and glitter. This is what is most familiar to the ordinary Englishman, who reads of Rajpoot princes, encrusted with diamonds and rubies from head to foot, visiting England with great pomp and state, and who sees in the illustrated papers pictures of durbars of the Governor-General or of the splendid presents sent to the Queen by Rajahs in celebration of her jubilee. The condition of the millions in India is the opposite extreme, and there is no parallel at all in European nations to the disproportionate distribution of wealth which prevails in India and the East. There the poverty of the many is even more extreme than the wealth of the few. In the towns, skilled labour earns from 1s. 9d. to 2s. 3d. per week; ordinary labour, 1s. 6d.; in the villages still less. The great mass of the people engaged in agriculture have to live entirely off the produce of their heavily-taxed holdings, and it is, of course, difficult to form any calculation of their average income.

An estimate was made a few years ago by a very able finance minister, now our ambassador at Egypt, Sir Evelyn Baring, placing the average annual income of the people of India at a trifle under £2 per head. This estimate was checked by Mr. Dadabhai Naoroji, a distinguished native statistician, who maintains that the average income does not reach more than about 28s. per head. We grumble enough about poverty and bad trade in England, but the best authorities tell us that the income of the inhabitants of Great Britain and Ireland is about £30 per head, or something like twenty times as much as the average income of India. The income tax returns show that in India there is no well-to-do middle class such as we have in England. In India this tax begins on incomes of £50, and only produces £200,000, affecting only 300,000 persons—a remarkable illustration of the poverty of the country. In England we commence at £150, and it produces £12,000,000. All my own observation confirms these estimates. I have visited many of the villages, as well as some of the larger towns. I found that the people, as a rule, lived only on the lowest quality of cereals—rice, millet, sorghum, peas, beans, and lentils, the finer grains, such as wheat and barley, being sold to pay rent. A man or woman pays at most 2s. or 2s. 6d. for a year's clothing, and in the north of India the suffering from cold in winter is very great. The houses are small clay huts without furniture, and very few families sit down to more than one meal a day. It may be truthfully said that the great part of the population of India live on the very edge of famine, and that a year of drought, flood, blight, or locusts brings about the death of millions of these poor miserable ill-fed folk. The terrible famines which come upon vast districts of India are mainly due to drought during one or more seasons. There is generally some reserve stock in most farmers' hands that carry them over a single bad year, though even then the pinch is felt seriously by families dependent upon weekly wages. But two dry seasons bring on universal starvation and the death of whole communities, unless the Government steps in. In the Behar district, in 1873-4, the people were only saved from perishing by the expenditure of about seven millions sterling by the Government on public works and the importation of a million tons of rice. In 1876-7-8 a terrible famine arose in the land. The harvest was short in 1875. In 1876 the main food crop perished throughout an immense tract of country, and prices at once went up to famine rates. By the end of the year the people were dying by thousands, and for nearly two years the Government were engaged in one long struggle with famine. Friends I have met in India have given me pitiful and heartbreaking descriptions of the awful scenes they witnessed during this terrible time. The Government had to spend about 12 millions sterling to feed the starving populace, for at one time, in Madras alone, upwards of two millions and a half of people were fed by the Government, two millions gratuitously. The famine commissioners estimated that five and a quarter millions of people were slain by this grievous famine, and, taking into account the diminution of births, the population was reduced by at least seven millions. Cholera alone swept away half a million. The famines of the last 30 years have carried off over 12 millions of people. This chronic poverty, reducing the stamina and working power of the vast body of the natives of India, rendering them unable to resist small local or larger general famines, is therefore one of the great social problems with which its Government is always face to face. Much has been done within the last ten years by means of improved communication, increased irrigation work, and the migration of population to lessen the risk and diminish the force of famines.

These poor people of India are probably the most overtaxed people on earth. The greater portion of the Indian exchequer is not revenue in the sense of taxation at all, but consists of receipts from State railways and irrigation works, and the large revenues from the opium monopoly, which is really paid by China and not India; the revenues from intoxicating liquor are also voluntary taxes, which no native need pay unless he likes, though the Government, by the way in which they are stimulating their revenue from this demoralising source, are undoubtedly doing much to increase the poverty and misery with which they are waging a never-ending warfare. The actual revenue of India, which is raised by taxation, is about £40,000,000, not much more than half that raised in the United Kingdom from one-fifth of the population. The burdens of taxation in India are therefore only one-tenth per head of the amount raised in this country. But it must be borne in mind that while the average taxation per head is only one-tenth that of England, the average income is only one-twentieth. The actual burden of taxation therefore is just double that which we ourselves have to bear. Half the taxed revenue of India is derived from land. The State in India is virtually the landlord, and the British Government carry on the same system of land tenure which they found prevailing amongst the various native states when they conquered or annexed them. They have, however, abandoned the ancient method which still prevails in some of the native states of taking the rent in the shape of a certain share of the produce,

2 C

which has the advantage of distributing the burden fairly on good and bad harvests, the rent thus rising and falling with the crop which the land produces. Instead of this a rent in money, levied without regard to good or bad seasons, is exacted from the tenants. The collection of this land tax or rent forms the main work of Indian administration. The average rent is from 2s. to 3s. 6d. per acre. This appears to us absurdly low, but in face of the vast difference in values between England and India it is really as high or even higher than rents at home, and is equivalent to a rent of at least 25s. for the same class of land in England. In many parts of India, however, the small farmer is in much worse condition than those holding direct from the State. In the old days of the East India Company they were too much engrossed with conquest and aggression to attend to the details of land revenue, and they farmed it out in great districts to men who gave them a lump sum, and who then got what profit they could out of the peasant. These men gradually slipped into the position of landowners, and in Bengal the Zemindar, as he is called, was raised in 1793 to the status of a proprietor holding his land at a quit-rent payable to the State. From time to time the hardships of the peasant cultivating under the Zemindar have been guarded against by the legal recognition of occupancy rights or fixity of tenures, but in vast districts of India individual proprietary rights in the soil have superseded the ancient State rights, and from all I could learn, the peasant under the Zemindar has a much worse time of it all round than the Ryot, who holds direct from the State.

The collection of a fixed rent, regardless of season, from an ignorant and improvident peasantry, has led to the existence of one of the great curses of India, the village money-lender, who comes in to the aid of the Ryot when he cannot make up his rent in poor years. Once in the clutches of the usurer, he never gets out of them again, and I heard fabulous estimates of the total aggregate indebtedness of the peasant to these village money-lenders. Everywhere in India I heard from natives the strongly expressed opinion that the only salvation for the peasant lay in the Government collecting the revenue from land in the shape of a share of the actual produce, rather than by a fixed rent in money. But none of them could tell me how they proposed to collect so great a revenue by such a cumbrous and antiquated system over such an enormous area as British India. The land tax of India is re-assessed every 30 years. It appears to me no sensible relief to the grinding poverty of the peasant is possible, except from some permanent reduction of the land tax, and by the securing of fixity of tenure and a fair rent to those under Zemindars with shorter periods of re-valuation. The condition of these Zemindar tenants is much akin to that of the Irish tenant farmer before the 1870 Land Act, and in Bengal, owing to the rapid growth of population under British rule, and the insurmountable objection to emigration on the part of the Bengalee peasant, the Zemindars have been able to rack-rent their miserable tenants, until their incomes have grown to many times the amount they were when their quit-rent to the State was fixed. The Indian Government are not blind to this state of things, and the Bengal Ryots Act, passed a year or two back, will confer fixity of tenure and tenant right on some millions of people, small cultivators under Zemindars. The overcrowding of these Zemindary districts may be judged by the fact that out of ten millions of holdings in Bengal, six millions pay a less rent than 7s. 6d. per annum for their land, and that in some districts the population runs as high as 500 to the square mile. All the land is occupied, and the population steadily increasing, so that the social problem of how to provide land for the agrarian population of India, is one that drives the Irish question into insignificance by comparison. Yet these Indian Ryots are just as much our fellow subjects as the farmers in the West of Ireland, and their patient endurance surely deserves as much consideration from the Government of India as the noisy clamour of the Irishman obtains from the Government at Westminster.

I will now pass from the question of the poverty of the people to that of education, which, in my opinion, after the necessities of life, is the most urgent social question in any country. Public instruction in India is directly organised by the State, assisted by grants in aid from the Imperial revenue, under careful inspection. A department of public instruction exists in every province, under a director, with a staff of efficient inspectors. A network of schools extends all over the country, beginning with the indigenous village school, graduating upwards to the highest colleges and the three great universities of Calcutta, Madras, and Bombay. All receive pecuniary help from the State, under the report of regular and well-organised inspection. A series of scholarships stimulates the energies of the best scholars and opens an easy path to the universities for the children of the poor, along which a goodly number travel. There are in all British India 141,000 schools of all sorts, of which 78,000 receive Government grants, with a grand total of students of about $3\frac{1}{2}$ millions. Ten years ago there were only 60,000 schools, with 1,800,000 scholars, so that the figures have more than doubled in that period. It is quite probable that in twenty or thirty years there may be as large a number of children in school attendance, in proportion to population, in India as in England. Everywhere, in my intercourse with natives, I found an intense desire that education should be stimulated and made universal. There are over 5000 students in training schools for masters and mistresses, and the position of schoolmaster is a very coveted one amongst the better class of Mahommedans and Hindoos.

The three Universities of Calcutta, Madras and Bombay were all incorporated thirty years ago on the model of London University. They are examining bodies, giving no instruction, and confer degrees in arts, law, medicine, and civil engineering. There is a fourth university on a similar plan, but including the teaching element, in Lahore, for the Punjab. Some idea of the influence and power of these universities may be obtained from the statistical abstract relating to British India published every year. From that book I find that during the last ten years 70,000 students entered the three great universities, of whom no less than 26,000 passed, 600 graduating in law, 1160 in medicine, and 400 in civil engineering. These universities are fed by over 100 colleges all over India. The colleges are divided into two classes, those which specially teach the art course of the universities and those which devote themselves to medicine and other special branches of knowledge. Some of these colleges are entirely supported by Government, others only receive grants in aid, these latter being chiefly missionary colleges. There are about 10,000 students in all these colleges.

The colleges are recruited from the higher schools, of which at least one, called the Zila or district school, is established at the headquarters station of every district in India, and there are many others, chiefly under missionary influence, which receive grants in aid. In these schools English is not only taught, but is the actual medium of instruction. All these schools educate up to the standard of the entrance examination at the universities, and in them are usually trained the candidates who seek employment in the many branches of Government service now open to natives. There are about 600 of these schools, with an attendance of about 70,000 scholars. Below the high schools are a series of middle schools spread all over India in the smaller towns and large villages, which provide an education calculated to supply the requirements of the lower middle classes. Some of these teach English, others confine themselves to the vernacular. They number about 4000, with an attendance of about 200,000 pupils. The lower or primary schools complete the system of education in India. They are to be found almost everywhere, and teach the rudiments of learning in the vernacular of the district. These are almost all the outcome of the last fifteen or twenty years, and their remarkable extension form the best guarantee of and testimony to the success of that educational system of India, which owes so much to the efforts of Sir George Campbell and Sir Richard Temple, whose names are never mentioned by educated natives without profound respect and gratitude. Before Sir George Campbell's administration, the primary inspected schools in Bengal numbered only 2451, attended by 64,000 pupils. In 1885 they had increased to 63,000 schools, attended by 1,300,000 students. To have been the means of increasing the school attendance of a great province twenty-fold is an achievement of which any statesman may well feel proud.

It is not possible to pass from this subject of education without recognition of the enormous services rendered, especially in the higher branches of education, by the various missionary societies. There are various opinions, favourable and unfavourable, with regard to missionary successes in the conversion of the heathen, but there can only be one opinion, and that a favourable one, with regard to the educational work of the missionary in India. There are now upwards of 200,000 pupils in the various schools and colleges of Protestant missions, this number having increased every ten years for the last forty years, at the following rates :—1851, 64,000; 1861, 82,000; 1871, 128,000; 1881, 196,000; 1888, 250,000 estimated. There would be no female education at all in India but for the efforts of devoted Christian women in connection with our missions. They now maintain more than 1200 girls' day schools, and the total number of female pupils under Protestant mission teaching in India has increased from 11,000 in 1851 to something like 80,000 in 1888.

The whole future of India largely depends upon education. The cultured natives who have passed through the schools and colleges of India are already showing themselves keenly alive to social reforms. The Brahmo-Somaj movement, of which the well-known religious teacher, Keshub Chunder Sen, was the founder, and which is an attempt to combine Christian morality and teaching with the pure theism of the ancient Hindoo religions, is stimulating a number of much needed changes in the social habits and customs of the natives of India, in which its adherents receive the help of many cultured Hindoos and Mahommedans. These gentlemen advocate the abolition of infant marriages, and the re-marriage of widows, with a view to relieving those many millions of widows, whose life is a living death, and whose husbands have died while they were babies. They also advocate and obtain wholesome changes in pernicious caste rules, encourage female education, oppose the extension of the liquor traffic, and generally show a warm interest in social reforms, which had no existence in native society thirty years ago. The Government of India does not undertake the direct instruction of the people. It simply stimulates and encourages education by grants in aid to all voluntary schools, whether originated by Mahommedans, Hindoos, Municipalities, European missionaries, or any other agency that satisfies the standard of efficiency. This wholesome rivalry is at the bottom of much of the stimulus which education has received in recent years, and I hope that the nobler and higher teaching which is or ought to be given in missionary schools may be widened until it affects the whole future of education in India.

I found amongst educated natives a great demand for the establishment of technical schools in all the large towns and cities. At Jeypore, the capital of one of the native Rajpootana States, I visited an admirable technical school, where instruction was given in many of the native arts of India, and which seems destined to rescue these arts from decay and extinction. More than one native industry is competing successfully with English and European manufactures, and the leading cotton spinners of Bombay, where there are now seventy or eighty first-class mills, assured me that in ten or twenty years India would manufacture for herself all that she now buys from Manchester. These mills have already pretty well driven Lancashire out of the China and Japan market for cotton yarns, which form a solid portion of the cargoes of the direct P. and O. line from Bombay to Hong Kong. The banks of the Hooghly at Calcutta are black with the smoke of jute mills, and there is no doubt that India is on the road towards recovering by machinery the great hand-made manufactures which Manchester in time past destroyed. No jealousy of India's competition with England must stand in the way of her Government doing everything practicable in the way of technical education to enable India to recover her home manufactures by adopting modern processes.

All this stimulated educational system is producing a fresh social problem of steadily increasing intensity, which sooner or later must be faced and grappled with. The British nation, when they took over the government of India from John Company, entered upon an ancient, primitive, but decaying civilization, of which the religion was the only vital remnant, with no education of any value, except that which was identified with the priestly caste alone. I have briefly described to you the splendid system of higher education which we have established under British rule during the last 30 years, and which is now turning out every year 10,000 or 15,000 young men as highly educated as English University graduates, many of whom visit England and Scotland, acquiring British habits of thought and criticism. These men find their way into the Indian Civil Service, the learned professions, become schoolmasters, lawyers, doctors, civil engineers, merchants, station masters, bank clerks, and what not. They are settling down all over India, rapidly creating an intelligent cultured native opinion, finding expression in a widely read vernacular press, which criticises and judges the actions of the Government, and discusses every social problem affecting the welfare of the Indian people. They all speak and understand English as well as we do, and in my journey through India I constantly met with young Hindoos content with salaries of 30s. or 40s. a month, who were perfectly familiar with Herbert Spencer, Mill, Carlyle, John Morley, and all the English classics. All the time I have been in India I have sought as much as possible the society of these educated natives. I felt I could see enough of Anglo-Indian officials at home, but that I might never have the opportunity of visiting India again, where alone native opinion could be gathered up. In the many interviews I had with educated natives, both Hindoo, Mahommedan, and Brahmo-Somaj, I was deeply impressed with their mental grip and great intellectual attainments. There was no attempt to mislead, a total absence of prejudice, and a tone of great moderation, with a desire to see both sides of every question under discussion. I found intense loyalty to British rule as the only Government possible to India, although almost every native had plenty of hostile criticism as to the methods and results of British administration.

In a very few years the educated native will become a tremendous force in Indian society, and already he is knocking loudly at the official door for some share in the responsible government of his native land. How far this demand is to be met is a social problem that is causing grave anxiety to successive Governors-General, and that will have to be seriously faced before very long. These educated natives have already learnt the power of combination. Three years ago they formed themselves into a powerful organisation, not unlike in its character and formation our own Social Science Congress, which meets annually at some great centre for conference on matters affecting the welfare of native India. Three of these great representative congresses have been held at Bombay, Calcutta, and Madras, attended by 1200 or 1400 of the picked natives of India, Hindoos, Mahommedans, Jains, Parsees, and Christians meeting together with perfect harmony and great enthusiasm. The proceedings are conducted in English, and although I have not had the opportunity of attending one of these congresses, I have carefully read their proceedings, and, as far as possible, in my intercourse with a great many natives who have been members of them, have endeavoured to find out what are the hopes and wishes of this united and representative body of educated Indians. I expect to be present at the Allahabad congress this winter.

When India becomes generally educated, the national system being based upon English ideas and English aspirations, it will be impossible to deny to those who by education are fitted for it, their share in the privileges and responsibilities of the Government of the country. It cannot therefore be wondered at that the few who have already reached that standard feel that at any rate they ought to possess some direct means of making the opinions and convictions of India felt by the Government. This important element in Indian society does not desire, as has been often unjustly stated, the overthrow of British India; they know only too well that in the outburst of anarchy which would follow such an event, they at any rate would be the first to be crushed. What they wish is that the Government should be more at touch with the people, and that the educated portion of the native races should have some voice in determining the policy of the Government, and above all should get a solid share in the administration, and of all the posts and offices which could be filled by natives as effectively and much more economically than by English. India is virtually ruled by a British Bureaucracy which is admittedly the finest civil service in the world, appointed by a severe competitive examination. This bureaucracy is directed by the Viceroy and local governors, assisted by councils which they themselves select. An Indian civil servant goes out to India for 25 years' service, four of which are holiday, and at the end of that time, when he is in the prime of life, retires with a minimum pension of about £1000 a year. This is, of necessity, a very costly civil service. Large salaries have to be paid to induce the pick of young Englishmen to enter for the competitive examinations, and the pension list, beginning at so early a date, is, of course, exceptionally heavy. The salaries and expenses of civil departments reach a total of 11 millions, of which less than two millions are paid to natives. Of course, in the earlier days of British rule, before English education had permeated the country, it was impossible to govern according to Western ideas, except through the medium of Englishmen. But natives now contend, and with some reason, that they ought to be much more largely admitted into the civil service, and if all the appointments which could be filled by natives, without entrenching on the actual British administration and government of the country, were so filled it would effect a saving of some three or four millions sterling in the item of salaries alone. They have a further grievance in the fact that the examination for the higher branches of the civil service is conducted only in England, and that natives, unless they undertake the risk and expense of a journey from India—which to the pious Hindoo would involve the loss of caste—cannot enter the higher civil service at all. They demand, in my opinion with great justice, that a fair share of these higher appointments should be allotted to natives, that the examination should take place in India, and that the successful candidates only should be expected to go to England for two years for study at one of our national universities.

But the main reform on which these educated natives insist is that the legislative councils of India, instead of being close bodies of nominated and official members, shall be opened to a certain number of elected representatives. They do not demand that the whole, or even a majority, of these councils should be elected. They are willing to leave the main power of government and administration with the European Executive. They would be content if one-third of the legislative councils could in some way or other be elected by the natives, so that their views could be stated publicly, the Budgets discussed, and the Government interpellated on questions of executive administration. This demand is the inevitable result of the spread of English education, with its idea of liberty and political rights, ideas fostered and encouraged to the utmost by a free native press, of great editorial ability. It is a demand to which, sooner or later, the Government will be compelled to yield. The main difficulty is to find a constituency to elect. The mass of the people of India have no more idea of representative government than the inhabitants of a baby farm, and the educated demand for representative institutions only exists in the great centres of population. I discussed this matter with a party of educated gentlemen in Bombay, most of whom were members of the Annual Congress already referred to, and they proposed that the large municipalities like that of Bombay or Surat, the Bombay Chamber of Commerce, the universities, an electoral college of Mahommedans and another of Hindoos, might easily furnish a constituency that would meet all the necessities of the situation. I am, however, quite convinced that to satisfy in one way or other this legitimate demand of the educated Hindoo for some share in the government of his native land, would be of as great advantage to British rule in India as it would be to these educated natives and all they represent.

The natives of India are also very urgent in another demand, which appears to me equally reasonable. The legislative Councils of India are, of course, subordinate to the Indian Council in India, presided over by the Secretary of State. This home council consists of fifteen experts on Indian questions, and is composed of retired Indian civil or military servants, who have returned home. Their functions are to advise the Secretary of State for India. The original draft of the Act creating this council was drawn by Lord Beaconsfield, then Mr. Disraeli, who, with great foresight, inserted a clause reserving four seats at this council for natives of India. His colleagues, however, objected, and it was struck out. Educated India anxiously demands that this wise proposal shall be adopted to-day, and that four or five natives, who have distinguished themselves in Indian administration, and enjoy the confidence of their co-nationalists, shall be added to the Indian Council as vacancies arise. These native gentlemen are also very anxious to see some of their number enter the House of Commons, and many of you are familiar with the names of Lalmohun Ghose, Dadabhai Naoroji, and other native Indians, who have contested English constituencies, so far, I regret to say, without success. Briefly, what educated India desires is, representation in all the departments and governing bodies which control the destinies of their country. If they had fair play in the civil service, representation on their own legislative councils, and on the Indian Council at home, and if it were possible to induce some English constituency to accept one of their number, they would be more than content, while the advantage to Indian society, of being able to discuss every grievance publicly in all the governing bodies which rule their destinies, would be beyond all measure.

My visit to India has been shorter than I had intended, but my holiday is curtailed by the intelligence that Parliament is meeting earlier than usual, and I have had to hasten home. India, however, is now so easy of access, that I have decided to spend next winter there, and see it with greater leisure and deliberation.

We left Bombay in the P. & O. steamer "Assam" on Monday, January 19th, and after a pleasant and uneventful passage, broken only by a three hours' stay at Aden, we reached home by Brindisi on Sunday night, February 5th, after an absence from England of five months, two weeks, and three days.

ADEN.

www.ingramcontent.com/pod-product-compliance
Lightning Source LLC
Chambersburg PA
CBHW030543300426
44111CB00009B/844